PUBLISH
LIKE A PRO

SOUTH AFRICAN EDITION

PUBLISH
LIKE A PRO

THE COMPLETE GUIDE TO SUCCESSFUL AND PROFITABLE SELF-PUBLISHING

VANESSA WILSON & GEORGINA HATCH

Quickfox Publishing

For all the authors who have entrusted us
with their books and their dreams.

Published by Quickfox Publishing
www.quickfox.co.za | info@quickfox.co.za
PO Box 50660, West Beach, Bloubergrandt, 7449
Cape Town, Western Cape, South Africa

**Publish Like a Pro: The Complete Guide to
Successful and Profitable Self-publishing**
Print edition ISBN 978-0-6399466-0-3

Copyright © 2018 Quickfox Publishing
First edition 2018

ePub edition ISBN 978-0-6399466-1-0
Kindle edition ISBN 978-0-6399466-2-7
PDF edition ISBN 978-0-6399466-3-4

All rights reserved. No part of this publication may be reproduced, stored in a retrieval system, or transmitted, in any form or by any means, without the prior written permission of the publisher.

Editors: Michelle Bovey-Wood, Rachel Bey-Miller
Proofreader: Nadine Dove
Book and cover designer: Vanessa Wilson
Production assistant: Lindsay Coetzer
Typesetting and production: Quickfox Publishing
Printed by RSA Litho, Cape Town, South Africa

Credits
Cover and chapter icons: Keep Calm and Vector
Photographs: Vanessa Wilson pp. 111, 112, 159, 162, 163
p. 102 Source unknown, used under fair use; p. 142 © Wordy.com, used with permission; p. 143 Adapted from *How to Get Published in South Africa* by Basil van Rooyen, Southern Book Publishers (Pty) Ltd;
p. 167 www.printisbig.com

DISCLAIMER
All information provided in this book is done so in good faith and was correct at the time of going to press. The authors, the publisher and its representatives cannot be held liable for any losses, financial or otherwise, that may result from using information provided in this book.

TABLE OF CONTENTS

SECTION 1 SO YOU WANT TO PUBLISH A BOOK?..................................15

Introduction: why write a book? 16

CHAPTER 1: ARE YOU A TRADITIONALIST OR AN INDEPENDENT?............ 18
The traditional approach 19
The independent option 21
Who owns your work? 23
Potential earnings 24

CHAPTER 2: THE WRITE STUFF – GETTING IT TOGETHER 30
First things first 31
Planning ahead 36
Beginning and ending 37
What's in a name (or title)? 40
Keywords are key 42
The end is not the end 43
Making it easier for publishers 45
Protecting your copyright: proving ownership 48

CHAPTER 3: YOU HAVE A DEAL! 50
The finishing touches 52
What if you don't have a deal? 53

SECTION 2

GOING THE INDEPENDENT ROUTE 55

CHAPTER 4: TYPES OF INDEPENDENT PUBLISHING 56
Independent publishing models 58
    Custom publishing 58
    Vanity publishing 62
    Self-publishing/print-on-demand 65
    Subsidy or partnership publishing 69
Decision time 72
Choosing your service provider 73
Consultation is key 75
    The consultation 75
    The manuscript evaluation 77
    The publishing budget 78

CHAPTER 5: OPPORTUNITIES, CHALLENGES AND PITFALLS 81
Do you have what it takes? 83
Tips on funding your book 87

SECTION 3

BOOK PRODUCTION PROCESSES – THE NUTS AND BOLTS 91

CHAPTER 6: AN OVERVIEW OF BOOK PRODUCTION 92
The publishing process 93

CHAPTER 7: THE EDITORIAL PROCESS 96
Editing 97
    Types of editing 99
    Substantive or complex edit 99
    Standard edit 100
    Light edit 101
    Proofreading 101
Editorial permissions 103
    Obtaining permissions 104

CHAPTER 8: ADDING PHOTOGRAPHS AND ILLUSTRATIONS TO YOUR BOOK 108

Reviewing image quality.. 109
    Resolution and image size 109
    Scanning.. 112
    File formats 112
Artwork considerations... 113
Using online image libraries 114
Image permissions... 116
Commissioning an illustrator.. 119
Commissioning a photographer.. 123

CHAPTER 9: PREPARING YOUR MANUSCRIPT FOR PUBLISHING 126

CHAPTER 10: DESIGN, TYPESETTING AND LAYOUT 131

Book interior design and style sheet set-up............................. 132
Typesetting and layout.. 135
Your cover story... 137
Page proofs and final sign-off 139

CHAPTER 11: ISBN ASSIGNMENT, LEGAL DEPOSIT AND BARCODES 146

ISBN assignment 146
    Registering an ISBN in your name.................................... 148
    Applying for an ISBN in South Africa 148
Legal deposit in South Africa 150
Barcode generation 151

CHAPTER 12: ALL ABOUT PRINTING – LITHO OR DIGITAL? 153

Litho printing.. 154
Digital printing 157
Choosing your printing specifications 159
    Hardcover or softcover?... 160
    Binding options... 162
    Choosing paper for your book interior 165
Obtaining a print quote 171
Preparing your book for printing.. 176

CHAPTER 13: EBOOKS IN A NUTSHELL 182
What is an ebook? 182
Ebook formats 184
Digital rights management (DRM) 189
Creating your own ebook – the danger of automatic
file converters 190
Preparing for ebook publishing 192

CHAPTER 14: THE PRODUCTION TIMELINE: PLANNING AHEAD 198

SECTION 4   TAKING CARE OF THE PENNIES 203

CHAPTER 15: BUDGETING AND BOOK PRICING 204
Your publishing budget 207
Working out your cost price per book 208
Setting a retail price 213
Calculating your breakeven point 223

SECTION 5   DISTRIBUTING, MARKETING AND SELLING YOUR BOOK 225

CHAPTER 16: DISTRIBUTION – CUTTING THROUGH THE CLUTTER 226
The state of bookstores 227
Selling to libraries 232
Selling to schools and tertiary institutions 233
Other channels of distribution 234

CHAPTER 17: ONLINE DISTRIBUTION PLATFORMS 235
Amazon Kindle Direct Publishing (KDP) 237
Apple iBooks Store 239
Smashwords 241
IngramSpark 242
US tax withholding 244
Expanding your market by exploring other book formats 245
   Audiobooks 245
   Large-print and Braille books 247

CHAPTER 18: PROMOTE, PROMOTE, PROMOTE! 250
Create a media kit 251
Develop your book pitch 254
Hold a launch party 255
Work your network 256
Make your worth known 256
Events are an event 257
Engage social media 259
Create a website 262
Enter publishing competitions 263
Attend book fairs and expos 264
Fortune favours the brave 267

CHAPTER 19: IT'S ALMOST, BUT NOT QUITE, THE END 268

SECTION 6

APPENDICES 271
Appendix A: Chapter 1: The write stuff 272
Appendix B: Keywords and title names 274
Appendix C: An example of prelim pages for non-fiction 276
Appendix D: A sample imprint page 278
Appendix E: Proofreading and editing marks 279
Appendix F: Publishing budget template (professional) 280
Appendix G: Publishing budget template (simple) 282
Appendix H: Publishing timeline template 284
Appendix I: The Advance Information (AI) sheet 286
Glossary and index 288
Acknowledgements 299
About the authors 300

FOREWORD

So, you want to write a book? You have a great idea, a compelling message or a unique story. But the simple truth is that writing a book is hard work and requires an enormous amount of determination and perseverance. The media and publishing world is saturated with instant information; news; books; social media; blogs; trends; magazines – and it's very difficult to even get noticed. Slush piles of honestly written and well-crafted manuscripts that will never move off the table of the literary agent or the publisher pile up and remain untouched, despite having the potential to fill that special niche in the market.

So for many authors, self-publishing is the way to go. This book, written by two experienced and reputable publishing professionals, will help you to avoid pitfalls along the way to producing a quality product with the potential for success. For many traditional publishers, profit is often the driving force and the super-seller mentality reigns supreme. Some real gems are missed along the way and although it is a daunting task to sell directly to your readers, there is huge potential to be tapped.

I have been involved in the book trade for more than 40 years as a book selector for a National Library Service and as a selector for the Leisure Books and Leserskring catalogues and online book selling business. Yet, this very professional and practical guide has opened my eyes to the enormous amount of work that goes into producing a book. I never knew! That is exactly why this book would make such a compelling difference in the life of a budding author. To produce a high-quality, self-published book is of paramount importance for the serious author who has a lot to offer and needs to be heard.

I have known co-author Georgina Hatch for more than 20 years. We met when she was the Publishing Director of a major South African publishing house, and after that as an independent editor, running her own editorial service business, Write It Right. She has assisted a number of authors, who preferred the independent route, to produce and bring their books to market. Nothing escapes Georgina's eagle eye and she offers solid advice on funding and promoting the book as well.

Vanessa Wilson, founder and Director of Quickfox Publishing, is a production and independent publishing wizard. She goes into great detail to explain the nuts and bolts of every aspect of the production process, offering additional advice on budgets and pricing, ebook publishing, production timelines and online distribution. Every type of publishing is dissected.

There are some works on self-publishing in the international arena, but for authors in South Africa, this very comprehensive and detailed book will make their job so much easier. I have not seen anything else as all-encompassing as this practical and useful book. I encourage all would-be authors to read it and learn!

Lana Barnett
CEO Leserskring/Leisure Books

SECTION

1

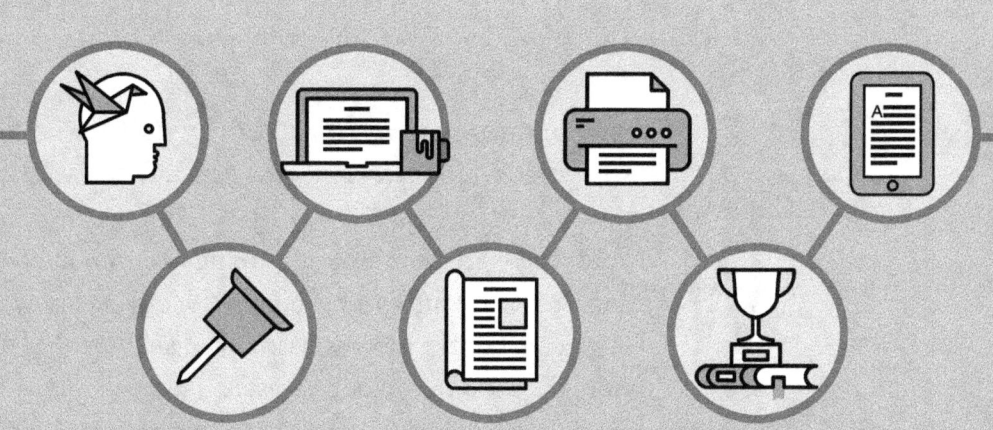

SO, YOU WANT TO PUBLISH A BOOK?

INTRODUCTION: WHY WRITE A BOOK?

"There is nothing to writing. All you do is sit down at a typewriter and bleed."

Wise words these are from Ernest Hemingway, who knew a thing or two about writing books. Typewriters may be long gone, but the process hasn't changed. Writing a book is all about the proverbial blood, sweat and tears.

According to a recent survey carried out by the *New York Times*, 81% of people feel they have a book in them and should write it. Their reasons range from wishful thinking to plain weird. So before you read any further, ask yourself: "Why do I want to write a book?" If your answer is any of those outlined below, it may be wise to find another way to achieve your goal:

- I want to be famous.
- I want to make a pile of money.
- My mum / dad / sister / uncle / dog will be proud of me.
- It will be my legacy to the world.
- I love writing, so why not?

These are all perfectly valid reasons for *wanting* to write a book, but they are unlikely to sustain you during the marathon that is book-writing, or guarantee you success as an author. For every famous writer, there are thousands of others who are being choked by a cloak of invisibility. For every wealthy writer, there are throngs who make nothing and are sometimes forced to subsidise their books. Here are some valid reasons for *actually* writing a book:

- You have a genuinely unique story to tell that will be of interest to other people.
- You have a powerful message which, through the telling, will be of benefit to others.
- You're an expert in a particular subject and wish to share your expertise, establish yourself as an authority in your field, and differentiate yourself from your competition.
- You believe that people will pay to read your story or message.

Many people believe that publishing a book is simple – just write the story and send it off to a publisher or obtain the help of an independent author services company and, hey presto!, you have a book. If only it were so straightforward.

A traditional publisher will not accept your book unless they can make money from it, no matter how brilliant its content; and the independent publishing route – despite being a quicker and easier route to getting published – presents many challenges of its own. While you may not have to bleed to get your book published, you will certainly have to sweat, and there may be a few tears along the way. **Never fear, we are here to help.**

This book is intended to guide you through the process of publishing your book while still hanging on to your sanity. We explore the entire publishing process, step by step. Within these pages, you will find survival tips, practical advice, technical know-how and specific instructions. We also cover most of the questions authors have asked us about publishing, book production, distribution and marketing. We hope you find this book not only highly informative, but also practical and a trusted partner on your publishing journey!

1

ARE YOU A TRADITIONALIST OR AN INDEPENDENT?

Firstly, let's take a long, hard look at the publishing industry in South Africa. South African publishing houses focus on three broad market areas: academic, education and trade.
1. Academic (or higher education) publishing provides learning materials for the tertiary education market.
2. Educational publishing is aimed at the schools market, from pre-school to Grade 12, and provides learning materials for learners and support materials for teachers.
3. Trade publishing provides the kinds of books that you find at bookstores in your local shopping mall. This includes fiction and non-fiction.

As academic and educational books are traditionally commissioned by specialist publishers, the focus of this book will be on trade publishing. However, the content is useful for all publications, so please keep reading.

According to a survey carried out by the Publishers' Association of South Africa (PASA), locally published books constitute

42% of the annual turnover of the South African publishing industry. Of this, fiction constitutes 36% and non-fiction, 64%. The turnover from imported books is the exact opposite – 64% comes from fiction and 36% from non-fiction. This tells us that the bestselling fiction in South Africa – in other words, big-name, top 10 titles – is imported.

Of the books that are published locally in the trade sector, adult books account for 82% of turnover and children's books for just 18%. English-language books constitute 54% of turnover and Afrikaans 45%. The English titles are predominantly adult non-fiction (62%) whereas the Afrikaans sector is fairly evenly spread across children's books, adult fiction and adult non-fiction.

What these statistics tell us is that more books are imported into the country than are published locally. Of the books that are published locally, non-fiction sells better than fiction.

The South African publishing industry is fairly small. At the time of writing, there were approximately 23 traditional publishers active in the trade sector, but this is shrinking all the time owing to mergers and, sadly, some closures.

To understand the local industry and decide which publishers to approach for your book, it's important to discern and comprehend the differences between traditional book publishing and independent book publishing.

THE TRADITIONAL APPROACH

Traditional publishing is for books that are guaranteed to sell several thousand copies. Traditional trade publishers receive hundreds of manuscripts per month, and with fierce competition and high production and distribution costs, they need to be selective about what they take on. Their clear intention is to make a profit, so they will only publish a book if they are convinced it will sell and make money for their company. This is truly the bottom line.

The publishing company's shareholders, sales executives and marketing team need to believe in the books they publish before they back them financially. The sales executives, in particular, need to be convinced that they can sell the book into various outlets, including bookstores, and that their valiant efforts will be supported by a promotable author who will work well with the organisation's marketing team.

Once a deal has been agreed upon, the traditional publisher will control all aspects of book production. Although the author will be consulted, the publisher will be responsible for:

- Evaluating the book and determining its sales potential.
- Financing the book.
- Editing the book.
- Designing the interior and book cover.
- Commissioning illustrations and photographs, if necessary.
- Obtaining text and image permissions, if necessary.
- Typesetting and proofreading.
- Printing the book.
- Converting the book into an ebook.
- Marketing and publicity.
- Book sales.
- Local and international distribution and stock control.
- Financial administration and author royalty payments.
- General project management.

In other words, the publisher will take on full financial, production and marketing responsibility for the book. In return for its investment, it will retain the bulk of profits made from selling the book. The publisher will also control what happens to the book: what it looks like; when it's published; where it's sold; and how long it will remain in print.

On the upside, traditional publishers have the resources, contacts and marketing experience to get the book out there and selling, and they take on all the financial risk in doing so. Furthermore, the publisher is likely to have access to a broader, international book-buying market that authors publishing independently may not have. The author earns a royalty from all sales without the need for any further involvement, apart from publicity appearances organised by the publisher.

On the downside, the author has no control of the book while the publishing contract is in place. You will be consulted during the production process, but ultimately the final decisions rest with the publisher. So how your book looks, how it's marketed, how it's sold, and how long it remains in print will not be your decisions.

Traditional publishing is best suited to authors who believe their book has widespread appeal and can be sold via conventional bookstores. It's also suited to authors who prefer to hand over their book in its entirety and have no further involvement in its production and marketing; authors who have little to no direct access to their potential readers; and authors who lack the funds to publish independently.

THE INDEPENDENT OPTION

Publishing independently, usually referred to as self-publishing, means that the author takes on many of the responsibilities that a traditional publisher would normally handle, from choosing a publishing team and funding the project, to making pricing decisions and marketing the book. The author is also responsible for finding suitable distributors and making most of the final decisions relating to the project.

Because authors have full control, they can customise the publishing process according to their needs. They can also keep a book in print for as long as they choose to do so. Most importantly, they retain all the profit from book sales.

As daunting as some of the author's responsibilities sound, there are service providers who can assist with many of the publishing and distribution functions, often as a seamless, one-stop service. The most important decision an author will need to make is which service provider to partner with to help them turn their book publishing dreams into reality.

A good publishing service will offer at least these basic services:
- Manuscript evaluation.
- General publishing and distribution advice.
- Editing and proofreading.
- Cover design and interior formatting.
- ISBN assignment.
- Book printing.
- Ebook conversion and distribution.
- Access to bookstore marketing and distribution services.
- Access to online book distribution services and retailers.
- Project management.

Some may offer additional services, such as:
- Translation.
- Ghostwriting or overwriting.
- Illustration.
- Photography.
- Obtaining permissions for image and content reproduction.
- Sourcing images.
- Organising book launches.
- Basic marketing, such as social media posts, publicity and press releases.
- Developing author websites.
- Designing promotional material such as book launch invites, posters, flyers, roll-up banners, and Facebook images.

Self-publishing is best suited to authors who believe their book has niche appeal and can be sold via outlets other than traditional bookstores; authors who have easy and direct access to their potential buyers; and authors who have the financial resources for publishing and marketing. It's a major plus-point if the author has a ready-made sales network made up of clients, strategic partners and other interested parties. It's also better suited to entrepreneurial or business-minded authors who are not afraid to market, promote and sell their book.

WHO OWNS YOUR WORK?

The ownership of a book is governed by the copyright, which is a type of intellectual property applicable to certain forms of creative work, including books. It's a legal right created by the law of a country that automatically grants the creator of an original work the exclusive rights for its use and distribution. You don't need to register your copyright to have it.

It's a complex issue, but broadly speaking, if you write a book the copyright belongs to you, the author, unless you cede it to a third party, such as a traditional book publisher.

Traditional publishing

For as long as the publishing contract is in place, the traditional publisher will hold the copyright to your book. During this period you may not take the original manuscript or any of its content and publish elsewhere, unless this has been specifically written into the contract. Even then, it's likely that you will be restricted in how that material may be used or republished.

Once the contract has expired, you will again own the rights to the original content of the book, but the publisher will continue to own the copyright to the book in its published format. This includes the design, layout and edited version, as well as the electronic files and printing plates. Should neither party choose to renew the contract, you are free to publish the book yourself using your original manuscript. Alternatively, you may have the option of purchasing the existing electronic files or printing plates from the publisher. It usually works out much cheaper to buy the existing material than to start production from scratch, so be sure to enquire about that option if the publisher chooses not to renew your contract.

Independent publishing

When going the independent route, you own the copyright to your original work. This means that you are free to republish your book elsewhere and you are also free to write and publish other books using the same or similar content. However – and this is very important – while you retain copyright of your original manuscript, you do not necessarily hold copyright of the electronic files created to print the book. This is because the publishing service uses its own team to design the cover and format the book, and they, therefore, own the copyright to that specific layout and design. The exception is when the publisher performs the services on a work-for-hire basis, or cedes the copyright over to you. In this case you, the client, will own the copyright. It is therefore necessary, when considering a publishing service, to establish up front whether you will have ownership of the final electronic files.

> You can find out more about copyright and proving ownership of copyright on page 48 in the next chapter.

POTENTIAL EARNINGS

One of the main differences between traditional publishing and independent publishing is the author's earning potential.

Because the traditional publisher invests money in the book, the company rightly expects a financial return. Authors are compensated by way of a royalty payment of between 8% and 15% on the *net receipt* of the book. The net receipt is the trade price after bookseller discounts and VAT have been deducted.

Yes, in exchange for displaying your book on their shelves, booksellers require the retail price to be heavily discounted. Discounts can range from 40–55%; and what is left after tax and discounts is split between the author and publisher, albeit not on an equal basis. The author is paid his or her agreed royalty percentage and the book publisher keeps the rest. The publisher uses their portion to cover the costs of production, warehousing, distribution, and marketing. The publisher must also cover operational costs and make a profit.

Let's look at an example: If a book has a retail price of R250 and the bookseller deduction is 45%, the net receipt is R137.50 minus 15% VAT, which equals R120.61. If an author is being paid a 10% royalty, the author will earn R12.06 for each book sold and the publishing house will retain R108.55. The publisher may seem to make a lot, but when you add up all the publishing costs, it's not much at all!

For as long as the book continues to sell, the author will receive a percentage royalty from each book sold, usually paid out twice a year. Once the publisher decides not to reprint the book and allows it to go out of print, the financial tap will be turned off.

In independent publishing, the author finances the publishing of the book and is therefore entitled to all the profits. By selling books directly to customers and bypassing bookstores, the author can make approximately 40–60% of the retail price after production and printing costs have been deducted.

Books can stay in print for as long as desired and, provided the author can pay the related production costs, content may be updated and new editions published as necessary.

The other advantage of publishing independently is that the author can secure bulk book deals with large companies and organisations. In exchange for the bulk sale, the author can offer to brand the book covers with the company's logo or customise the entire cover. There is tremendous flexibility to publishing independently, so authors can find innovative ways to make money from their books.

There is no get rich quick!

At this point, let's make one thing completely clear: whichever publishing route you choose to follow, you're unlikely to get rich from publishing a book, at least in the domestic market. In South

Africa, if you sell 3 500 to 4 000 books, your book is considered a bestseller. Of course, there are the rare exceptions to the rule. John van de Ruit's novel *Spud* (Penguin Books) sold more than 500 000 copies. Former South African national rugby coach Jake White's non-fiction book *In Black and White* (Zebra Press) sold more than 210 000 copies. These particular titles succeeded because of their originality, topicality, and widespread appeal to a general target market. But they are uncommon exceptions in a country that is noted for its less-than-average book sale success.

When it comes to earning potential, there is very little room for negotiation with traditional publishing houses, unless the author is a celebrity or major authority in their field. In that case, higher royalty payments can occasionally be secured. No doubt, you have read with envy about international publishing houses vying for the rights to publish a particular book, or about agents auctioning off the rights to a book. This rarely, if ever, happens in South Africa. In fact, book agents hardly exist in this country and most would-be authors conduct their own negotiations with publishers.

That's not to say that international sales are impossible. If authors feel their book has appeal outside of the domestic market, the services of an international book agent may be obtained. This agent will then approach publishers in other countries who might have an interest in publishing the book.

If the book is published by a local traditional publisher, the company will retain all domestic and foreign rights. If the publisher feels the book appeals to an international market and a deal is secured with an overseas publishing company, the South African publisher will be paid a fee and the author will receive a percentage return on this deal. There is no average return as each deal can be completely different depending on the market involved.

The main attraction of publishing through a traditional book publisher is that someone else funds the project and takes charge of services, such as sales, marketing and distribution. The disadvantages are that the author has to relinquish control of the publishing process and will earn less.

The main attraction of publishing independently is that the author takes control of the publishing process, retains ownership of the work and has the potential to earn more. The disadvantage is that all publishing costs are for the author's account and the author is responsible for driving marketing and book sales.

In conclusion

By now you should have a better idea of the advantages and disadvantages of using a traditional publisher and publishing independently. The table overleaf summarises the features of both types of publishing.

TABLE 1 Traditional publishing versus independent publishing

Traditional publishing	Independent publishing
It can take many months or years to secure a publishing deal.	You can publish your book straightaway; you simply need to find the right publishing service.
It costs you nothing to have your book published; if your book includes illustrations or photos, you might be required to supply those at your own expense.	You pay for publishing your book, so you must have enough money to cover all the production, printing and marketing costs.
There is no financial risk to you, the author.	There could be minor to considerable financial risk.
The quality of the final book that hits the shelves is likely to be high, and the product itself very marketable.	The quality and marketability of the final book is dependent on the service provider and the budget you have available to invest in professional services.
You don't have the final say over the production of your book, although your input will be regarded and accommodated where possible.	You have full say over the production process. If you are catering to a niche market that you know well, you can preserve the integrity of your content.
You earn a royalty of 8–15% of the net receipts (retail price less bookstore discount and VAT).	You earn 100% of the profits after all costs have been deducted. This can work out to be anything from 15% to 60% of the retail price depending on the channels you sell through and your initial investment; the highest profits come from direct-to-customer sales.
You have no control over the pricing or marketing of your book.	You have full control over every aspect of your book, including pricing and marketing.
The publisher decides whether to keep the book in print or not.	You decide whether to keep the book in print or not.
The publisher takes full responsibility for the marketing and selling of the book.	You take full responsibility for the marketing and selling of the book; you can enlist the help of professionals but this will cost you.
Better suited to authors who feel uncomfortable driving their own marketing and book sales.	Better suited to authors who feel comfortable driving their own marketing and book sales.
Suited to authors who have no access to their target market.	Well suited to authors who have easy or direct access to their target market.
Once your book has been published, the publisher will promote it for the first three to six months.	Once your book has been published, you can continue to promote and sell it indefinitely.
Popularity and demand for your book will dictate whether it is kept in the market after the publishing contract has expired.	Your book can remain in print regardless of the level of demand.

Traditional publishing	Independent publishing
Your book's success lies with the publishing company.	Your book's success lies with you and the resources you have available to publish and promote a good-quality product.
It can take up to a year, sometimes longer, for your book to be published and available in the market.	It can take 4 to 6 months for a trade-quality book to be published and available in the market. Some online platforms enable you to publish in less than a month, but this assumes that your manuscript is already well edited and good to go.
You are bound by contract, so you may not approach another publisher while your contract is in effect. You are usually also not allowed to rewrite or rework your content for publishing elsewhere, unless your contract allows it.	You are free to publish with whomever you like, whenever you like. You can also use some or all of your content for other products and books published through other companies.
At the end of the contract period, you may have the option to buy back the printing plates or book files to continue publishing the book yourself.	Depending on the publishing service used, you may or may not have ownership of the final print-ready files.

> **# TIP** Before you submit your manuscript for publishing
>
> If you want to approach a traditional publisher, first have your manuscript evaluated and then professionally edited to give yourself the best chance of being accepted. The less work a book requires to make it market-ready (work costs money), the more likely the publisher is to offer you a deal – if they believe the book will sell. It also presents your book – and you – in the best possible light. Publishing houses receive hundreds of manuscripts monthly, so you need to stand out in the crowd with a product that reads well and impresses.
>
> Finally, the more you can bring to the table, the better. An accurate analysis of your book's target market; the niche it fills; how it differs from similar books; its sales potential; and how you are able to help promote it, will also shine favourably upon your submission and increase the likelihood of your picking up a publishing deal.

THE WRITE STUFF — GETTING IT TOGETHER

Now that you know the difference between traditional and independent publishing, it's time to review just why you want to put yourself through the exquisite torture of writing a book. So, take five and ask yourself the following questions. Use the worksheet on page 272 to jot down your answers.

1. What are your reasons for writing your book?
2. What do you want your book to achieve?
3. Who is your target audience? Consider specifics, such as gender, age group, interests, concerns, and so on.
4. Have you identified and researched your competition? Are there similar books on the market already? Can your potential readers source the same information elsewhere?
5. What is your book's unique selling point (USP)?
6. What are your sure-fire marketing and promotion ideas?
7. With whom can you work to help sell and promote your book?

If you have already written your manuscript, well done! Read this section of the book to be sure you haven't overlooked anything important. If you're still thinking about writing your book, or have tentatively jotted down a few words and ideas, read on!

FIRST THINGS FIRST

Before you put fingertips to keyboard, you need a **topic** for your book. This has to be specific. If you are writing fiction, you need to choose a genre; if you are writing non-fiction, you need a topic. More and more, cross-over literary genres are becoming the trend, so there's no need to limit yourself to only one genre.

Some of the major literary genres and non-fiction categories are as follows:

FICTION:
- Romance
- Drama
- Humour
- Mystery/suspense
- Crime/detective
- Historical fiction
- Adventure
- Satire
- Tragedy
- Horror
- Fantasy
- Science fiction
- Short story
- Poetry/verse
- Picture book
- Comics/graphic novel

NON-FICTION:
- Biography/autobiography
- Memoir
- Textbook
- Reference book
- Journalism
- Business and economics
- Religion/spirituality
- Narrative non-fiction
- Photography
- Crafts and hobbies
- Self-help
- Parenting
- Health and wellness
- Sports and recreation
- Nature
- Computers and IT
- Technology and engineering
- Art and design

If you are struggling to find a topic, here is a simple formula that may prove useful:

Something you have an interest in + something you have knowledge about + something other people will be interested in reading about = YOUR TOPIC

If you have no interest in what you are writing about, chances are you won't complete your book. If you're bored with your subject matter, it will reflect in your writing.

"Write about what you know" is popular advice that is given freely. The easiest topic to write about is something of which you have knowledge or that you have experienced. Experience lends authority to the content, transforming it from mere theory into concrete reality. You cannot possibly know everything about your topic and will need to do some research along the way, but writing about what you know is a good starting point. Plus, your authenticity will be evident in your writing.

If you find your topic interesting, then others will, too, even if only a specific segment of the market. Sometimes, particularly in non-fiction, niche topics sell even better than fairly general ones. For example, most people, with the correct research, could put together a general manuscript about marketing. But what if you break the topic down and focus on a sector that you know something about and in which you have an interest, such as hair salons. You could then aim your marketing book at a buying sector that has an interest in the subject matter, such as owners of hair salons. Sometimes you have to open your mind and do things a bit differently in order to succeed.

If your choice of torment is writing fiction, the same formula applies. It makes no sense to write a sci-fi novel if the genre holds no appeal for you and you know nothing about sci-fi or the people who buy and read it.

Given that local fiction generates 34% of book sales in South Africa, success can be a steep uphill climb. Fortunately, local fiction authors such as Lauren Beukes and Deon Meyer are doing their utmost to transform this situation, and we are seeing an increase in quality home-grown fiction.

Fiction writing tends to appeal more to traditional publishers, but the manuscript has to be really marketable to be worthy of attention. Non-fiction writing, while of interest to some traditional publishers, is more likely to attract the interest of independent publishers – provided your content is good and your topic holds appeal.

When choosing a topic for your book, take the following factors into consideration:

- Timeliness of the topic: Is your subject matter evergreen or is it a topic that is 'hot' right now but might not be this time next year?
- Market size: Can you find stats that back your conviction about the level of interest in your topic?
- Availability of current information: Can people find out what they need to know about your topic in other ways, such as the Internet or books that are already on the market?
- Level of expertise: Can you introduce readers to new elements of your topic? Will your book appeal to those who are already well-versed in your particular subject matter?

Does anyone care?

Now that you have a topic for your book and you are convinced of your ability to write knowledgeably about the subject, you have to ask yourself the hardest question of all: will anyone actually want to read about the topic? This soul-searching question goes hand-in-hand with what you would like your book to achieve. Whether your book is fiction or non-fiction, you would probably like it to:

- Inform
- Inspire
- Provoke
- Entertain
- Motivate
- Sell!

All of the above are possible, as long as your book has a target market: a potential segment of consumers who are willing to part with their money to buy and read your book. Please note that your *target market* may not be the same as your *target audience*.

The audience is who you write for, but the market is those who will buy the book. For example, you may choose to write a non-fiction book about how men can learn to become more romantic in their personal relationships. In this instance, your *target audience is men* who will benefit from the advice contained in the book. But your *target market is women* who will see the value of the book and buy it for the men in their lives. So, women who are in a relationship with a man are your *primary market*, but hopefully men (at least those who are not too shy to buy the book) could become a *secondary market*.

It's worthwhile to identify more than one secondary market for your book. In other words, identify people who may not be your target audience or market, but who may also purchase the book for reasons of their own. Continuing with our example, other people who may wish to buy a book about encouraging romance in men include relationship coaches, life coaches, psychologists, and even divorce lawyers.

When considering the primary market for your book, it pays to be as specific as possible. Picture the people who will buy your book. Ask yourself questions such as:

- How old are they?
- Are they male or female?
- What concerns do they have?
- Are they looking for solutions to specific problems?

So, working on a best-guess supposition, the buyer of your "how men can become more romantic" book will most likely be a woman in the 25–35 age group (the age group when relational priorities tend to take centre stage) who is concerned that her male partner is not sufficiently well versed in the rules of romance and who would like to find ways to encourage her partner to become more aware. She is probably well-educated, has an interest in pop culture and is active on social media.

Can you see how exploring the profile of your target market can enhance your writing ability? You can now, to the best of your ability, curate your content to appeal to the potential buyer of your book. You can also generate ideas for marketing and promoting your masterpiece, as you will know who to aim for and how to reach them. Research is time well spent.

Samuel Johnson said: "The greatest part of a writer's time is spent in reading, in order to write; a man will turn over half a library to make one book."[1] In other words, you cannot begin writing until you have thoroughly researched your topic and your target market. Nowadays we can easily access resources other than books in order to gather information. Bear in mind, though, that online sources can be highly suspect. Wikipedia, for instance, can be edited by anyone. Wherever possible, use academic, government or reputable sites rather than popular sites. Substantiate your findings by checking the information on at least two other authoritative sites.

When searching for information, we should also heed the words of Dan Brown, who points out that 'Google' is not a synonym for 'research'.[2] In other words, we cannot be lazy about our research. Simply repeating other people's theories and words is not research – it's repetition – and, if you're not careful, it can be considered plagiarism.

Researching a topic will undoubtedly involve reading other experts' advice and philosophies, but that should merely be a starting point. Research could include keeping abreast of current events that relate to your subject matter; interviewing others for opinions and input; surveying would-be readers; visiting locations that might be useful in expanding your knowledge; engaging with people via social media; sourcing suitable photographs / documents / images; and obtaining permission to use relevant information.

You may find it necessary to continue your research as you formulate your manuscript, but it pays to have the critical mass of information available to you before you start to write.

---

1   *The Life of Samuel Johnson, LL.D., Comprehending an Account of His Studies and Numerous Works, in Chronological Order, Volume 3*, by James Boswell (1740–1795), Wentworth Press, 2016.
2   Dan Brown, *The Lost Symbol*, Knopf Doubleday Publishing Group, 2009.

> **# TIP Organising your research**
>
> Make sure you store your research in one location that lends itself to organisation. This could include files; folders; boxes; computer folders; CDs; an external disk; cloud storage ... whatever works best for you. Whatever you do, be sure to acknowledge the sources in your book! This not only gives credit to others for their information and ideas, but also shows readers that you have executed the information-gathering expected of you as an expert author.

PLANNING AHEAD

Once you have completed the bulk of your research and feel that you're ready to commence writing, you need a **content plan**. For **non-fiction**, this is simply an outline or table of contents for your book. A content plan will help you structure your work in a way that makes sense. It will also help to keep you on track and alert you to any deviations or U-turns! How you do this is up to you, but it's best to keep it simple and easy to follow.

Many authors choose the straightforward method of writing chapter headings and then adding sub-categories that summarise what each chapter will include.

If you were the author of our make-believe example book on how to encourage men to be romantic, the outline for the first three chapters might look like this:

Chapter 1: What is romance?
<u>Sub-categories:</u> *Definition of romance; history of romance; what is romantic love?*

Chapter 2: Is romance important?
<u>Sub-categories:</u> *What the experts say about romance; why romance is deemed important to a relationship; the difference between love and romance*

Chapter 3: How do men view romance?
<u>Sub-categories:</u> *How men and women view romance differently; the problems caused by differing viewpoints; can men's view of romance be changed?*

As you can see, the outline helps to progress the content and develop the structure of the book. You can use different methods to create your content plan, such as mind-mapping, brainstorming, or by using special software, such as Scrivener. The important thing is that you have one.

For **fiction**, outlining your novel is more complex because too much rigidity can kill the magic of a book. Fortunately, there are many good online resources you can turn to for help.

BEGINNING AND ENDING

While planning your book, try to give careful thought to how you are going to begin and how you are going to end. In fiction, you need to pull your readers in from the beginning and hook them with your first sentence. So, choose a powerful scene to set the tone of your book and snake-charm your reader from the first sentence.

The ending of your novel should be a natural conclusion to your yarn. It should logically tie up the story line, resolve outstanding conflicts, and pull together any loose ends. It should satisfy the reader, evoke emotion, and leave people wanting more – of your next book!

In non-fiction, the beginning and ending are referred to as the **introduction** and **conclusion.** A good introduction should introduce the topic of the book; allude to the what's in it for me (WIIFM) message; and give some background on why you are the best person to write this particular book. Don't introduce your book by listing facts and statistics; rather tell your readers a brief story that provokes their immediate interest and confirms that they were right to buy your book.

As with fiction, the conclusion of a non-fiction book should tie up all the loose ends. This is where you summarise what has been said; reinforce the main ideas; remind readers how you have helped them to solve their problems; and help them further by advising them what to do next (a call to action).

Just because it's a non-fiction book doesn't mean that your conclusion shouldn't arouse a response. You are passionate about your subject matter, so let this shine through right to the end to instil some excitement in your readers.

> **# TIP** Introduction and conclusion
>
> If you think like your reader when you're writing the introduction and conclusion of your book, you should find the job much easier. Your introduction will help develop the relationship between you and your readers. Your conclusion will determine if that relationship continues. What readers say when they put your book down matters more than what they say when they pick it up.

How long is a piece of string?

You may think it's impossible to plan the finished length of your book or estimate how long it's going to take you to create it. You could be right! However, with a non-fiction book it is possible to plan ahead and create a **writing schedule** that will help you complete your book within a specific period of time.

Assuming that the bulk of your research has been done and organised, use the **content plan** that you generated to create a writing schedule.

- You already know how many chapters you are going to write – now allocate a specific number of words to each chapter. As a starting point, give each chapter the same word count.
- Break this down further into the number of words per sub-category. Allocate each sub-category the same word count.
- Write your first chapter according to your pre-set word count and note how many hours it takes you to write it.
- Multiply this time by the total number of chapters in your book.
- Add in a few extra hours for unforeseen circumstances.
- Add in an additional number of hours for polishing your manuscript.

So in theory, if your total book content is planned at 50 000 words, with 10 chapters of 5 000 words each, and it takes you five hours to write each chapter, then the total time to write your book will be 50 hours. Add in another 10 hours for safety and you're looking at 60 hours from starting to finishing writing the content of your manuscript.

Remember that this does not include the time required for research and fact-checking, or for reviewing your manuscript! The amount of time these activities will take depends on your topic and your attention to detail.

Discipline takes effort

Some people take months to write a book; others take years; while others need only a few weeks. In theory, writing non-fiction books should take less time to write than fiction. This is because authors generally write about subjects on which they are an authority, and the book is based on fact. How long *you* take to write your book depends on your own urgency (or your publisher's deadline), your level of knowledge, and personal discipline.

However, if you want to complete your manuscript within a reasonable period of time, it's best to create a writing schedule and commit to it. A schedule gives you a sense of how many hours it will take you to write your book. It's up to you to find those hours in your calendar and block them off. Setting a goal is vital, otherwise any time you have will be wasted on procrastination.

Your schedule should also take into account time needed for other aspects of your life, such as work, family commitments, and leisure pursuits. It's all good and well to set aside the time, but you must be able to use that time to write without being interrupted or distracted. Inform others about your deadline – accountability to others is the best motivation! Stay focused and remain committed. Nothing is as rewarding or satisfying as typing the words "*The End*".

WHAT'S IN A NAME (OR TITLE)?

In order to send your book's details to publishers or agents, you will need a title for your book. At last, we can hear you say! Most writers are keen to decide on their title as soon as possible – our advice is, don't! By all means play around with ideas and bounce them off people, but leave the final decision about your book title until you have completed it. And even then, don't be completely wedded to your decision, because the publisher might make other suggestions that would make better commercial sense.

The title

The title of your book will be one of the most important marketing decisions you will have to make, along with your book's front and back cover design. The title is what will entice people to look twice at your book, particularly if you're publishing online and an attractive front cover is not immediately available. The title is the first piece of information a potential reader gets about your book. It impacts on their judgement of your book and their purchase decision.

Whether your book is fiction or non-fiction, your title must:
- Grab people's attention.
- Make an impact.
- Be easy to remember.
- Provide an idea of what your book is about.

Grabbing people's attention is pretty obvious – you need a book title that excites, entices and intrigues. You can do this by being provocative or controversial, or simply by making a promise.

Advice on creating the title for your book can be found on many good writing and publishing websites. Also visit multi-book author Scott Berkun's website[3] for some helpful pointers.

---

3   http://scottberkun.com/2012/the-truth-about-picking-book-titles

George Orwell's *1984* is proof of how a brilliant title can affect the success of a book. Orwell's original title was *The Last Man in Europe*, but his publisher thought *1984* was catchier. And how right he was! Orwell was a serial title changer: he also dropped the subtitle from his classic *Animal Farm*, which was originally going to be *Animal Farm: A Fairy Story*. There is no doubt that the change of titles influenced both sales and marketability.

An attention-grabbing book title may not necessarily be memorable. It's easy to attract attention for an instant, but it's harder to attract attention *and* be memorable. You need people to *remember* your book title so that they know what they are looking for when they decide to purchase. Play around with ideas and test them out over time. Jane Austen's novel *Pride and Prejudice* has remained a classic due, in part, to its title, and we are grateful she did not stick with her original choice of *First Impressions*. F. Scott Fitzgerald originally wanted to title his book *Among Ash-heaps and Millionaires*, but ultimately changed it to the much more succinct and memorable *The Great Gatsby*. Margaret Mitchell's first choice was *Baa, Baa Black Sheep*. Literary history thanks her for finally settling on *Gone with the Wind*.

In terms of the information a title should convey, an informative book title is not especially important for a work of fiction. However, it's essential for non-fiction. The title must indicate what the book is about, without being boring. If, on hearing your book title, people still ask what the book is about and need a lengthy explanation, your title has failed.

The subtitle

The subtitle of a non-fiction work usually serves to place the title in context and add more information about the subject matter to lure and persuade book buyers. Both title and subtitle should adopt the same style and tone. A good example is the bestselling book *The 4-Hour Work Week* by Timothy Ferris, which boasts the subtitle *Escape 9-5, Live Anywhere and Join the New Rich*. Both are catchy and promise to divulge the secret of how to escape the work-day rut, live in your version of paradise, and get rich.

Words that work well in non-fiction book titles suggest that they will reveal something new and even resolve some problems. Consider these words to start your title:
- How (to)
- Steps (to)
- Secrets (of)

KEYWORDS ARE KEY

Keywords help people find your book, so it's a good idea to include them in either your title or subtitle if your work is non-fiction.

A keyword is used in metadata as a reference point for finding other words or information. When people search for items online, they enter a specific word into the search engine to initiate the search. It stands to reason that if, for example, people are searching for a book on chemistry, their keyword will be 'chemistry'. Omitting keywords from your non-fiction book title or subtitle would be a huge mistake that could condemn your book to online obscurity.

Amazon offers these tips for choosing a keyword for your book title:

1. **Make a list of words** customers are likely to use when searching for something to read that is related to your particular topic.
2. **Test these words** by slowly typing them into the search bar, one letter at a time, and take note of the prompts that appear with the words on various search engines. Typically, you want the first word that pops up, as that is the most widely used search term.
3. **Cross-test the words at Google Keyword Planner** to see if one word or phrase is more popular than the other.

4. **If necessary, add keywords to your book's title**, since the title is most influential on search results. For non-fiction especially, your title must be related to search terms.

Use the worksheet in Appendix B on page 274 to jot down some keyword ideas for your book. Then experiment with titles using one or more of these keywords.

THE END IS NOT THE END

When you've finished writing your book, your work is not yet done. You will need to spend a significant amount of time and effort reviewing your manuscript. Revision differs from editing – a professional will carry out the latter but only you, the author, can revise what you have written to see if the content is really worth reading; it says all you wanted it to say; and whether a reader will understand what you have said.

It's useful to wait a while before revising your book, even if it's just for a few days, and then approach it with a fresh and open mind. When you reread it, resolve to be brutally honest with yourself about whether you have kept your promise to your readers.
- Will it grab and hold their attention?
- Will it identify their concerns?
- Will it resolve those concerns?
- Will it offer them something new that they've not previously considered or contemplated?

At the revision stage, you're concerned with the content and structure of your book rather than the commas and semi-colons. Some authors like to read their work out loud, which can help the revision process because it gives them an indication of how it will sound to the reader.

Next, get down to the nitty-gritty of fact checking. You are responsible for the accuracy and veracity of the content, not your editor or publisher. You might be sued or taken to court because of errors or misleading information in your book. *And don't kid yourself that no-one will challenge you – it happens, even here in South Africa!*

Don't forget to acknowledge all sources and obtain permission to use all copyrighted information that you have included in your book. You can find out more about this in Chapter 7.

Before you rush off to find a publisher, you still need to **prepare your manuscript**. A messy manuscript is a sign of a careless mind and could make publishers think twice before accepting.

Technical tips for preparing your manuscript

- Do a spelling and grammar check. You'd think this was obvious, but it's amazing how many authors don't!
- Use double-line spacing throughout and margins on both sides of your A4 pages.
- Use a legible font – 12pt Arial, Times Roman or Courier are good options.
- Make sure your pages are numbered correctly.
- Start each new chapter on a new page.
- Indicate chapter headings clearly.
- Remove extra spaces between words, sentences and paragraphs.
- Clearly mark and caption all images.
- If you're preparing your manuscript for independent publishing, refer to Chapter 9 for extra information pertinent to the independent publishing process.

Once you've done this, read your manuscript again, revising as you go along. It may be helpful to ask a few friends, family members or colleagues to read your revised manuscript and comment on the flow of the narrative, content appeal, suitability of language level, completeness of information, and so on. Beware of asking too many people for their input as this might lead to confusion and frustration. Entrust your manuscript only to those who are qualified to give an opinion and whom you trust to give constructive criticism.

MAKING IT EASIER FOR PUBLISHERS

Book publishers are busy people who are constantly inundated with hundreds of manuscripts from hopeful authors. There is no way they or their editors can possibly read through each and every submission, so you need to help make their lives, and decisions, easier. Don't send them your full manuscript and expect them to read it – they won't. Send a **covering letter** with a **book synopsis** and **three sample chapters**.

Your synopsis

A synopsis is a two- or three-page snapshot of your book. It tells the publisher about the book and highlights why it will appeal to book buyers.

Begin with a brief summary of no more than 100 words that will grab the publisher's attention – think of the sort of thing you would read in the blurb on the back cover of a book.

For **fiction**, write a section of no more than 500 words describing how your story flows and unfolds, and what is interesting or exciting about it. Describe the setting for your story, give some information on the characters pivotal to the plot, and highlight any particularly dramatic turning points.

For **non-fiction**, write a section of no more than 500 words outlining what your book will reveal; why your content will be different from other books on the same subject; and why you are the best person to write this book. Publishers of non-fiction need to see if there is a gap in the market for your particular book. It will help if you can also outline any marketing opportunities you can bring to the table.

Your covering letter

Your covering letter should be no more than one page in length, economically written and to the point. The suggested content is:

1. The first paragraph introduces you as the writer and includes your experience, previous books published, and any other relevant personal information.
2. The second paragraph briefly describes your book, why you wrote it and what is unique about it.
3. The third paragraph outlines the plot (fiction) or subject matter (non-fiction).
4. The fourth paragraph explains that you have enclosed the first three chapters as sample chapters.
5. The fifth paragraph thanks the publisher for taking the time to consider your work. Invite them to contact you for further information and include your contact details.

Although your covering letter should be brief, it should ooze confidence and energy. The aim is to excite the publisher and convince them to read your synopsis and sample chapters.

 # TIP How to find a publisher in South Africa

STEP 1	Search the Internet for publishers that specialise in your genre. The Publishing Association of South Africa (www.publishsa.co.za) features a list of South African publishers in the Members section of its website.
STEP 2	Visit the publishers' websites and follow their manuscript submission guidelines.
STEP 3	It can take up to three months for a publisher to get back to you, so you may want to send your letter and sample chapters off to a few publishers. If a publisher shows interest, you should disclose at the first meeting that you have sent the manuscript to other publishers for consideration.

TIP How to find an international publisher

Large international publishers don't accept author submissions directly, so you will need to approach a literary agent first.

STEP 1 Search the Internet for literary agents who specialise in your genre.

STEP 2 Visit their websites and follow their guidelines to the letter! Non-compliance will usually result in immediate rejection – no questions asked – with little to no further opportunity to resubmit your enquiry.

STEP 3 You will need to submit a query letter before sending your manuscript. If your query letter grabs the agent's attention, the agent will request three chapters of your book. If those three chapters interest them, they will request the entire manuscript. This can be a daunting process, so take the time to do proper research on how to write a compelling query letter. You have only one opportunity to capture their interest. In short, you need to share the title of your book and the word count; summarise your story or content; add your biography and credentials; then follow the agent's guidelines for submission.

STEP 4 Follow up politely after 10–12 weeks if you've heard nothing from them, but do **not** start harassing them. They receive hundreds of submissions every month and badgering them could end up harming rather than helping your submission. In the meantime, send your query letter off to other agents. Some agents may be good-mannered enough to respond with an answer, whereas with others, silence can be taken as a 'No'. Accept it and move on.

TIP Author support and workshops

If you're new to writing, it's helpful to know that you don't have to battle alone – there are many workshops and writing courses available to help you hone your craft and create a well-written book. There are also numerous informal writers' support groups and forums. A simple Internet search will provide some options. The Centre for the Book, which is a division of the National Library of South Africa, also co-ordinates national book-related activities, such as book discussions, poetry readings, writing workshops and conferences in an effort to promote reading and publishing of books in all of South Africa's national languages. They also offer publishing grants to deserving authors.

PROTECTING YOUR COPYRIGHT: PROVING OWNERSHIP

The act of putting your thoughts into words, whether on paper, in digital format or as a voice recording, gives you copyright of that content. There is nothing you need to do to establish that copyright. Should there ever be a dispute over copyright, you will simply need to prove that you have the earliest existing version of that work. That is all.

Electronic manuscripts

To establish earliest ownership of a manuscript that exists in electronic format, save the original manuscript to CD or memory stick and file it away safely. All electronic documents have a file date, which you can see when you display your files in a file manager like Windows Explorer. Every time you save the document, a new date is created that overwrites the existing date. For this reason, **always** save the document with a new file name *before* making changes to it so that you don't overwrite your previous versions and their file dates. In this way, you will have copies of your manuscript as it evolves, along with the corresponding file dates – ample proof of ownership of each version of your book.

Handwritten or typed manuscripts

If you have a physical copy of your manuscript, known as a hard copy, you have three options available to you:
1. **Mail it to yourself:** Place your manuscript in an envelope, seal the flap with sealing wax, then address and post the envelope to yourself. Sounds pretty crazy. But wait. When it returns, DO NOT OPEN IT! File it away safely, preferably in a fireproof safe or a safety deposit box. The post office stamp has a date on it and the fact that the envelope has not been opened proves that the contents have not been tampered with and that you have the earliest copy.

2. **Scan and save your manuscript**: Scan your manuscript using a desktop scanner and save it on to disk. If you don't have a scanner, you could use one owned by someone you know and trust. After testing that the file copied successfully, delete the scan on their computer.

   There are also many free scanning apps that you can download on to your smartphone or tablet from your device's App store that will do the job. It may prove more laborious, but it's a free and safe solution.

3. **Make a voice recording of your work**: You can do this using a voice recorder on your smartphone or on your computer using software that you can download from your App store or the Internet. Remember to copy your voice recording on to a disk and file it away safely.

Although you no longer need to use the copyright symbol © to protect your work, it's a good idea to include it on your copyright page, for example, "Copyright © 2018 Author Name. All rights reserved." If you do this, an unauthorised user cannot claim ignorance and you may be awarded a larger settlement. The year is the year of first publication, and the name can be your name, a pen name, or the names of additional copyright owners.

A sample copyright page has been provided in Appendix D on page 278.

 # TIP Before you send your manuscript off

It is highly advisable to follow the guidelines for establishing file ownership *before* you start sending your manuscript out to potential publishers and service providers!

 # TIP Cloud storage file dating

If you are storing your file on a cloud server, be sure to check that the server has not changed the date of the original file to the date of the upload. It must retain the last edited date, which may be days, weeks or months before you actually get to uploading it. Similarly, check that the file date does not change when the file is downloaded from the server on to your hard drive. Test it first by uploading, then downloading your file to see what happens; if the file date changes, this method of storage is not suitable for copyright protection. Rather keep your original file on a memory stick, hard disk or CD.

3

YOU HAVE A DEAL!

Imagine you're one of the fortunate few whose manuscript is accepted by a publisher for its wow content, topicality, expertise, killer title and sales potential. Once you've finished celebrating, you need to consider what happens next.

Regardless of whether you've opted for traditional or independent publishing, your work is not yet over and your publisher is going to expect you to assist in promoting and marketing your book. If your book is non-fiction, the publisher will ask you to provide a **foreword** and some **testimonials**. These two inclusions provide important credentials for your book to persuade people to buy it and read it.

The foreword

A book foreword is a marketing tool for the book. Ideally, it should be written by someone who knows you and is considered an authority on the subject matter of the book. The foreword introduces you as the author; explains the relationship between you and the writer of the foreword; conveys the influence you have in your specific area of expertise or field of interest; and explores the impact the book is likely to have on the reader.

Asking someone to write a foreword is quite a big ask – the person must read your manuscript and then comment intelligently on its content. Here are some guidelines that you can pass on to the person who is doing you this huge favour. The ideal foreword:

- Is no longer than three pages.
- Establishes the credentials of both the foreword writer and the author.
- Provides an appetiser that tempts readers to explore the rest of the book and prepares them for the content.
- Explains how the book has impact and why it should be read.
- Is written in an appealing way using language that is appropriate for the reader.
- Is clear, to the point and devoid of waffle!

> **# TIP Writing a foreword**
>
> The author of your foreword should understand the message of your book. Reading the contents page and one chapter alone is not enough. Taking detailed notes while reading the book will assist with the foreword content.

Testimonials

Testimonials are words of praise that have been written about your book. These are then published in the book, usually on the front and back covers, and sometimes on the first few pages.

They are endorsements from other people that will hopefully convince potential readers that your book is a good buy. Ideally, they should come from other experts in your field, clients, or if you're lucky enough to know any, celebrities. These short affirmations should focus on the value of your book and what it delivers.

Testimonials are equally important for works of fiction and non-fiction. Often they can come from other authors who appreciate your book and aren't afraid to put their appreciation into words.

As soon as you know your book is being published, start thinking about specific people you could approach for testimonials. Your publisher should be able to provide you with a sample of your book in draft form for this purpose.

> **# TIP** Sending your book off for testimonials and endorsements
> Be sure to give your potential endorsers plenty of time to respond to your request, read your book and write the testimonial. Ideally, you should give them 4–8 weeks advance notice of your preferred deadline.

THE FINISHING TOUCHES

All books include what is known as front matter and end matter. These are simply the information pages that are published at the beginning and end of your book. Here is what is typically included on those pages:

FRONT MATTER	
Half-title page	Name of the book.
Title page	Name of the book, author, illustrator and publisher.
Imprint page	Details of the publisher, edition, ISBN, copyright, professional credits, image sources.
Acknowledgements	A note of thanks to anyone who assisted with the book.
Dedication	If the book is dedicated to a particular person/people.
Preface or Introduction	Introduction to the book.
Table of contents	List of chapters with their page numbers.
Foreword	Endorsement or testimonial written by someone who knows you and is credible as an authority.

BODY	
Text	Main part of the book written by the author.
END MATTER	
Appendix	Extra information at the end of a book (if relevant), such as reference material, charts, worksheets, and maps. The appendices in this book are a good example.
Glossary	Alphabetical list of definitions and pronunciations of special or unusual words (if relevant).
Bibliography	List of sources used to glean information or generate ideas, that are not referred to directly in the book.
Index	The last pages of a non-fiction book containing an alphabetical list of subjects covered in the book, and a list of page numbers where they appear in the book.
Resources	List and accreditation of resources used when writing the book.
About the author	A short biography of the author.

The front cover of your book will be fabulously and professionally designed by your publisher and will include your killer title, subtitle, a sincere and enthusiastic testimonial and, of course, your name. The back cover will usually feature more testimonials, book reviews, a blurb, an ISBN, a barcode and a small photo of you, the author. If you have secured a publishing deal, your publisher will take care of these things for you. If you are going the independent route, you can find out how to put these little extras together as you make your way through this book.

An example of front matter has been provided in Appendix C on page 276.

WHAT IF YOU DON'T HAVE A DEAL?

No advice about book publishing is complete without mentioning the word all authors dread hearing – rejection. We all have to deal with rejection at some point in our lives, whether it's from a parent, a lover, a colleague, and yes, maybe even a publisher. As we said at the beginning of this book, publishing is a business that operates along traditional commercial lines with profit as the guiding light and decision-maker. Publishers need to make money from your book and will opt for books with content that *they* believe will sell, which does not always equate to content that is excellent.

You can try to pre-empt rejection by refining your research in the first place and submitting your manuscript only to publishers you know might be interested. There is no point in submitting your sci-fi novel or book about plumbing to a publisher that produces only children's books. It also helps to send your manuscript to a specific person and to follow the submission guidelines precisely. It is well worth investing time and effort to write a winning synopsis and introductory letter.

Nothing in this world is guaranteed, particularly in book publishing. If you find yourself on the receiving end of a rejection letter, try to take a constructive approach.

- Accept and understand it. It's hard to get published and there are myriad reasons for rejection, many of them external.
- Learn from it. It may be that your manuscript was considered unsuitable or simply not good enough. Try to find out the reason for the rejection.
- Bounce back from it. Accept feedback, move on and improve. Adjust your manuscript, revise it, rewrite it, do whatever it takes to get your book published.

Remind yourself that even if your book has been rejected, you have been brave enough to take action, unlike thousands of other would-be authors whose manuscripts languish in computer storage or locked drawers because they don't have the courage to send them out into the world.

Think of those who tried and failed but carried on trying. The first of J.K. Rowling's *Harry Potter* books was rejected by 12 publishers before finally being accepted. Agatha Christie endured five years of publishing rejection before someone acknowledged her skill. Jack Canfield and Mark Victor Hansen, authors of the *Chicken Soup for the Soul* series, received 140 rejections before being published. Don't give up.

SECTION 2

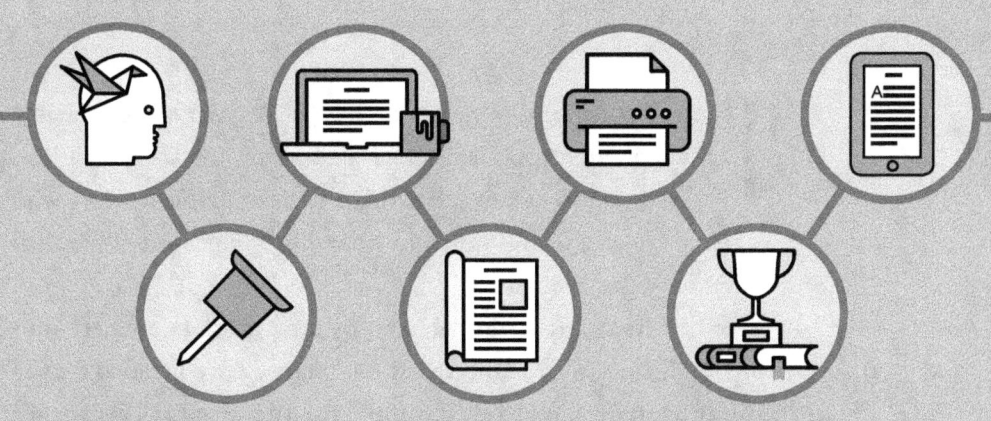

GOING THE INDEPENDENT ROUTE

TYPES OF INDEPENDENT PUBLISHING

If you've done any online research, you'll have noticed a variety of independent publishing services vying for your business. Trying to figure out exactly what these companies offer – who is reputable and who is not, and what you will get out of the deal – can be somewhat tricky.

The Internet has significantly lowered barriers of entry into the publishing sector, and many companies have jumped on the bandwagon. Some are in it simply for the money. This makes it difficult to distinguish between biased guidance based on the company's desire to make money from you, and unbiased advice based on the financial viability of publishing and the probability of success in the market.

As in all business sectors, there are good guys and bad guys. Unlike traditional publishers who make money from sales and carefully vet a manuscript before making an investment, companies that help authors self-publish their own books make the bulk of their money from the services they provide. Their business does not rely on your book sales to survive, so the quality of your manuscript and whether your book has the potential to sell is of little interest to them. Many of them also sell expensive marketing packages along with their publishing packages. Unless you have a solid product with good sales potential from the outset, you will simply be throwing good money after bad.

While authors are rarely able to do a good job of publishing independently without the help of service providers, the challenge is to find a company that will provide honest feedback and publishing advice up front, even if it means potentially losing the work because they believe the small fortune needed to whip the book into shape is unlikely to be recovered.

While money can buy almost anything – including top-notch editorial and design services to create a product on par with those produced by traditional publishing houses – book publishing remains governed by economics. So the question begs: will you sell enough books to recoup your investment? Authors frequently overestimate their potential sales and underestimate the costs of production, marketing and distribution.

If cost is no issue and you're willing to pay whatever it takes to publish your book, even if you don't make a cent back, then you may be less concerned about the service provider with whom you partner.

Most authors, however, fall into a third group: you want a professional product, but you also need to recover your investment and, if possible, make a profit. If you are such an author, finding the right service provider is essential to your success. So it's really important to know exactly what kind of company you're dealing with and the *real* price of the various publishing options available to you.

INDEPENDENT PUBLISHING MODELS

Despite the many descriptors for a company that offers publishing services – author services company; publisher; custom publisher; independent publisher; self-publishing service; vanity press – when you peel away the layers and drill down, there are essentially four basic independent publishing models. They are:
- Custom publishing
- Vanity publishing
- Self-publishing/print-on-demand publishing
- Subsidy or partnership publishing

The difference between these models lies in the quality of the books they produce, and whether there is a screening process prior to publishing.

Custom publishing

As the name implies, custom publishing services are highly customised and tailored to the needs of each book and client. Here, the author secures the assistance of a publishing team, usually represented by a company, to help publish the book. The members of the team are appropriately qualified in their particular field and usually have experience in a traditional publishing environment. These members specialise in different aspects of publishing; from manuscript evaluation, editing and translation, through to design, illustration, image and permissions sourcing, printing and ebook conversion. The range of services offered differs markedly from one custom publishing company to the next. Some may offer a full one-stop solution, while others offer selected services only. Also, many custom publishers don't offer sales, marketing or distribution themselves, but they usually have established partnerships with third parties who can provide these important services.

A respectable custom publishing company is often just as selective as a traditional publisher in terms of what they publish.

The company's imprint will appear on the spine of the book and it will be judged accordingly. A good custom publisher will publish books that they feel have market potential, and will help authors develop their books to the required standard. Its books will be of high editorial, production and print quality, and content will be intelligent, readable and consistent.

With this model, the author pays the full professional price for the services. In return, they own the product in its entirety and enjoy all profits from its sale. There are often no contracts and no author obligations. The author usually owns the final print-ready files, however, this detail should be clarified up front before any work begins. Non-ownership will have financial repercussions down the line should the author choose to reprint or publish elsewhere.

With this option, the author can also choose to publish under his or her own brand or company name instead of the service provider's imprint.

Custom publishing companies will usually quote on a job-by-job basis, based on the author's requirements, the type of book being published, and the size of the print run.

The author has full flexibility when it comes to production, printing, print finishing and binding, making this the best – and usually only – option for specialised or customised publishing projects. The author also has full control over distribution outlets, publishing rights and merchandising. This service is also better suited to larger print runs of a few hundred to a few thousand books. Some custom publishers can also assist authors with add-on products, such as game boards, card decks, CDs, packaging, and promotional materials.

Custom publishing is usually more expensive at the outset than package-deal options owing to the higher-quality production services. However, the printing cost per unit is usually lower because of the higher print volumes. This is the most suitable option for bookstore distribution. It is also the most cost-effective option over the longer term if large quantities of books are printed and sold, or there are repeat print runs.

Custom publishing is particularly suited to non-fiction books. It is also best suited to authors or businesses that require a professional, hands-on service accompanied by expert advice. Typical authors include workshop facilitators; motivational speakers; companies producing commemorative or business books for clients; public personalities; trainers and educators; academics; corporate coaches; authors with a large social media following; lodges and hotels producing souvenir books; chefs; and entrepreneurial authors.

How it works

1. **Evaluation**: Most good custom publishers will evaluate your manuscript to determine the quality of the content and writing, as well as its viability in the marketplace. If the book has potential, they will draw up a publishing budget. If not, they may refer you to an editor or editorial coach to help you improve your manuscript for publishing.
2. **Editing and production**: When you have made the necessary corrections and your manuscript is deemed ready for publishing, it enters production. Production includes everything from editing and design through to the delivery of an ebook and final printed product. Most custom publishing companies will make the book available for sale through online retailers, but if they can't, they will usually refer you to someone else who can. Some companies will help you get your book into local bookstores and libraries. They may also help you with your website development, social media campaign, and marketing material.
3. **Ownership**: You would typically own the print-ready files produced for the cover and book inner. You can distribute your books as you see fit, or warehouse them with a national book distributor. You can also republish in other countries, sell publishing rights to local and foreign publishers, and reprint your book using another service provider.

4. **Earnings**: You keep all the profits from the sale of your books. For sales made directly to your customers, you earn the equivalent of the retail price less your publishing costs. For sales made through bookstores, you earn approximately 30% of the retail price. If you sell publishing rights abroad, you keep the full advance plus all royalties generated from sales.

> **# TIP** Investigating potential custom publishing companies
>
> When looking for a publishing partner, review samples of books they've worked on and speak to some of their clients about their experiences with the company. Also ensure that key team members have had experience in a traditional publishing environment, as this will ensure a professional product that meets traditional publishing standards. Be mindful of authors who start publishing businesses to help other authors. While they may be sympathetic to your struggle and have your best interests at heart, many do not have the required editorial, production and printing expertise. Remember, these are specialised skills that should be performed by suitably qualified people.

BEWARE: Some custom publishing companies may retain the rights to the final print-ready files, allowing you to have full rights only to the original manuscript. You must ensure that all rights to the final files revert to you since you have paid the full production cost, known as work-for-hire. This won't be applicable if the publisher has subsidised production, in which case you may also be bound to them by some kind of contract.

Also, not all custom publishing companies will act with the author's best interests in mind. Some of them are more concerned about selling their services than about whether the book will sell well enough for the author to recoup their costs. These companies usually don't assess the manuscript beforehand or conduct a proper consultation with the author before taking on the project and accepting the author's money. If this is the case, the company could be considered a 'vanity publisher'.

> **ⓘ DID YOU KNOW?**
>
> Custom publishers are sometimes referred to as independent publishers; however, all non-traditional publishing models in which the author invests in their own production and printing are independent publishing solutions, also known as self-publishing.

Vanity publishing

Vanity publishers provide an attractive option to authors who are desperate to see their work in print. There are many companies who are willing to indulge your vanity as an author – at a price!

Almost without exception, the conditions for being published have absolutely nothing to do with the content or quality of the manuscript. Vanity publishers will publish *anything* – even a badly written book – as long as they can make money selling their services to you. So while custom publishers will usually have the author's target market and potential sales in mind, the vanity publisher's market is *you, the author* – how much you can pay for the publishing process and how many copies you can buy from the vanity publisher to sell to your customers.

Vanity publishers usually offer publishing packages with relatively low entry-levels costs, which forms part of their appeal. However, their package pricing assumes that the manuscript has *already* undergone a full editorial process and is polished and ready to publish.

Pricing is usually tiered, with entry-level costs as low as US$399, and the more expensive packages reaching US$5999, or more. The lower-cost packages carry minimal risk to authors who have a limited budget but require some help with their cover design and layout. Vanity publishers may be considered good value for money, provided the author has a well-written manuscript that has already been professionally edited and proofread. However, the more expensive packages at the top end of the vanity press market don't necessarily provide the same value for money, and authors would be better advised to consider a reputable custom publishing solution instead. It may work out to be the same price, or less, and you retain full ownership of all your files and enjoy cheaper printing costs over the longer term. You're also likely to end up with a better quality product.

Vanity publishers can become alarmingly expensive for additional services, such as editing, indexing and editorial author assistance. A vanity publisher will offer a whole range of services to help you get a weak and poorly-written book into better shape. A few will even rewrite the text and research content for you – but more often than not the investment you make cannot be recovered. They don't tell you this. If a book needs that much work, a traditional publisher, by comparison, will simply send a rejection letter to the author. A good custom publishing company will also likely express their reservations about the viability of such a book. It's not that books cannot be rescued – all books can be whipped into shape if the author has the money – it's just not economically viable to do so.

On the plus side of the vanity publishing fence, the publishing process is made easy for the author. There is almost nothing for the author to do except cough up the moola, hand over the manuscript, approve the proofs, and promote the books. It's a fast and easy model, with international distribution included in the deal.

Unfortunately, publishing abroad is an unsuitable option for local bookstore distribution. Some overseas vanity publishers offer bookstore representation as part of their service, but this normally involves displaying your book in bookstores on a shelf or stand dedicated to that particular publisher. The obvious disadvantage is that your book is featured alongside other books from that publisher that may be of poor quality, even if yours isn't. "You are known by the company you keep" is sadly true in this instance, as most vanity publishers have a dubious reputation in the book trade due to their lack of quality control.

Some vanity publishing companies offer marketing services. These are often very expensive and there is little proof that the sales warrant the investment. Without a good, solid product, you will be wasting your money. If you're thinking about signing up for one of their pricey marketing packages, you'd be well-advised to get an objective, third-party evaluation of your book or ebook to see if it's worth the spend. If your book gets the green light, do some online research to find out how other authors have benefited from the company's marketing services. Ideally, you want sales figures. If you're not impressed, you have the option of sourcing your own publicist or social media expert.

Finally, if establishing yourself as a serious author or respected expert in your field is paramount to you, and you rely heavily on media reviews for promotion and recognition, then overcoming the vanity publishing stigma may prove difficult and counterproductive, and this option should be pursued with caution.

How it works

1. **Production and publishing**: The author chooses and pays for a publishing package, hands over their manuscript, and the company starts production. The most basic package will include cover design, interior formatting, ISBN assignment, barcode generation, and possibly a sample book or two. It will also include distribution through online stores, including Amazon. The more expensive packages offer add-ons, such as editing, author copies, a hardcover edition, a press release, an advert in a local publication, a social media plan, and so on. Once the proofs have been approved by the author, the company forwards the book information to various retailers and distributors for inclusion in their catalogues and on their websites.

2. **Order fulfilment**: Orders placed via the company's bookstore and other retail channels are sent to the printer, and books are printed and shipped to the purchaser. The company sometimes establishes relationships with printers and distributors in other countries; orders originating in those countries are then forwarded to the printers there for fulfilment to reduce delivery times and costs. Authors can

purchase copies in bulk at a discounted price for their own direct-to-customer sales; however, international shipping costs need to be considered.
3. **Earnings**: The author receives a percentage of each sale after printing and retail discounts have been deducted.

BEWARE: Although these companies say that you retain the copyright to your work and that you can republish your book anywhere you choose, they fail to mention that the copyright pertains only to your original manuscript. This means that if you want to print or republish your book elsewhere, you will have to start the production process all over again. Reprinting elsewhere using formatted book files received from the vanity publisher is not permitted.

Self-publishing/print-on-demand

Although the term self-publishing is usually used to describe the process of publishing independently, we are using it here in the context of someone who is preparing their own manuscript and taking that manuscript to a printer, or using a print-on-demand (POD) service. It also refers to authors who manage the entire publishing process themselves and subcontract individual service providers, such as editors, designers and printers.

Managing the process yourself and taking your files to your local printer is probably the least desirable way of publishing independently. Authors – usually with no experience in publishing, editing or design – either try to perform these specialised functions themselves, or they subcontract professionals without knowing how to assess the contractors' competencies and whether they're getting a professional job. Authors rely entirely on what the contractors say they can do. Unfortunately, not all editing is good editing, just as not all doctors are good doctors.

The self-publishing author also lacks insight into the technicalities of production and printing: from choosing the book size, paper type and binding method most appropriate for their genre, to optimum page counts for the best pricing and binding method chosen; binding methods bookstores will and won't accept; how to structure a book for economical full-colour printing, and so on. This is just the tip of the production and printing iceberg and a few of the myriad decisions that need to be made in a publishing and production workflow.

Ironically, authors usually choose this route to save money, but the learning curve can be very steep and expensive if they don't know what they're doing.

Print-on-demand services have made it easy and cheap for authors to self-publish, reducing almost all of the risk involved when it comes to printing. In other words, badly written and produced books need no longer result in thousands of copies lying in a garage somewhere gathering dust. Difficult decision-making is also eliminated because most print-on-demand platforms have highly simplified production processes offering very limited paper and finishing options.

Print-on-demand platforms provide an online, guided publishing process that the author follows to set up the book for printing. The author can choose a book interior layout and cover design template. The author then chooses paper and cover finishing options, adds the book content, sets the price and distribution options, and even assigns an ISBN. In other words, the author sets up their own book, which can then be printed on demand as and when orders are received. They can also turn their print edition into an ebook, or upload an MS Word document for ebook conversion, at the click of a button.

Print-on-demand is an attractive option for many authors because set-up and publishing are usually free. Print-on-demand companies make their money by charging a printing fee per book. If they have an online store, they retain a percentage of the list price on copies sold. If they distribute to other retailers, they retain a percentage of the retailers' sales, too. They also sell bulk copies to authors at a discounted price, earning a percentage of the manufacturing cost on each copy sold. Some print-on-demand companies also make money cross-selling other products and services, such as marketing and publicity plans, cover design, book interior formatting, and professional ebook conversion, to name a few.

International print-on-demand services are an excellent option if you've published your book locally and want to make it available to customers abroad. It takes care of your international distribution requirements quickly and easily.

It's probably true to say that most authors choosing the self-publishing or print-on-demand route are either budget-strapped or too afraid to invest money in their books. If it's the latter, perhaps they don't have enough faith in their writing or their book's potential to sell. Or they could simply be risk-averse.

Whatever their reasons, we don't endorse this type of publishing if certain basics are not in place, such as solid content, good writing *and* professional editing, because it erodes the credibility of the independent publishing industry. It also makes it difficult for talented authors – those who have invested years honing their skills – to overcome book buyers' reservations toward self-published books. It's bad for the industry. And book buyers are being ripped off by paying the same price for a book produced by an author who has invested nothing in production, as they do for a book produced by an author who has invested tens of thousands of Rand to create a quality product. It's just not fair.

Having said this, we've been in the business long enough to know that authors with no money will continue to publish this way, so we've provided suggestions on how to improve the quality of your book when preparing your manuscript for printing, or when using a print-on-demand or ebook platform.

Amongst the plethora of low-quality, self-published books, there are some real gems whose authors are talented or visionaries – or both – that *should* see the light of day and not be held back by budget constraints.

How it works

1. **Account set-up**: Authors register an account on the company's online platform. They then upload their book files using a guided process and complete all the necessary book information. Authors manage their titles and track their book sales and earnings from their account portal.
2. **Printing and shipping**: Book information is forwarded from the print-on-demand service to various online retailers. When a book is purchased, the retailer forwards the order to the print-on-demand service, who then prints and ships the book to the customer. Print-on-demand books are printed only as and when they are purchased. If the book is an ebook, the retailer provides the customer with a download link or the book is push-delivered to the customer's e-reading device. Authors can also print books in bulk at a discounted price for their own direct-to-customer sales.
3. **Author payment**: The print-on-demand service generates a sales statement at the end of each sales period. The author's royalty is the amount remaining after printing costs and bookstore discounts have been deducted from the selling price.

> **# TIP** Consider where your print-on-demand company is based
>
> It becomes very expensive for South African authors to order books in bulk due to the high shipping costs, since most print-on-demand services are based abroad. Print-on-demand publishing is therefore **not** suited to local bookstore distribution in South Africa because printing and shipping costs will exceed what the author earns from bookstore sales.

BEWARE: Some print-on-demand companies offer templates to help you prepare your book inner and cover for printing. If you don't have the time or you would like a more polished-looking book, you can use the professional services offered by these companies and their affiliates. However, these services may end up costing more than those offered by service providers closer to home due to the currency exchange rate. Production time is billed in USD and every change over and above what was originally quoted is billed to the author. These changes can mount up very quickly, resulting in a hefty bill, despite the 'affordable' original quote. Unless the book is solid and has been well edited, designed and formatted, this form of publishing rarely makes the grade for positive media reviews and bookstore interest.

Publishing rights: You retain the rights to republish your book elsewhere using your original files – you are not bound to the print-on-demand service.

If you have uploaded your own PDF files, you can republish elsewhere using those files.

Subsidy or partnership publishing

There is one final form of publishing out there, and that is subsidy or partnership publishing. This is a hybrid of traditional publishing and independent publishing: the author and a publishing house enter into an agreement to jointly finance and share the profits of a book.

This form of publishing allows the publishing company to print more titles and produce books with less financial risk. In most cases, the partnership publisher also retains copyright of the printed work.

It goes without saying that securing a partnership publishing deal can be difficult because the publisher needs to be convinced that the book will sell and that they will make a return on their investment. They will evaluate your manuscript to determine its sales potential in the market. Some partnership publishers specialise in certain genres, such as medical or academic publishing, and their marketing and distribution are targeted at those markets. It would be wise, therefore, to research partnership publishers who specialise in your genre so that they can leverage their existing networks and, in so doing, maximise your book's success.

Partnership publishing implies that both parties bring something to the table. The partnership publisher will usually provide production input, such as cover design and typesetting, as well as distribution, marketing and sales support. The author is normally responsible for covering the costs of artwork, editing and, very often, printing. Other partnership publishers are willing to fund all the production, but require the author to commit to buy a certain number of copies. The partnership model is based on the ideal that each party brings an equal, or close-to-equal, share to the project. However, the contributions required differ from company to company.

This is an attractive model for many authors, because a publisher who invests in a book and shares the financial risk is more likely to put in the time and effort to make the book a success, and will not publish just any manuscript.

In South Africa, the only option for subsidy publishing at present is through mainstream traditional publishers, which means that your manuscript will undergo the usual manuscript submission process. When making your submission, you should state your willingness to invest in the production of your book and submit a very basic business plan that includes how you intend to drive sales. The more you can bring to the table, the better: you are submitting a proposal to a potential business partner! Cookery books and full-colour coffee-table books are popular candidates for subsidy publishing.

How it works

1. **Assessment**: Your manuscript is assessed to determine if it's a viable book. Well-known or respected authors, or authors with easy and direct access to their target market that are willing to put time into marketing their books, will stand a better chance of being accepted for a partnership publishing deal. If your project has been given the green light, you will receive a proposal detailing your required investment, and what you will make on sales.

2. **Production and distribution**: If you agree to the deal, production will begin. Once completed, the publisher sets up distribution and starts marketing the book.
3. **Author royalties**: What you earn depends on the company model and how much you invested. You will usually receive a percentage of the net profit after all distribution and bookstore discounts have been deducted. You will have the opportunity to buy books from the publisher at a deeply discounted price so that you can earn a profit on sales you make directly to your customers.

Publishing rights: Because the partnership publisher is investing in your book, there may be certain limitations in terms of your publishing rights. You will most likely have to sign a contract with them granting them rights for a specific period of time. For this reason, it's vital that you research your options well and are completely happy with the publisher with whom you form the partnership, as well as the terms of your agreement with them.

BEWARE: When choosing a subsidy publisher overseas, it would be wise to research the company first. What do other authors say about them? How easy are they to get hold of? Do they have a good track record? Do they deliver on their promises? How big is the business? And *are they good at paying author royalties?*

While no business is immune to tough times, smaller businesses are more vulnerable as they often lack the financial backing to pull them through. If your overseas company doesn't pay as promised, it's not practical to pitch up at their offices and refuse to leave until you have answers. You will have to either kiss the money goodbye or engage in costly legal action.

Larger publishers have proper systems in place and adhere to audited accounting processes, making them more accountable.

In South Africa, payment is less of an issue because subsidy publishers tend to be well-known traditional publishers.

DECISION TIME

Print-on-demand or self-publishing may be a way to dip your toes in the water, but be aware of quality issues that could limit the credibility and selling potential of your book. If you go this route, you must, at the very least, have your manuscript evaluated and professionally edited. You should also engage the services of a book cover designer, or purchase a professional, pre-designed book cover.

> Find out more about pre-designed book covers on page 138.

Vanity publishing is a middle-of-the-road option – somewhere between self-publishing and custom publishing. If your publisher is overseas, printing and shipping costs usually end up being too high for bookstore distribution or book sales through third parties. If you decide to go this route, you'd be well advised to find a vanity publisher closer to home where you can save on bulk book delivery. Some South African vanity publishers may be able to help you with bookstore distribution, but stores will only be interested if the quality of your book is good enough. You should also consider manuscript evaluation and professional editing before you start the publishing process to ensure a higher-quality product.

Subsidy publishing is still a bit of an unknown entity in South Africa, so deals may be difficult to secure. Such publishers are highly unlikely to part-finance a book unless it has the potential to be a bestseller or, at the very least, do very well. Approaching a traditional publisher and offering to part-finance the book may elicit some interest – particularly if you've published other successful books, or you have a good product backed by a solid marketing and business plan that includes you driving a fair number of sales. There are quite a few subsidy publishers overseas, and if you are looking for a strong international footprint for your book in a niche market, approaching one of them could be a good option.

Custom publishing is the way to go if you want to be in control of your own publishing venture and income, and your aim is to publish a book that reads well, looks good, elicits media interest, boosts your brand, and is well-suited to bookstore distribution. It's often the only suitable option for projects requiring large print runs or different printing and finishing options. However, this type of publishing is not suited to all authors or projects as the financial risk is higher. If your book is not adequately promoted, it may take a long time for you to recoup your costs.

CHOOSING YOUR SERVICE PROVIDER

As with all ventures, it pays to do your research before choosing the publisher with whom you would like to work.. They are not all the same, and you could still end up paying a lot of money for an inferior product that has no market appeal or potential.

Many mass-market publishing services use cheap resources to make publishing more affordable for authors. For instance, English editing is frequently done by editors in foreign-language countries, such as India. It's unlikely that an editor for whom English is a second language, living in a country in which English is not commonly spoken, is going to understand the nuances, subtleties and unique expressions of the English language. This holds true for any language. These so-called editing services usually correct grammar, spelling and punctuation only. The editors don't engage with your content, remove ambiguities, tighten the narrative, liaise with you to fix structural and characterisation issues, check logic and flow, or make editorial recommendations. Your book is, and remains part of, one long sausage factory in which production follows a cookie-cutter formula designed to push your book through the system as quickly and cost-effectively as possible.

This is not to say that you shouldn't use the cheaper, mass-market publishing services. Some offer a very affordable entry into the book market and are a good choice for certain authors and books. But you should be aware that editorial quality is likely to suffer unless you invest heavily in your editing beforehand.

These companies also create the perception that if you publish with them, your book will be made available to millions of people around the world through their global distribution platform of tens of thousands of retailers. By implication, you stand to make soaring sales with that kind of exposure. If only it worked that way!

However, with low financial investment, there is also low risk, making it a safe way to test the market. It's also a great way to help you grow and fine-tune your skills as an author.

At the other end of the spectrum, there are publishing services that will offer you the publishing advice you need and ensure that your book meets the stringent quality standards of the book trade and the media. Their services are professionally priced, but you're more likely to end up with a product that you feel confident promoting and that the media is willing to review. Remember, though, that *expensive* does not always equate to *quality*. You don't want to spend money unnecessarily or overpay for services. So within this echelon, further research is needed to ensure that the publishing company you have set your sights on can truly deliver a quality product.

Tips to help you with your research

- Look at books the publisher has already produced and evaluate their quality.
- Does your book fit in with the publisher's chosen genres?
- Is the company website professional and functional? Is the content well-written and edited? Any company offering editing services should reflect the quality of those services on their own website.
- Does the company have an online store through which you can sell your book, or can they offer you such a platform?
- Check their track record, asking for references if necessary.

- Speak to other authors about their experiences with the company. Does the company offer good customer support and deliver on their promises? You need easy access to your publishing team and timeous responses to your emails.
- Does the publisher have established links with partners in the supply chain, such as distributors or retailers?
- If you're considering an overseas provider, factor in the time difference and customer service hours. Do these customer service hours work for you?
- Consider the shipping costs if you plan to order books in bulk. Expensive shipping costs can make publishing overseas non-viable.
- When comparing quotes from different service providers, be sure to include all the important publishing functions in your comparison. We have provided templates in Appendix F on page 280 and Appendix G on page 282 to help you with this so that no expenses are overlooked.

CONSULTATION IS KEY

If you're serious about the quality of your book, find a publishing company that conducts an initial consultation and some kind of manuscript evaluation or project assessment. No valid publishing venture can begin without a basic assessment of your book and its potential in the market. You should also be advised of the process and what will be required of you, the author, to make your project a success. This is responsible publishing.

The consultation

Prior to the consultation, you may be asked to provide a brief synopsis of your book, details of your intended target market, and what you can bring to the publishing table.

With your agreement, and for a small fee, the publisher will arrange a consultation during which you will be able to discuss your book in more detail. This no-obligation process is designed to investigate the publishing viability of your book. It will encompass the following aspects of publishing:

- Your target market and its potential buying power.
- What differentiates your book from others of its kind.
- Where you see the book being sold.
- How you see the book being marketed.
- The work that remains to be done on your book.
- Book and cover design.
- Print quantity and printing options.
- Estimated production costs.
- Ebook potential.
- Marketing and promotion.
- Sales and distribution.

This consultation is well worth the investment because it provides a valuable opportunity to brainstorm your publishing options, evaluate your book's potential sales appeal, and identify areas in which your book may still need work.

It also affords you the opportunity to get a feel for the people with whom you may be working. If red lights flash, you can address your concerns or walk away. Remember, they aren't the only service providers in town, so don't be afraid to shop around.

Finally, to get the most from your consultation, it's best to go prepared. Have the necessary information to hand, write down a list of your questions, and know something about the publishing terms and processes involved so that you don't get lost in a maze of jargon. Use the information in this book to become an active participant in the future of your book!

The manuscript evaluation

After the consultation, the publisher will ask one of its expert editorial team members to perform a manuscript evaluation. The evaluation, which is carried out for a fee, is a vital step in the publishing process as it provides invaluable input into what you have written. It can also be given to your editor to help guide the editing process. The evaluation should also guide the price set for the edit, as it will determine the depth of intervention needed on the manuscript.

Your manuscript is professionally assessed from the viewpoint of both a publisher and a reader. Depending on the length and complexity of the manuscript, you can expect a five to ten-page report that focuses on the following key areas:

1. A synopsis of the strengths and weaknesses of the manuscript.
2. A general readability assessment of the manuscript, focusing on language, grammar and tone, using examples from your text to illustrate points.
3. Commentary on narrative outline, word choices and sentence structure.
4. An assessment of ambiguity and contradictions.
5. An overall assessment of structure – how your book fits together, with examples and questions highlighted for the author.
6. A characterisation assessment (if applicable).
7. An assessment of suitability for the target audience, highlighting strengths and areas for improvement.
8. General comments and input. This includes an assessment of the current state and readiness of the manuscript to proceed to publication, and its viability in the marketplace when the recommended work has been completed.

If a rough publishing cost has already been provided, it will be adjusted to accommodate the recommendations of the evaluation and any additional work that may be needed.

> View the list of services that should be included in your cost estimate on page 22.

The publishing budget

> Refer to pages 173 and 174 for an example of how to calculate the page count using your word count.

If both parties agree to move forward, the publisher will draw up a formal cost estimate, or publishing budget, for your book. This will be based on the final expected number of words and pages, book format, print options, and so on. Your publishing service may also provide an estimate of how many books you will have to sell in order to cover your production and printing costs.

The publishing budget will change if the final page count or job specifications change. Page counts are based on the word count of the manuscript. The average novel fits 320–350 words per page, and the average non-fiction book fits about 300–320 words per page. Of course, this will change depending on the size and type of book, as well as the interior design.

> Find out more about budgeting and costing in Chapter 15.

The higher the page or word count of the manuscript, the more it's going to cost to publish. You can use the publishing budget templates in Appendices F and G on pages 280 and 282, respectively, to work out your publishing budget. It may be easier to do this once you've read through the book and have a better understanding of the different processes involved.

How to request a quotation

Vanity publishing costs can be easily obtained online by browsing the websites of vanity publishers. Custom publishers, on the other hand, rarely offer package pricing, as their services are tailored around the specific requirements of your book. They may have standard forms online for you to complete, or you may make initial contact via email. If you send them an email, be sure to include the following information:

- **Book title**: This can be a working title if not yet finalised.
- **Number of words**: You can provide an estimated word count if your manuscript is not complete. The word count is used for the editorial quote and to calculate the estimated number of pages – known as the extent – of the formatted book. The extent is used to calculate your production and printing costs.

- **Representative sample chapters**: These are used to assess the editorial work required and the formatting costs. Send at least three chapters.
- **A synopsis of your book**: This gives the publisher an idea of the genre and basic storyline, and will help guide the costing for editing and design.
- **The intended target market for your book**: The editor will assess this in terms of the work required to make the book fully accessible to your intended target market; the designer will use it to guide the cover and book inner design.
- **Your intended distribution methods**: This will help the publisher advise on suitable print quantities and production processes, which in turn will affect the publishing cost.

Find out more about the publishing process in Chapter 5.

The custom publishing company will firm up your publishing budget once they've received final copy from you, confirmed your word count, and assessed exactly what they will be working with. Once you and your publisher have come to an agreement regarding cost, payment terms, and the services you'll be using – and your deposit has been paid – the publishing process will begin.

ⓘ DID YOU KNOW?

A custom publishing quotation can take a few days to complete as pricing is obtained from various departments and service providers. Once the preliminary pricing is in, your consultant will assimilate everything and prepare a final costing and publishing proposal. This can take many hours, so do be cognisant of this when requesting your quote. Only request a quote if you are genuinely interested and ready to move ahead. If you are simply shopping around for pricing to get a feel for the market and to see whether custom publishing is financially viable, mention this to the service provider. They should be able to provide you with a rough estimate of the investment required without having to go to enormous effort.

> **# TIP Before you begin: self-publishing payment terms and admin basics**
>
> Familiarise yourself with your publishing service's payment terms to ensure that you have the funds ready as and when required. Different companies have different payment policies. Some require a 50% deposit before work begins, the balance being due on completion, after your account has been reconciled. Others may ask for full payment up front. Always request invoices for everything you pay as they are needed for tax purposes. Also keep the receipts of all project-related expenses, including stationery, paper, project-related travel (a log book is required), computer expenses, photocopy charges, and even the coffee you drink while writing and reviewing your book! When your book starts making money, you will be taxed on your profits. Your profit is what's left over after all expenses have been deducted. Your invoices and receipts are proof of these expenses.

Your preliminary research is now complete and you should be able to tick off the items in this list:

- ☐ You have found a suitable publishing partner.
- ☐ You have consulted with your publishing partner to discuss your project and the way forward.
- ☐ Your manuscript has been evaluated and is now ready for production.
- ☐ You have worked out your publishing budget and have the money available to fund your project.
- ☐ You have determined that your project is financially viable – what you spend can be recovered from projected sales at a price that book buyers are willing to pay.

It's now time to look at some of the ins-and-outs of independent publishing and whether you're cut out for the road ahead.

OPPORTUNITIES, CHALLENGES AND PITFALLS

With traditional publishing, you, the author, tend to take a bit of a backseat. Not that you are unimportant – of course you are, you are the creator of the work, after all. But once the traditional publishing machine gets into gear and the production line starts rolling, you may find yourself becoming a bystander and while your publisher makes all the decisions.

Independent publishing is very different as you are *expected* to become actively involved in many aspects of the publishing process.

Before you even think of publishing independently, ask yourself the following questions:
- Am I willing to work hard?
- Am I willing to put in the time and effort required to make my book a success?
- Do I like being involved in the nitty-gritty?
- Am I able to accept and act on constructive criticism? Publishing is a collaborative and negotiable process.

- Am I willing to work with others? Producing good books requires team work, not one-man-bands operating in an uncoordinated fashion.
- Do I have existing sales channels or networks?
- Can I market and promote my book?
- Can I afford to carry the publishing costs until my book starts turning a profit?

Although a good independent publisher will assist you through the process from start to finish, the success of your book ultimately begins and ends with you.

Good candidates for independent publishing

We now know that independent publishing is easier for authors who already have a network to which they can sell books directly, bypassing third-party sales outlets and recovering costs quite quickly. This is why independent publishing is particularly suited to non-fiction. For example, authors who are considered an authority on a particular subject, and who regularly conduct workshops in their area of expertise, have a captive audience to whom books can be sold. Obviously, it helps if you are already a proactive marketer well-versed in brand YOU. Your book will simply become an extension of your brand, helping to meet the needs of your target audience.

Companies that produce books on subjects related to their particular market niche are also ideal candidates for independent publishing. Imagine a bank publishing a book about money management, or a firm of lawyers producing a book about the legal rights of consumers. Such companies have an existing client base to whom their books can be marketed and sold. They might also have a network of business partners who are interested in the topic. Swift financial recovery and profits are practically guaranteed.

What's particularly attractive about independent publishing is that the author can set the retail price of the book without having to discount to their clients – any discounts offered can be at the author's discretion. Depending on the project – and assuming the book is professionally produced – most authors can recoup their financial outlay by selling 250–350 books directly to clients. *However, the sale of these books is dependent on the effort the author is willing and able to invest.*

If you don't have an existing pool of potential customers upon which you can expand, then the sales process of your book will be slower and more difficult, particularly if your subject matter is niche. At the very least, you need to be a competent self-marketer.

On the upside, independently published books, even those of a specialist nature, can often have a longer life span than traditionally published books because authors tend to promote and sell their books long after publishers have abandoned them to move on to the next title.

DO YOU HAVE WHAT IT TAKES?

The commercial sales chain remains influenced by traditional book publishers who are able to use their business muscle to get their books in-store. It's not geared to the author who chooses to publish independently. If you succeed in getting your books into retail outlets, the quantity taken will still be small and the sell-through minimal. Unless your book sells well and consistently, securing repeat orders from bookstores is difficult. Therefore, you'll need a fair amount of marketing, publicity, and persistence to keep the orders rolling in. This tells us that if you choose the independent option and you want your book to be successful, **most of your sales will have to be generated through your own efforts.**

As with all ventures, independent publishing carries financial risk in terms of production and printing costs. South Africa has a small book market when compared to the rest of the world, so your profits are not going to make you rich. However, all things considered, the risk is small compared to many other investments. You can easily recover your costs if you are *prepared to do the work*. If you get it right – if you choose a good publishing partner and you invest the energy required to promote your book – then the rewards of independent publishing are many.

Over to you

Now that you've read about what is required to publish your book successfully, complete this questionnaire to find out if you have what it takes.

TABLE 1 **Establishing your suitability as an independent publishing candidate**

ARE YOU A GOOD CANDIDATE FOR INDEPENDENT PUBLISHING?	Score
Choose the most applicable statement in each section and transfer the score in the brackets to the right-hand column.	
1. How much access do you have to your target market? • I have easy and direct access to my potential customers. (5) • I have a reasonable amount of direct access to potential customers. (4) • I have some access to potential customers. (3) • I have limited access to potential customers. (2) • I have no access to potential customers. (1)	
2. How comfortable do you feel about promoting and selling your book? • I feel extremely comfortable. (5) • I feel fairly comfortable. (4) • I feel somewhat comfortable. (3) • I feel somewhat uncomfortable. (2) • I can't think of anything worse. (1)	

ARE YOU A GOOD CANDIDATE FOR INDEPENDENT PUBLISHING?	
Choose the most applicable statement in each section and transfer the score in the brackets to the right-hand column.	Score
3. Will you be playing an active role in direct-to-customer sales? • I will be playing a very active role in direct sales to my customers. (5) • I will be playing a fairly active role in direct sales to my customers. (4) • I will be somewhat active in direct sales to my customers. (3) • I will have little involvement, if any, in direct sales to my customers. (2) • I will have no involvement in direct sales to customers. (1)	
4. How critical is online distribution to the success of your book? • Not critical – I have other ways and means of selling the book. (5) • Somewhat important – I have direct physical access to my customers but also a good online following through social media and my website. (4) • Very important – I have a large online following and lots of potential customers abroad. (3) • Extremely important – I will be relying entirely on online distribution to sell my book and I have only a few followers. (2) • Extremely important – I will be relying entirely on online distribution to sell my book and I currently have no followers. (1)	
5. How critical is bookstore distribution for the success of your book? • Not important – I have other ways and means of selling the book. (5) • Fairly important – I will be relying on bookstore sales for some of my sales. (4) • Somewhat important – I will be relying on bookstores for a lot of my sales. (3) • Very important – I will be relying on bookstores for most of my sales. (2) • Extremely important – I will be relying entirely on bookstore sales. (1)	
6. How much money are you willing to invest in your publishing? • I will spend what is needed to create a high-quality product. (5) • I have a reasonable budget. (4) • I have to be careful about what I spend my money on and prioritise the most important services. (3) • I have a very tight budget. (2) • I have no money available – I'll have to find sponsorship. (1)	
7. How much time do you have available to market and promote your book? • I have all the time I need, or easy access to others who can help. (5) • I have some time available and a fair amount of access to others who can help. (4) • I have some time available and some access to others who can help. (3) • I have limited time available and/or limited access to others who can help. (2) • I have no time available and/or no access to others who can help. (1)	

ARE YOU A GOOD CANDIDATE FOR INDEPENDENT PUBLISHING?	
Choose the most applicable statement in each section and transfer the score in the brackets to the right-hand column.	Score
8. What is your level of confidence in your book? • I totally believe in my book – I think it's a really good product. (5) • I feel mostly okay about it and I'm willing to do what's necessary to improve on it. (4) • I'm not really sure – but I'm willing to have an evaluation done and put in extra work until I feel happy with the product. (3) • I'm not sure and/or I don't really feel like doing more work on it. (2) • I don't feel confident and/or I don't know if it's worth spending money on publishing. (1)	
9. How comfortable are you about taking a financial risk on your book? • I'm not afraid to take a financial risk and/or the money's not important. (5) • I'm a bit worried about the financial risk but think it's worth it in order to realise my dream. (4) • I'm worried about the financial risk but feel more positive than negative about my book's potential for success. (3) • I'm worried about the financial risk and I'm not sure my book is worth losing money over. (2) • I don't want to take a financial risk and/or I can't afford to lose my money. (1)	
TOTAL SCORE	

Reality check

Add the scores in the right-hand column to create one final total, then find out what your total score shows about your suitability as an independent publishing candidate.

36–45: What are you waiting for? Start publishing already! You are the perfect candidate for independent publishing and you're more likely than most to make a real success of it, recover your costs fairly quickly, and make a profit.

27–35: You may have to step outside your comfort zone and be willing to explore new markets and connect with potential customers. With determination and ongoing promotion, there's no reason why you shouldn't be able to recoup your costs and make a profit.

18–26: Think before investing heavily in your book, unless you have money to blow or want to publish simply for the satisfaction of it. Consider a professional manuscript evaluation to see if it's worth forging ahead and spending the money. If marketing is your issue, perhaps you should consider sending your manuscript to a traditional publisher who can promote it properly. Alternatively, try an online print-on-demand and ebook publishing service to publish with minimal risk.

9–17: Self-publishing is not the recommended route for you. You'd be better served approaching a traditional publisher if your book is good enough and has market appeal, and this is confirmed in a manuscript evaluation. If you're really desperate to publish and you're willing to spend the money, even if you don't make it back, try an online print-on-demand and ebook publishing service, or a vanity press.

TIPS ON FUNDING YOUR BOOK

Book publishing remains an unrealised dream for many authors because they cannot afford the full cost of publishing. Here are some tips that might assist you in raising the necessary funds if you find yourself in this position.

Approach friends and family: This might be the first choice for some authors and the last choice for others. If your friends and family have encouraged you to write a book, they may be willing to offer you their financial support. If they do, then it's best to approach this funding as a business agreement. Draw up a proper loan document that details repayment terms. A written agreement makes it a binding agreement and not just a verbal agreement between pals. It also shows your level of professionalism, and your intention to repay the loan.

Grants and awards: You may be fortunate enough to be paid to write and publish your book! Some foundations and organisations offer publishing grants to individuals who meet their guidelines. Research local angels, such as The National Arts Council of South Africa[1] and the National Library of South Africa[2]. Some writing competitions also offer publishing deals and prize money. Do an Internet search for relevant competitions and be sure to enter them.

Sponsorship: You may be able to interest a corporate enterprise or company in sponsoring the production or printing of your book. Approach companies whose interests are aligned with the topic of your book and who might benefit from an association. The book cover and foreword can be branded with the sponsoring company's logo, serving as a marketing tool for the company and an added incentive for their sponsorship.

Crowdfunding: This is the practice of funding a venture by raising small amounts of money from a large number of people, typically through the Internet. Instead of traditional investors, crowdfunding campaigns are funded by the general public. There are numerous platforms through which entrepreneurs can ask for capital, such as Kickstarter[3] and Publishizer.[4] Here in South Africa we have Jumpstarter[5] and Thundafund[6], among others.

Crowdfunding is safe for investors because if you fail to meet your financial target through the crowdfunding platform, investors receive their money back.

---

1 http://nac.org.za/funding/literature
2 http://www.nlsa.ac.za
3 https://www.kickstarter.com/discover/categories/publishing
4 http://www.publishizer.com
5 http://www.jumpstarter.co.za
6 http://www.thundafund.com

Pre-orders: Allow potential customers to pre-order your book. Create marketing material using a mock-up of the cover and a description of the book, then let buyers know when the book is expected to become available. Provide added value by personally signing all pre-order copies or by giving customers an early bird discount for orders placed in advance.

This option should *only* be considered if the production of your book is complete and paid for, and you would like to fund, for example, your printing costs. You must have backup finance available if you fail to meet your pre-orders target.

When it comes to funding, it can literally pay you to explore all available options. Think outside the box. Brainstorm ways in which you can provide extra value to customers who purchase your book. Explore the Internet to find out how other people are raising money for their ventures. It's amazing how many ways there are to raise funds.

> **# TIP   The benefits of a business plan**
>
> As with any business project requiring a financial investment, you should formulate a basic business plan. This business plan can be used, and will most probably be necessary, to secure sponsorship. More importantly, it will help you put your project in perspective, work out the financial viability of publishing, formulate a solid marketing plan, set a suitable retail price, make sales and profit projections, and remain directed and focused to ensure that your project is a success. Examples of business plans can be downloaded for free from the Internet.

Proceed with caution!

How you fund your book is up to you. We endorse any of the safe methods mentioned above. However, we cannot endorse any option that will leave you in severe financial debt, such as funding your book via your credit card or raising a second bond on your house. Books rarely sell as quickly or as well as authors think they will. It always pays to proceed with caution and consider the personal financial implications of funding your book publishing venture.

When obtaining funding in advance, you have an obligation to fulfil all your commitments and book orders, by the dates promised. We therefore don't advise going ahead with your project until *all* the necessary funds have been raised or secured, and you can be certain of seeing the project through to the end. **Don't rely on book launch sales to pay your printing or other production costs, as these sales cannot be counted on and may end up being much lower than expected!**

And finally, in the interests of best practice, we also recommend that funds received in advance be kept in a separate bank account with a suitable project name. As an example, it would make sense for us to open a bank account for this book in the name of 'Publish Like A Pro'. A separate bank account will help investors feel more secure in the knowledge that they are depositing funds into a proper project account rather than a personal account where the funds may end up being spent on everything *but* publishing. More importantly, if you fail to secure the full funding needed, or your project falls through or is postponed for whatever reason, the funds are safe and can be easily returned to the rightful owners, if necessary.

To work out how much money you'll need for your publishing venture, you must know more about publishing budgets and how to set up a realistic budget for your book. This is covered in Chapter 15. But first, you need to know about production processes and what goes into making a good book. So, read on.

SECTION

3

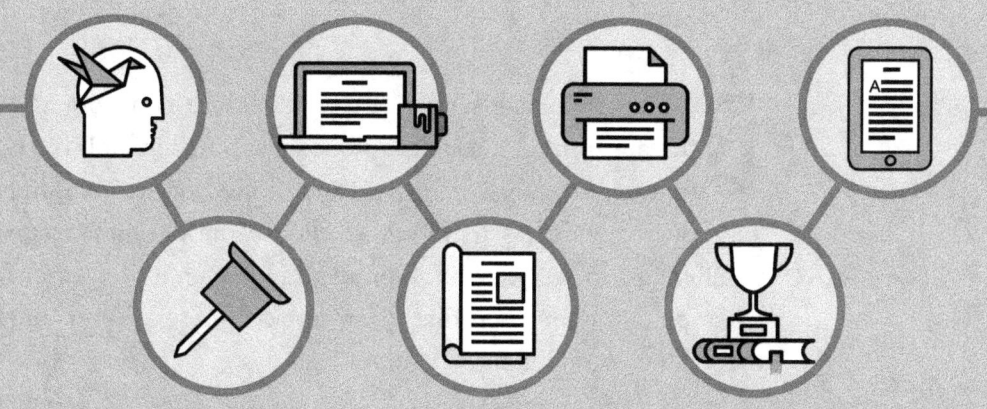

BOOK PRODUCTION PROCESSES — THE NUTS AND BOLTS

6

AN OVERVIEW OF BOOK PRODUCTION

By now, you may have noticed that there is a common thread running through this book and a word that is often repeated – *quality, quality, quality*. When you are investing your own money, it's tempting to choose the cheapest route possible just to see your book in print. However, it's important to stop and remember that your book represents **you** and everything you stand for.

There are no short cuts

In the past independent publishing was synonymous with poor quality because authors didn't invest in professional editing and design. Editing and design are art forms and the expression 'you get what you pay for' is very apt when it comes to these skills. Settling for anything less than excellence destroys credibility, as well as customer trust. It also annihilates your chances of marketing the book through mass media. Media, such as magazines and newspapers, won't touch books that are clearly of low quality, never mind review or feature them on their pages. In fact, members of the media are more critical than most: hundreds of books compete for the same review space on their pages each month, and as experienced writers and journalists, they are constantly exposed to high-quality books by major publishing houses. They instantly recognise professional quality when they see it.

Bookstores are reluctant to stock books that are not supported by adequate marketing and publicity. And some publications won't review your book if it isn't readily available in bookstores. So even if bookstores are not your primary channel of distribution, you might still require a bookstore presence to secure reviews in certain media. From this perspective, publishing a book that meets industry standards is non-negotiable.

Establishing consumer confidence in you, the author, and what you have to say is vital if you hope to publish more books down the line. Consumers take trade-quality books for granted. After all, that's all that's been available on the market, before self-publishing became a popular option. You can bet your bottom dollar that customers who have a bad or disappointing experience will not give you a second chance when you release your next book.

THE PUBLISHING PROCESS

When you choose the independent publishing route, there are processes that need to be followed and boxes that must be ticked to ensure a quality product.

Figure 1 on page 95 shows a typical publishing process, from start to finish. Following this process will ensure the greatest likelihood of achieving a trade-quality product. Each of the stages in the publishing process have been dealt with extensively in other chapters, so we won't elaborate on them here, except to say that the order in which the stages are completed can differ slightly from one publisher to the next.

For instance, you'll notice that the *Commissioning artwork* stage (Step 5) comes after *Editing* (Step 4). In an independent publishing workflow, the stage at which the artwork is created is somewhat flexible. The author might commission it before or after editing. It may even be ready before the manuscript is handed over for evaluation (Step 2).

Our recommendation is to wait until *after* the editing stage, especially if information in the text is going to be used in the artwork. In a traditional publishing environment, artwork is typically commissioned *after* the first set of page proofs have been generated. The typesetter, while laying out the book, includes 'placeholders' for the images showing the editorial team where the images should go in the layout, as well as the size and orientation (portrait or landscape) that the images must conform to. The editor then commissions artwork to the sizes indicated and within the budget allocated. In some cases, it's the commissioning editor who supplies the image sizes, orientation, and location to the typesetter. Each publisher has their own preference and way of working. Some traditional publishers may even require the author to supply all artwork and photographs before publishing begins.

The *Typesetting* stage (Step 7) includes all technical processes required to make up the book, such as scanning artwork and photographs if they haven't been provided in electronic format; retouching and colour-adjusting photographs where necessary; formatting text; laying out the content; creating tables, graphs, charts and diagrams; and ensuring that technical production and print requirements are met.

Marketing and publicity (Step 13) has been placed at the end of this timeline. With independent publishing, authors typically start marketing when their books are complete and distribution has already been set up. In a traditional publishing environment, marketing often begins as soon as the cover design has been finalised. Bookstore and pre-sale orders are already waiting to be fulfilled by the time the books have come off the press and reached the distribution warehouse.

CHAPTER 6 | AN OVERVIEW OF BOOK PRODUCTION

FIGURE 1 A simplified custom publishing process

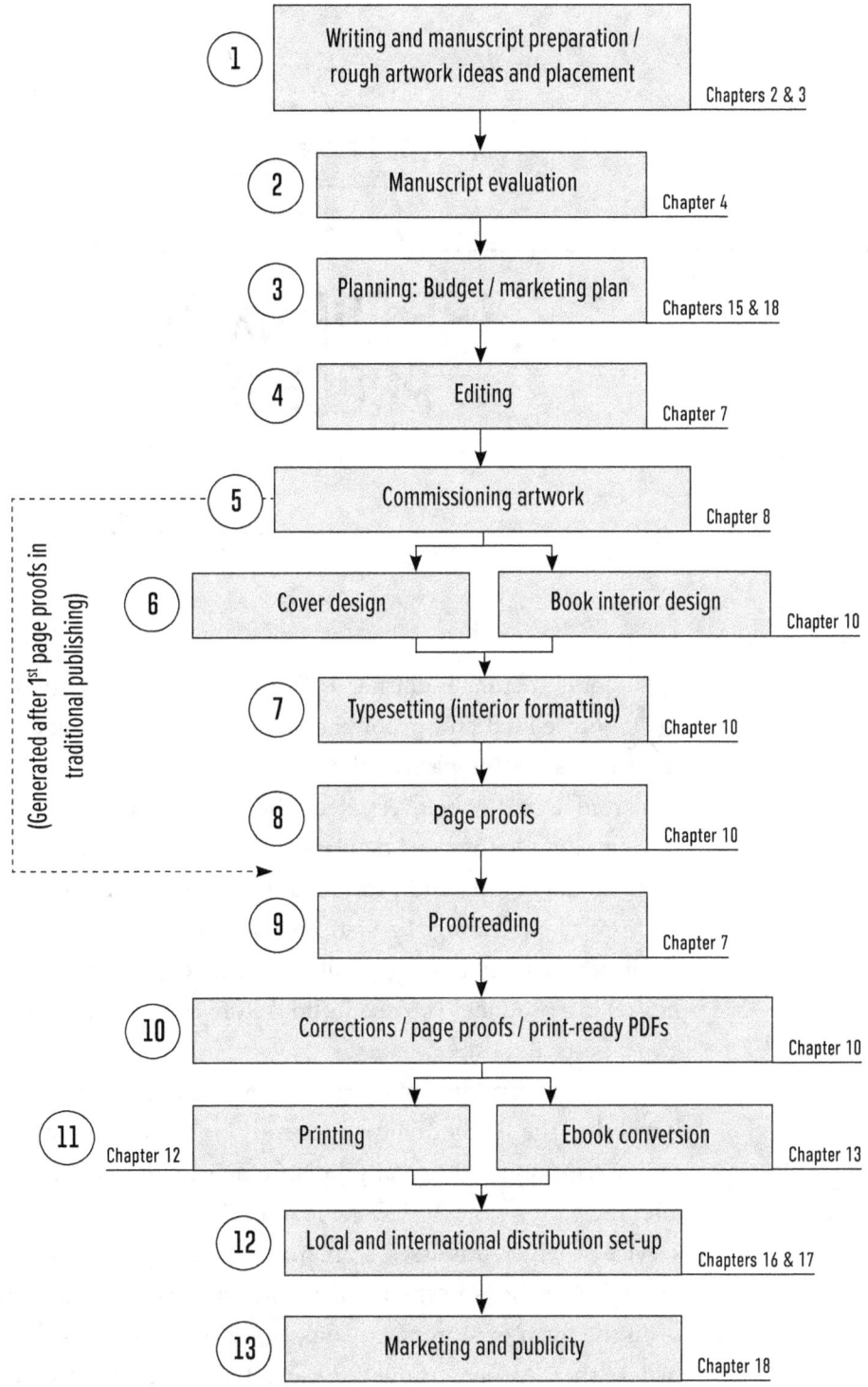

THE EDITORIAL PROCESS

A good custom publisher will insist on having your book both edited and proofread. We have devoted a good few pages to this part of the production process because its importance cannot be overstated. There's not an award-winning or bestselling author on the planet whose books don't undergo professional editing and proofreading. It's par for the course in traditional publishing. In fact, books published by traditional publishers usually undergo multiple edits to produce the slick, bestselling products you see in bookstores or on the *New York Times* bestseller list.

Your manuscript may require a complex, standard or light edit. The type of editing depends on the condition of the manuscript and will usually be specified in the cost estimate after the editor has assessed the manuscript. Depending on your service provider, this assessment might be done by way of a brief perusal of sections of the manuscript, usually at no cost to you, or in the form of a proper manuscript evaluation, for a fee. We believe that a proper evaluation is vital to ensure that the editor and author address all the issues in the manuscript, and that the editorial budget accurately reflects the amount of work required to produce a clean, publishable manuscript. You don't want to be saddled with an unexpected bill for extra editorial work.

EDITING

Editing is a specialised skill and should be performed by an experienced book editor. Editing books is very different from, say, editing a magazine or a newspaper in which articles are short and self-contained. Expecting a magazine or newspaper editor to edit a book – unless they have experience doing so – is akin to expecting a 5km-runner to run a 42.2km marathon with no additional training.

Avoid the temptation to have your newspaper editor brother-in-law perform the main edit on your book. By all means, engage his help to get your manuscript into the best possible shape before you hand it over for production. This will make the editing process quicker and easier and therefore less costly. And yes, definitely get his help if you're on a low-to-zero budget and will be using a print-on-demand or low-cost publishing solution. It's also an excellent idea to enlist his help at the proofing stage as every set of eyes helps, and any help you get is better than no help at all. However, he might not have the legs to carry you all the way to the finish line when it comes to producing a professionally edited book akin to those produced by major publishers.

Also avoid the temptation to assume that overseas editors are better than local ones just because they're more expensive and they're based overseas.

As publishing consultants, we frequently come across manuscripts that authors have paid a fortune to have edited abroad, sometimes by professors of English at well-known universities who are published authors themselves, that needed extensive editing back here in South Africa to get them into proper shape. There are a few lessons in this: 1) Professors of English teach

English – *teaching* is what they do for a living. Book editors edit books – *editing* is what they do for a living. 2) Even if professors of English *do* have a few published books under their belts, their books have *always* been edited by a professional book editor who earns a living editing books all day. 3) There are specific English language conventions and idioms that are unique to a South African audience – our use of 's' instead of 'z' being just one of them. And finally, 4) It's important to know what kind of edit you are paying for. Different levels of editing address different issues in the manuscript.

The editorial process can take anything from a few weeks to a few months to complete, depending on how busy the editor is; how long the book is; the level of editing required; how quickly you respond to the editor's queries, if any; and how many editing phases the manuscript requires.

If it's a complex edit with many queries, this will obviously delay the process. It's more cost-effective to take the time needed to get your manuscript into the best possible shape before handing it over for editing. Also, be aware that most editors will not be able to start your job immediately. They're usually working on other jobs that they need to complete before they can tackle yours, so you'll need to factor this into your publishing timeline.

Once the editing is complete, the editor sends the edited manuscript back to you to review – usually with changes marked and highlighted so that you can see their insertions and deletions – and approve or reject the changes. The editor may be in touch with you during the editing process to ask for clarification or to request further elaboration. Alternatively, they may leave notes

> Find out more about publishing timelines in Chapter 14.

 # TIP Choosing an editor

When choosing an editor, it's reasonable to request an edited sample chapter of your book to assess the editing before you hand over the entire job. This may or may not involve a small cost, but if it does, it's worth it. Editing is one of the more expensive book production services – and the most important – so it's best to make sure that you're happy with the editor and the quality of their work.

and remarks in the manuscript for you to address, and then integrate your additions and comments into the final manuscript before handing it over for typesetting.

Types of editing

There are four main levels of book editing, each attending to different issues in the manuscript and carrying a different cost. Terminology defining these levels may differ depending on where you are in the world. Americans, for instance, use the terms line editing and copy editing, whereas in South Africa, we use the terms substantive editing and standard editing.

Editors in South Africa often perform multiple levels of editing as part of the same edit. A substantive edit, for instance, will include everything that a standard edit includes and more, as it works with the manuscript at a much deeper level. And a proofread may turn into a light edit. While not cast in stone, and bearing editorial fluidity in mind, the information that follows illustrates the basic editorial functions so that you're aware of what you're getting and can budget for your editorial requirements accordingly.

Substantive or complex edit

Sometimes called a 'developmental edit', this is the **most intensive form of editing**. In addition to all the standard editing functions, a complex or substantive edit also focuses on the manuscript's intended use and target market, as well as the internal organisation, style and flow of information or narrative. It ensures completeness, accuracy, consistency, conciseness, readability and, most especially, clarity. The aim of a professional edit is to ensure that everything is so clear that it cannot be misunderstood. Paragraphs may be rewritten, expanded upon or condensed, and text moved from one section of the book to another if it makes better sense there.

This is the most expensive form of editing because the editor engages with the material at the deepest level – also checking for factual accuracy and copyright, referencing material appropriately and pre-empting a range of potential issues including legality of content. Ultimately, the accuracy and legality of content is the author's responsibility, but it's important that the editor raises any red flags about potential issues.

A substantive edit is almost always followed by a standard or light edit due to the extent of the work undertaken. It's impossible for an editor working at this level to ensure everything is perfect. The editor is also required to make many judgement calls during the editing process. A fresh set of eyes – and a new perspective – are called for. As an author, you can well appreciate this: simply think back to when you stopped writing for a while and then went back to your manuscript to carry on. Invariably there were things you ended up changing because you saw room for improvement, or you spotted mistakes or repetition that you hadn't noticed before. So it is with editing.

Standard edit

A standard edit is the *minimum* level of editing required for publishing. A standard edit – sometimes called a copy edit – is the most common level of editing. It checks for grammar, punctuation and spelling. It also checks for factual errors; syntactical problems; word usage; language style; consistency; repetition; ambiguity; hyphenation; tautology; capitalisation; number usage; logic; and general flow of content.

The editor will flag contradictions, timeline issues and factual inaccuracies; standardise heading levels; check table and figure numbers to ensure that they run sequentially; and check that tables, graphs and artwork correlate with the text.

In a traditional publishing environment, particularly academic and educational publishing, the book designer will provide the editor with a marked-up sample of the design specifications, which the editor uses to mark up the entire book. This is rarely, if ever, done in an independent publishing environment.

> **ⓘ DID YOU KNOW?**
>
> In a traditional publishing environment, editors are often required to mark up the text. This means that they will indicate level 1, level 2 and level 3 headings, captions, the start and end of special text boxes and text features, quotes, and so on. This ensures that when the book is typeset, the hierarchy and structure of the content is accurately and consistently maintained throughout. An example of how text is marked up can be found in the Did You Know? box on page 129.

Light edit

A light edit is similar to a standard edit, except that far less work is involved and it's **typically performed on a manuscript that has already been edited**. In involves a further check on grammar, spelling, punctuation, incorrect word usage, needless repetition, consistency of language and punctuation, and ensures correct cross-referencing. It's practically mandatory after an extensive edit, as it provides a fresh second-eye check to iron out any issues or mistakes that were missed or arose as a result of the extensive edit. It may also be necessary after a standard edit, depending on how complex the standard edit ended up being. It's extremely rare to come across a manuscript that requires only light editing. When that happens, the author is usually an experienced writer or editor.

Proofreading

This is often done *after* the book has been typeset and the first set of page proofs have been produced. By now, the sentence structure, flow, development, and content should already be sound, but the manuscript still needs another check for punctuation, spelling, table and figure numbers, typos, as well as errors that may have crept in during typesetting.

Proofreading also checks for consistent use of regional English (e.g. British English vs. American English), consistency in currency (e.g. USD vs. $), consistency in how numerals are written out (e.g. 100,000 vs. 100 000), how dates are represented (e.g. 1 January 2016 vs. January 1, 2016), and so on.

If you are publishing an academic book, or any other book in which credibility depends on a high level of accuracy and detail, engaging the services of a specialist proofreader, rather than an editor who proofreads, is recommended.

> **ⓘ DID YOU KNOW?**
>
> You may be wondering why an extensive or standard edit doesn't leave you with a perfect manuscript. That's because editors are human, too. An extensive or heavy edit involves a level of engagement in which the editor eventually becomes too involved, much like the author, and starts seeing what they expect to see, not what is *actually* there. It's the same reason that authors cannot edit their own work. Our brains are amazing organs that are very good at filling in letters and words. We see what we *expect* to see.
>
> **Aoccdrnig to rseearch at Cmabrigde Uinervtisy, it deosn't mttaer in waht oredr the ltteers in a wrod are, the olny iprmoatnt tihng is taht the frist and lsat ltteers be in the rghit pclae. The rset can be a toatl mses and you can sitll raed it wouthit a porbelm. Tihs is bcuseae the huamn mnid deos not raed ervey lteter by istlef, but the wrod as a wlohe.**
>
> **NO71CE H8W YOU C4N RE4D 7H1S ES81LY W17HOUT H4VING TO R3ALLY 7H1NK A3OUT 1T?**
>
> This should give you a new appreciation for editors and proofreaders! It explains why errors still manage to creep through, despite reading and correcting your book countless times.

Jumbled letter order (bold) collected on the Internet, 2018. Original source unknown.

In reality, most books require at least two edits and a proofread, and even that may not be enough. The book, the complexity of the subject, and the nature of the editing performed will all have an impact on the number of revisions that may be needed. This is quite normal, and in a traditional publishing environment, multiple revisions are common, with various people (fresh eyes) reading the manuscript at each stage.

Editorial services will likely make up the largest portion of your production costs. At the very least, you should budget for a minimum of *two* editorial phases: a standard edit and a proofread. If the manuscript requires substantive editing, then three editorial phases may be the necessary minimum: a substantive edit, a light or standard edit, and a proofread.

EDITORIAL PERMISSIONS

It's entirely normal for authors to research other similar published works or online information when writing their books. No-one can know everything, even if they are a specialist in their field, and a well-researched book is an authoritative book.

What authors cannot do, however, is quote someone else's work word for word, sentence by sentence – at least, not without obtaining permission from the copyright holder to do so. The copyright holder can be either the author or the publisher. Reproducing copyrighted work without the necessary permission is known as *copyright infringement.*

Provided you are using very *short* extracts from other people's work, it may not be necessary to seek permission – this is known as 'fair use'. The problem is that there is no standard rule for the number of words you are legally allowed to copy. Some claim it's 150 words, others say it's 300, and yet others maintain that you can use as much as 10% of your total word count. Our advice is to use as few copied words or extracts as possible and **always credit the source!** Using other people's work without crediting them – in other words, passing the work off as your own – is called *plagiarism* and is a form of fraud. Plagiarism is taken very seriously in the publishing industry.

There are other instances when you may not need to seek permission, but it's a complicated business.

Generally, you don't need permission to publish someone else's words in the following cases:
- The work was published before January 1, 1923, in which case the copyright has expired.
- The work is in the **public domain**.
- You mention the title of a work or its author as a **stated fact** (also applies to songs and poems).
- The work is licensed under **Creative Commons** guidelines; this enables free distribution of an otherwise copyrighted work and should be clearly stated in the book itself.
- You are following **fair use** guidelines – quoting just a few lines from a full-length work. But this can be something of a grey area so the guidelines should not be abused or you might find yourself in legal trouble.

Obtaining permissions

When you want to use material in a way that cannot be classified as fair use, you need permission from the copyright owner. This material could, for example, include several verses of a song or poem, or entire paragraphs from a book. Always err on the side of caution and get the go-ahead before you publish. You may sometimes have to pay for permission to use the extract, but rather pay a small fee than be sued for copyright infringement.

When it's not practical to obtain permission, for example, you cannot track down the author or publisher, then consider not using the content at all unless the doctrine of fair use can be applied.

It's common practice nowadays for people to trawl the Internet when doing research. The attitude towards re-using information published via digital media is a little more relaxed, provided the source is credited. Bloggers, for example, may view it as a marketing opportunity if you quote from their blog and acknowledge them as the author. But it's always best to check their copyright policy just in case. You are still at risk when copying information from a digital source.

Obtaining permissions can sometimes be a tedious process that involves time-consuming research, lengthy communication, and occasional head-butting. Fortunately, there are people out there who can do it for you, if your budget allows. Some custom publishers will offer the service for a fee. There are also specialised companies and freelancers who will obtain permissions on your behalf – naturally, also in exchange for payment. If you have the time and you want to save money, it's best to obtain the permissions yourself.

How to obtain permissions

1. Find the contact details for the copyright holder. If the work is still in print, this will usually be the publisher, but if not, it could be the author. If it's a publisher, the company will usually have a rights or permissions department you can contact, the details for which can be found on their website.
2. Compile a **permissions letter** that provides the following information:
   - Your name, address and contact details.
   - Details of the work for which you require permission, including author, title, year of publication, ISBN, and exactly which portion of the work you wish to use; also, the nature of how it will be used. Some copyright holders may request to see the formatted pages on which their work is quoted so that they can assess the context of its use. They may also want to see the imprint page.
   - Details of the book you will be publishing, including the title name, publisher, publication date, print quantity, and price.
   - Audience to whom the work will be made available.
   - The rights that you require – for which country, in which language, and in which format (print, digital, or both).
   - A promise that you will acknowledge and credit the copyright holder and permission granted.
   - A request for the copyright holder to provide permission in writing, either by email or letter.

View an example of an imprint page in Appendix D on page 278.

> **# TIP** Permissions timeline and filing permissions received
>
> Obtaining permissions usually takes time and you may be redirected to different people or publishers, so make sure you complete this process well before your publishing deadline.
>
> Remember to safely file away or store your permissions when you receive them. These should form part of the permanent archives pertaining to your book.

> **# TIP** Copyright for artwork, quotes, bible verses
>
> **ARTWORK:** Copyright also applies to photographs; cartoons; charts; line drawings; graphs; maps; and screen shots, so make sure that you have permission to use these items. Obtaining image permissions is covered on pages 116–118 in Chapter 8.
>
> **QUOTES:** Many authors use quotes from well-known speakers, celebrities, leaders, and other authors. These are considered safe to use and permission is not required, although the source of the quote must be credited, even if it's 'Anonymous'. Quotes should also be represented word for word. Where there are conflicting versions of a quote, choose the version from the most reputable source. If you cannot quote the text accurately, word for word, rather paraphrase the quote and do **not** place it in inverted commas, for example: Napoleon Hill reminds us that we can only grow and become strong through continuous effort and struggle. (The actual quote is: "Strength and growth come only through continuous effort and struggle.")
>
> **BIBLE VERSES:** Different publishers own the copyright to different translations of the Bible. Most translations give permission for a limited number of verses – usually around 200 – to be quoted word for word, provided your quote makes up less than a certain percentage of your own book. Look up the publisher of the specific Bible translation you'd like to use and follow their usage and credit guidelines. The World English Bible (WEB) is an updated version of the American Standard Version (1901) and is a translation that has been put into the public domain. As such, there is no copyright and it's freely available for use, in any form, without needing to credit WEB. However, if you choose to credit World English Bible (WEB) or use the name, you must faithfully copy the verses as they appear in the WEB.

> **# TIP Inserting a copyright credit in your book**
>
> When you receive permission to reproduce copyrighted work, the copyright holder may have specific requirements regarding how they wish to be credited. Ensure that this is done. If they have not specified a format, you can do the following:
>
> **TEXT CREDITS**: If you're using content with **permission granted**, insert "© [Copyright owner's name], used with permission" alongside the content being credited (see page 142 for an example).
>
> If you're using content under **fair use** guidelines, insert: "© [Copyright owner's name], used under fair use" or "© [Copyright owner's name], with thanks".
>
> If you're using **Creative Commons** content, you can find guidelines on how to credit the copyright holder supplied with the content. Do as requested.
>
> If you are quoting something from the **Internet**, reference the website and then provide the date you accessed it, for example: Source: www.quickfox.co.za, 18/08/2018.
>
> Some publishers also provide credits on the imprint page. If you do this, remember to include the page number that the content appears on, for example: "Page 142 © [Copyright owner's name], used with permission", and if more than one source needs to be credited on that page, include the article name as well: "Page 142: Proofreading and editing marks © [Copyright owner's name], used with permission".
>
> **PHOTOGRAPHIC AND ARTWORK CREDITS**: Photographic and artwork credits are often provided on the imprint page, accompanied by the page number on which the photograph or artwork appears, for example: "Keep Calm and Vector (Shutterstock), cover; Vanessa Wilson pp. 111, 112, 162, 163". Sometimes image credits also appear in small text alongside the photograph or artwork in the book itself, for example: "Copyright © [Copyright owner's name]". This method of crediting is typically found in magazines and journals, but less often used in books. The most important rule when crediting images is to use the method requested by the copyright holder.
>
> View the imprint page of this book for an example of how credits can be included.

Once your book has been polished editorially and all relevant permissions have been obtained, it's time to move to the next stage – adding illustrations and photographs. If this is not relevant to you, skip to Chapter 9 on page 126 to find out how to prepare your manuscript for publishing.

ADDING PHOTOGRAPHS AND ILLUSTRATIONS TO YOUR BOOK

If you're including illustrations or photographs in your book, it's your responsibility, as an author publishing independently, to source your own material, unless you specifically request this of your publisher.

Custom publishers should be able to assist or at least point you in the right direction, offering their input and advice along the way. Only some vanity publishers may offer this service, whereas print-on-demand publishers don't get involved at this level at all.

Depending on the type of book you are publishing, traditional publishers will either ask you to supply your own photographs, or they will arrange the photography or commission an illustrator. The costs may or may not be deducted from your royalties.

When including images in your book, it helps to follow some basic guidelines to ensure that your images meet professional production standards. This will prevent unnecessary expense and delays further down the line.

REVIEWING IMAGE QUALITY

Image quality from a production perspective is typically affected by the **resolution** of the image and the **size** at which the image will appear in the book. It's also affected by how the images are **scanned** and converted into an electronic file, and how that file is **saved** and used. Let's look at each of these factors.

Resolution and image size

Resolution is measured in 'dpi' (dots per inch) or 'ppi' (pixels per inch). A dot is the same as a pixel – dot is a term used in the printing environment, whereas pixel is a term used in a web-based environment. Dpi is a measurement of printer resolution that indicates how many ink dots the printer can place on one square inch of paper. The higher the dpi, the sharper the image. **Image size**, on the other hand, refers to the image's *physical dimensions*, measured in millimetres (mm), centimetres (cm), or inches (in).

The image resolution for all photographs should be at least **300 dpi at the size they are to appear in the book**. So, a photo that measures 10 × 15cm in your book should have a resolution of 300dpi at that physical size. Although digital printing is more forgiving and can tolerate images as low as 200dpi without a noticeable drop in quality, we recommend the professional minimum of 300dpi. Line art should be 600dpi.

Images can be **resized** and **resampled**. Resizing and resampling images can compromise your image quality if they are not used correctly.

- **Resizing** changes the image size *without* changing the resolution. Resizing is used to make very large images smaller, particularly when the original size is much larger than needed. This helps to keep file sizes down and prevents electronic documents from becoming slow and cumbersome to work with when they have lots of images in them. So a 20 × 30cm image at 300dpi can be safely resized down to

> A definition of terms can be found in the Glossary on page 288.

10 × 15cm at 300dpi. However, this does not work the other way around. You cannot make a small image bigger without degrading the image quality *unless* the image has a high enough resolution to compensate for the increase in physical size. If you don't know where to find the image resolution for your image, it's best to play it safe by **never increasing the size of your images**. Use them at the size they are, or smaller.

- **Resampling** *changes* the resolution of an image. This is normally done to accommodate the way in which the image will be used. For printing, the image would be used at 300dpi, but on websites, it would be used at 72dpi – the standard resolution for all Internet content. So an image of 5 × 10cm at 300dpi used for printing would be resampled to 5 × 10cm at 72dpi for use on the Internet.

However, you should **never** add pixels to a low resolution image to increase the dpi! Doing so will force the computer to artificially add extra dots to make up the higher dpi.

The easiest way to understand resampling is to think of pixels as gas in a container. If you double the size of the container, the gas spreads out to fill the container, leaving only half the number of gas molecules per inch than were there before. To get back up to the previous number of gas molecules per inch, you would have to add extra gas. What's the problem with that, you may ask? Well, when computers add pixels, they can only do so by analysing the colour of nearby pixels and inserting extra pixels of the same colour next to them. This ends up creating an artificial or blurry look to the image. You may not easily see the blur on a standard monitor, but you'll see it in a printed book, or when viewing the image on a high-quality monitor at 100% scale or larger.

> **# TIP** Two rules to remember when using images
> 1) Do not resize images upwards
> 2) Do not add pixels to Internet or other low resolution images to increase their dpi.

A high-quality image at 300dpi at 100% scale. Note the crisp detail and sharp lines.

A 72dpi version of the image **resized** upwards. Note the pixelation.

A 72dpi version of the image **resampled** to 300dpi. Note the blurriness.

Scanning

Scanning is the process used to convert a print, negative, slide or physical piece of artwork into an electronic file. For a trade-quality book, all images should be scanned professionally. Scanning is a specialisation on its own and prepress studios employ dedicated scanner operators who use sophisticated equipment to accurately capture the colour, sharpness and detail of images. Blemishes are removed, colour is corrected to match the original image or enhanced, if required, and files are saved in the correct format for a print or web workflow.

Unfortunately, home desktop scanners and all-in-one office copiers are not good enough to produce high quality image files. Home or office scanning should be reserved for projects that are non-commercial in nature.

File formats

Our discussion wouldn't be complete without looking at file formats and the potential pitfalls of working with images in JPEG format.

A JPEG is a compressed image file. Compression makes the file size smaller, so this format is ideal for images stored or used on the Web. However, the compression causes loss in image quality, especially when high compression settings are used. Repeatedly opening and saving a JPEG file results in severe quality loss over time, because you are essentially saving a JPEG of a JPEG.

When you download images from a photo library or your camera, first resave them in TIFF, BMP or PSD format using

A 'blocky' image from saving the image too often in JPEG format

an image editor, and then work on them. These formats don't result in deterioration when images are edited and saved. You will also have the originals to go back to, if needed.

You can tell that a JPEG has already lost quality when some parts of the image become blocky, especially around the edges of objects and lines. If you want to use a JPEG image, view it at 100% size on a high-quality monitor to see if it's suitable. If you can see any blockiness, the same effect will be visible on the final printed product.

> A definition of terms can be found in the Glossary on page 288.

> # **TIP** Using Internet images
> Images downloaded from the Internet are rarely of high enough resolution to use in a printed book. While the image may look good on your 72dpi monitor, it will not print well. The exception is when images have large physical dimensions at 72dpi and are of very good quality, or they have been downloaded from a professional image library.

ARTWORK CONSIDERATIONS

If you decide to add images to your book, there are certain factors that will affect your publishing costs and impact on your publishing timeline.

- **Full-colour images**: If you choose full-colour images, your book will be much more expensive to print. Unless you are producing a book that *must* have full-colour images, such as a coffee-table book or a children's book, you'd be well advised to keep colour images to a minimum or, better still, convert them to greyscale (black and white). Greyscale images will have little impact on your printing costs and should not significantly affect your production costs.
- **Placement of colour images**: If you must use colour images, think about grouping them together in sections of 8 or 16 pages for greater cost savings.

> Find out in Chapter 12 why grouping images together is more cost-effective for printing.

- **Spot colour graphics**: When you need to introduce colour in a litho-printed book, such as a corporate colour, or to make tables and artwork more appealing, consider using a spot-colour as a more cost-effective option. A spot colour is a premixed colour that uses a special code for identification. The two popular spot colour systems used in the printing business in South Africa are Pantone and Coates. If you go the spot colour route, the assistance of a graphic designer will be necessary. Spot colours cannot be used for digital printing.

> Find out more about litho and digital printing on pages 154 and 157 in Chapter 11.

- **Scanning costs**: Photos or artwork provided in hard-copy format will need to be professionally scanned. These costs must be factored into your budget, and the time needed to scan all your images must be added to your production timeline.
- **Artwork permissions**: If you use images that require permissions, factor in the time needed to obtain them. There might also be additional costs to consider.

USING ONLINE IMAGE LIBRARIES

If your image requirements are fairly generic, you can search for images from some good online image libraries offering royalty-free and rights-managed images.

A royalty-free image is one you have the right to use for multiple applications in multiple media without having to pay royalties or license fees for each use. This use is non-exclusive – in other words, the image library can sell the image to many buyers. This means that another author may use the same image in their book or on their cover. Reselling images in this way benefits you because it keeps the cost fairly low. You can expect to pay from $7.50 to $10 per A5 image at 300 dpi from a regular image library, and from $350 upwards per image from a specialised or high-end library that carries high quality stock images. An **extended licence** is required, at an additional cost, if you intend using the image as the definitive part of a product, for example, in a calendar, or on a mug or T-shirt.

When sourcing images from these libraries, opt for the largest size available if your image is to be printed full page, or the next size down if you need a half-page image or smaller. Some photo libraries provide the physical dimensions of the images. Always check these dimensions and the resolution (dpi) before purchasing and downloading an image so that the image meets the dimensions you require at 300 dpi.

Some popular royalty-free image libraries include:

- Shutterstock[1]
- iStock[2], a division of Getty Images
- BigStockPhoto[3]
- 123RF[4]
- VectorStock[5]
- StockPhotos.io[6]
- Pexels.com[7]

Most of these libraries offer credit packs, which enable you to purchase and download a set number of images within a specified period, such as a year. Unless you see yourself using most of the images in a pack, it makes more sense to ask your service provider whether they have an account with any of these libraries and, if so, to buy the images on your behalf and add the cost to your bill. You then supply your service provider with the image reference number and the low-res version of the image that you download from the image library website.

StockPhotos.io and Pexels.com are different from the other libraries in that they are free stock photo sharing sites holding

---

1 http://www.shutterstock.com
2 http://www.istockphoto.com
3 http://www.bigstockphoto.com
4 http://www.123rf.com
5 http://www.vectorstock.com
6 http://www.stockphotos.io
7 http://www.pexels.com

public domain and Creative Commons-licensed images. You are free to use these images, provided you follow their accreditation and usage guidelines.

Pay-per-use libraries, such as Getty Images[8], are usually high-end professional libraries that stock high quality or hard-to-come-by images that are either rights-managed or royalty-free.

A **rights-managed image** is one in which the licence grants very specific, limited use. The licence only covers the agreed use, so if you want to use the image in other ways, such as on a promotional banner or for a magazine article, you will need to purchase a new licence. The price is based on the intended use, the size at which the image will be used, and the quantity of products being produced.

Due to the strict control and limitations associated with rights-managed images – not to mention the much higher cost – fewer of these images are in circulation, so you're assured of a more exclusive image. You can expect to pay well upwards of $350 per image, but often you're looking at $500 or more. There is an option within the rights-managed category that grants you exclusive use of an image, but this is extremely expensive!

IMAGE PERMISSIONS

There are times when you may need to use an image or photograph from a source other than an online image library or your own illustrator. Common image sources include published books, magazines, newspapers, journals, and theses.

It is vital to obtain permission to use images and photographs that have been originated by, and therefore legally belong to, another person or company. In other words, if you didn't create

---

8   http://www.gettyimages.com

it, someone else did, and that person or their publisher must give their permission, in writing, for you to use it.

If you are using very old images, it's possible that copyright has already fallen away. These images may already exist in the Creative Commons repository, but not always. The natural copyright period differs from country to country, so you will need to research this. In some countries, copyright lasts for 50 years after the copyright owner's death, while in others, it lasts for 100 years after death. You will still need to ensure that the copyright has not been transferred to a new owner, such as a descendent, relative, or company.

If you're in any doubt about the copyright implications of photographs or artwork that you intend using, it's always best to seek legal advice. There are companies who specialise in this area of the law and can advise you accordingly. Consultations are normally quick, worthwhile, and don't necessarily break the bank.

> **# TIP Copyright when downloading images from the Internet**
>
> Don't assume that the website from which you downloaded an image is the original copyright holder. Websites frequently use images from other sites or sources that they have received permission to use, or paid to use. Consider purchasing your images from a royalty-free image library, or commission an illustrator or photographer to create unique images. This will save you a ton of hassle and wasted time trying to track down copyright holders.

A special consideration

Some illustrators and photographers will insist on retaining copyright to the work you commission them to create, allowing you limited use of the material. **You must therefore establish your rights concerning the use of the images**. Ideally, you want full copyright to, or at the very least unlimited usage of, the material that you've paid for – assuming you've paid a normal professional rate.

How to request permission to use copyrighted images

When asking a copyright holder for permission to use an image, you must attach the image to an email in which you provide the following information:

- A description of the image you intend using.
- The title of your book and a description of the content/nature of the book.
- Your name (author), as well as the names of your co-authors and contributors, if any.
- The name of your publisher or publishing services company.
- The media format of your book – print, ebook, or both.
- The context in which the image will be used, for example, to illustrate a section of text; to encourage debate among students; as a reference to the text.
- The estimated number of book copies you expect to have in circulation.
- A copy or PDF of the page in the manuscript where the image appears.

Ask the copyright holder how they would like to be credited. Make sure that this is done. Permissions should be given to you in writing and saved on a memory stick or printed out and filed for safekeeping in a permanent archive.

If you're unable to trace the copyright holder, it's advisable to replace the image altogether or to have something similar drawn up by an illustrator. **The illustrator should not copy the image exactly, as the concept/design of the image belongs to the original copyright owner.**

COMMISSIONING AN ILLUSTRATOR

You might find yourself having to commission artwork for your book. Finding and commissioning the right illustrator can feel very daunting.

The first thing you need to do is decide on an **illustrative style**. Do an Internet search for illustrative styles and you'll be amazed at what comes up! This will show you the possibilities and give you some ideas.

A good option is to browse illustrator websites or artist directories and view their online portfolios of work. If you want to keep it local, check out some of these sites:

- www.illustrators.co.za
- www.sacreativenetwork.co.za
- www.cartoonist.co.za
- www.artsquad.co.za
- www.safrea.co.za

> **# TIP** Illustrative styles and finding your illustrator
>
> It's better to find an illustrator who already illustrates in the style you are looking for than to ask an illustrator to match someone else's style. Illustrators generally don't like copying other people's styles and may even flat-out refuse to do so. When you let them work in their own style, you're far more likely to be satisfied with the end result.

Briefing your illustrator

It's important to brief your illustrator properly to prevent endless rounds of revisions. The better you communicate your vision and what you're looking for, the more likely the illustrator will produce something that is both spot-on and amazing.

Illustrators are creative, imaginative people and can often bring amazing elements to an illustration that you might not have considered, so try to avoid being too prescriptive. When briefing your illustrator, you must provide the following technical information:

- **The size and orientation of the artwork:** Give the dimensions and unit of measure (e.g. 5cm deep × 10cm wide), and whether it will be landscape or portrait.
- **Whether the illustration should run across two pages**: The illustrator must position important elements on either side of the book spine. You do not want the spine to split your main character's face into two! You must remember to check this when you receive the initial rough sketches from the illustrator.
- **Who the book is aimed at**: This will guide the illustrative style and complexity of the artwork. Remember to include the age group of your reader.
- **The format in which you require the artwork:** These days, electronic format is usually the norm. If your illustrator provides artwork only on paper, you will need to factor in professional scanning costs. Also, do *not* let your illustrator photograph and Whatsapp you the artwork with their smartphone to meet your electronic format requirements. Although pieces of artwork that are too big to scan *are* photographed, this is done professionally at high resolution using cameras with special lenses and controlled lighting.
- **A proper brief**, per illustration, of what you expect to see. If it's a children's book, your illustrator should read the story and illustrate accordingly within the parameters that you set. If you need a technical illustration or diagram, it's best to provide an example of what you want using a similar piece of artwork as a reference, and then mark your required changes on it.
- **Text areas:** If text is to overlay the illustrations – as is often the case in children's books – let the illustrator know how much text must be accommodated on each page. By specifying this information up front, the illustrator will provide text areas in

the illustration. These are areas in which the background is much lighter, with few to no drawing lines, so that the text can be easily read.
- **The deadline for finished artwork:** Illustrating takes time, sometimes a lot of it, so let the illustrator provide a realistic date for when the artwork will be complete, and then follow up with him or her at regular intervals. If you have a specific deadline, this must be communicated with the illustrator beforehand to ensure that they can meet it.
- **The format and colour in which the images should be supplied:** This could be TIFF, JPEG, EPS or PDF, although TIFF, EPS and PDF are best.
- **The colour format:** Specify the colour format required for each image – CMYK or black and white.

If you're publishing a children's book, you will need to prepare a book plan first in order to properly brief the artist and advise on the size of the text areas. A book plan is a 'rough' version of your book in which the text is split up on each page and presented at the size it will appear in the final book, accompanied by an artwork brief or rough sketch per page.

A professional illustrator will first provide a sketch of what they intend drawing and, if you're happy with the concept, they'll go ahead and then complete the illustration. Don't be alarmed when you see the sketch – it's **not** the final product! If you are using an artist who does not illustrate professionally, such as an art student or talented artist in your community, you must ask at the outset to see a rough sketch of all your illustrations before they go ahead with the finished art. You shouldn't be charged extra for this. This interim step is important because it's much easier to correct the concept at this stage than after the illustration has been completed. This is the time to assess whether the illustrator is on the right track and has captured the important concepts.

How much will you pay?

This is a difficult question to answer because it will depend on the illustrator and the amount of time it takes to complete the illustrations. When ordering in bulk – illustrations for your entire book, rather than just a few – you can negotiate better rates. Full-page, double-page, and book cover illustrations are generally more expensive, as are technical and medical illustrations. Full-colour illustrations will be more expensive than greyscale or black and white ones. Well-known illustrators will usually be more expensive than lesser-known illustrators.

For generic illustrations, you can try royalty-free online image libraries. You can source good science, medical and nature illustrations from Science Source[9], and ADAM Images[10], one of the largest medical illustration libraries. For other topics you can search online using the topic keyword and the word 'illustrations' to view libraries specialising in your subject matter.

---

9   http://www.sciencesource.com
10 http://www.adameducation.com

TIP Illustrations on a budget

For cheaper illustrations, try local art and graphic design schools. Most students are keen for the exposure and need to build up a working portfolio. Review the work they've done. Who knows? You may discover a talented gem. You could also try placing ads online – such as on Gumtree – stating your requirements and budget. Also ask prospective applicants to submit samples of their work with their applications. Finally, since artwork can be generated and sent from anywhere in the world, you could try an international portal. An excellent source of well-priced creative work that is usually delivered very quickly is www.freelancer.com. An Internet search will turn up others.

ⓘ DID YOU KNOW?

A greyscale or black and white (B&W) image is one in which there are varying shades of black. A black and white photograph is a good example of a greyscale image.

Line art are images that consist of just one colour in straight or curved lines usually on a plain background. There are no shades or hues. Zapiro cartoons are a good example of line art.

> **# TIP Commissioning illustrations**
>
> Before commissioning illustrations, get your custom publisher's feedback on your preferred illustrative style. Your publisher's professional designers and editors are used to conceptualising and commissioning illustrations for projects, and you can be sure that your final illustrations will be correct and suitable for production and printing. Some custom publishing companies will also source an illustrator, negotiate rates, and manage the entire process on your behalf.
>
> If you are using a vanity publisher or print-on-demand platform, we recommend you book a consultation with a publishing consultant to plan your illustrations and text before you commission your artwork.

COMMISSIONING A PHOTOGRAPHER

When stock photographs are not readily available for your book, you will need to commission a photographer. This is most often the case when producing cookery books, photographic coffee-table books, technical books, or books used to promote companies and their products or services.

It's important to brief your photographer properly so that you receive images that suit the requirements of your book and subject matter.

Briefing your photographer

You will need to provide your photographer with the following information:

- **How the photographs will be used**: This will give the photographer an idea of the kinds of photographs required, and the image size and resolution in which to supply them.
- **The orientation of the image**: Landscape or portrait?
- **If the photograph is to run across two pages**: The photographer will know to keep important visual elements off-centre to prevent them from being split by the spine. It will also help the photographer better compose the image.
- **Who the book is aimed at (target audience)**: This will help guide the photographic style and how the shot is set up.

- **The colour format**: Are the photographs needed in black and white, or full colour?
- **A brief of what you expect to see in each photograph**: We suggest that you enlist the help of your publisher or graphic designer for this. Photography can be quite expensive, so you need to be sure that the photographs complement or aid the design style of the book. In a traditional publishing environment, the graphic designer and photo stylist will usually be present at the photo shoot to help direct the photographer and ensure that the right shots are taken. If you're organising your own photography, you must have a solid concept of what you need or expect to see, page by page, *before* commissioning your photographs.
- **Whether a photo stylist is needed**: A photo stylist creatively sets up the scene for each shot. Stylists are typically used for cookery books, sales catalogues, and books on interior décor and fashion. Some photographers do photo styling themselves, or may work in tandem with their own stylist. But you should confirm this beforehand as you may need to find your own.
- **Text areas**: If text is to overlay the photographs, you must let the photographer know, advising him or her of approximately how much text-friendly space you need in each image, and more or less where it will be needed.
- **The deadline**: Photographers don't just take photos and then hand them over to you when shooting is over for the day. Once the photographer has reviewed and selected the best shots, there is still post-production work to be done, such as colour correction, touch-up, and saving the photos in a suitable format.

How much will you pay?

The cost will depend on the photographer you choose. Standard photographic rates can range from R4 000 to R8 000 per day, excluding travel. However, the more in-demand and well-known the photographer is, the more they could charge. It's therefore wise to be really organised and have as much ready as possible for the photographer on the day to prevent unnecessary expense.

> **# TIP   Photography for cookery books**
>
> In the case of cookery books, you will likely require your photographer over a few days as you will need to cook each dish before it can be photographed. It may, therefore, be worth your while engaging the help of cooking assistants to ensure that dishes can be produced quickly and in a steady flow. It also takes time to set up the right lighting and photo styling to create the photographic look you're going for.
>
> Then you need to consider your venue – it should easily accommodate your cooking assistants, provide enough equipment and utensils to create all your dishes, and be visually conducive to photography and the theme of your book. Tap into your list of contacts: do you know anyone who owns a lodge, restaurant or other venue with a well-equipped kitchen that could also serve as a visually-appealing location for your photo shoot?
>
> You may want to consider the services of a photo stylist to create just the right shot in terms of mood, colouring, composition and tone. The photo stylist will usually find all the props needed to do this, and will also position the props for the photograph. Remember, you will be cooking or overseeing the cooking, and it will save both time and money to have an extra pair of professional hands take care of the creative aspects of each shot. Your opinion and feedback will still be required before each shot is taken, but at least most of your time can be spent doing what you do best – preparing and plating your dishes.
>
> If you're not using a photo stylist, and your venue does not have props such as crockery, cutlery and table decor, you could consider hiring them from a catering hire company. Alternatively, you could use a professional food art studio. They usually come equipped with cooking facilities, utensils, props, and adequate space for both cooking the dishes and photographing them. Food art studios can be quite expensive though, so careful budgeting on your part will be needed if you choose to go this route.

PREPARING YOUR MANUSCRIPT FOR PUBLISHING

> Refer to the Glossary on page 288 for a definition of terms used in this chapter.

Your manuscript is now complete and you have all your artwork and photos ready. You've also obtained all permissions, where necessary. Whether you use an independent publishing service or choose to go it alone with a popular print-on-demand or ebook service, your manuscript will need to be prepared for publishing.

If you're using an online print-on-demand or ebook service, it's best to refer to the manuscript preparation and publishing guidelines provided by the platform you're publishing through. The guidelines in this chapter are aimed primarily at authors who are using a custom publishing service or vanity press.

Your manuscript

Make sure that you hand over the **final, most complete version** of your document. It is better and more cost-effective for an editor to work with the entire manuscript than to attend to dribs and drabs. A full manuscript helps the editor maintain editorial continuity and consistency, and allows for proper cross-referencing within the manuscript. It also facilitates a smoother production process and helps to prevent unnecessary costs and delays.

Rather take the extra time needed to get your manuscript into good shape, complete with front and end matter. The same holds true when you receive the manuscript back from the editor. Take time to go through it carefully before forwarding it on for production and typesetting. Making extensive changes once typesetting begins could result in additional costs and delays in production.

> Find out more about typesetting on pages 135–136.

One exception is the index. Indexing is only done right at the end of the production cycle once the page numbering is final.

When using a publishing service, don't waste time perfecting the formatting of your document – the typesetter will reformat everything from scratch, anyway. Just make sure that the organisational structure and heading levels are clear, and that special features, such as information boxes, extracts, and quotes, are easily distinguished from the main body text.

Your images and artwork

You can leave artwork and photos in your document as a reference for placement, but you must still supply all artwork and photos in a separate folder.

> Refresh your memory regarding image resolution and quality by referring to pages 109–110.

In a professional production process, images are first converted from RGB (red-green-blue) to CMYK (cyan-magenta-yellow-key) colour format, and then inserted into the typeset document. This is done because printing uses a CMYK colour model. Fortunately, you will not need to do the colour converting yourself, nor will you need to resize or resample your images – your publishing service will do this for you.

> Find out more about printing and printing processes in Chapter 12.

Your photos and artwork can be supplied in any popular image format: JPEG, TIFF, BMP or EPS. You can also supply vector illustrations. These have sharp lines and text that are infinitely scalable, and are typically created using vector software, such as

Adobe Illustrator or CorelDraw. To preserve the sharpness of the lines and text, supply these in PDF format in either CMYK or black and white.

 # TIP Indicating image placement in the manuscript

If you do not include your images in your word-processing document as a reference, you must clearly indicate in the document exactly where they will appear. The format to use in a text file is square brackets with an instruction, before or after the relevant paragraph of text. You can also include the preferred image size. For example, [Insert A/W 5.2 Nguni Cattle – half-page size]. Let your typesetter know that the square brackets include instructions that should be deleted once they have been implemented. If you are using square brackets in your manuscript that should **not** be deleted, rather use colour for your artwork instructions and inform your typesetter. In fact, all instructions to your typesetter can be in either a specific colour or included in square brackets, with the latter taking preference.

Find out more about how square brackets are used in a traditional publishing environment in the Did You Know? box on page 129.

Handing your material over

Here is a checklist of what you will need to supply to your service provider:

- Your completed manuscript in **one document.**
- A PDF of your manuscript showing the layout. This is needed because when the manuscript is moved from one computer to another, or opened in different versions of the same software, the text flow and appearance can change. The PDF provides a good reference to the original layout.
- A separate folder containing all your artwork in either JPEG, TIFF, BMP, EPS, PSD or PDF format. Artwork must be clearly labelled, either sequentially in the order in which it will be placed, or according to the page number on which it appears in the PDF of your manuscript. The artwork file names can also include a few keywords that clearly link the artwork to the text.
- A covering letter with special instructions, if any.

- A photograph of you, the author, and a short biography.
- The book cover image, if you are responsible for providing one.
- The cover blurb, if you will be writing one, and endorsements that you'd like to add to your book or cover.
- The ISBN number, if you applied for one yourself.

ⓘ DID YOU KNOW?

When your manuscript goes for professional typesetting, it is completely deformatted and all images are removed. It is then reformatted from scratch using the design templates and formatting styles set up for your book. You will help the typesetting process enormously by ensuring that headings, special features and other deviations from the normal body text are made clear.

The reformatting of your book also explains why, on receiving your typeset pages back, you may notice that some of the italic and bold formatting has been lost. While typesetters do their best not to miss anything, they are trying to follow your original document, deal with the technicalities of the software, and negotiate the practicalities and challenges of laying out the book.

In a traditional publishing environment, editors mark up manuscripts for typesetting using tags. Tagging entails putting simple instructions in square brackets directly in front of, or directly after, special features, headings, captions, and so on. For example:

[Heading 1]Using a publishing service
[body text]This will indicate the start of the body text. The end of the body text is not indicated unless another, different feature begins.[end body text]
[Insert A/W: computer connecting to an online publisher – 1/4 page portrait]
[start extract text]This indicates the start of extract text that will likely be formatted differently to the body text. Theoretically, only start tags are needed to indicate when a style change or new element begins. But to play it safe and ensure that there is [bold]no[end bold] confusion, the [italic]correct[end italic] way is to add an end tag too. An end tag is mandatory when tagging words within a tagged section, such as the bold and italic text in this paragraph.[end extract text]
[Heading 2]Your images and artwork

Although somewhat laborious, you can see that by using tagging, no text formatting on the author or editor's part is needed. The typesetter simply follows the tags and knows exactly what to do with the text. In fact, they can even search for specific tags and auto-format them – which is exactly what they do if the manuscript has been tagged correctly and consistently. Everything is formatted perfectly and efficiently. However, for tagging to work optimally, keeping the tag names the same and using them consistently is key!

TIP Sending images or large files to your service provider

STEP 1 It's preferable to place all your content and images into one folder and zip the folder to create one file. It makes sending and receiving your content much easier, and items won't become lost in multiple emails.

STEP 2 Some publishing services will provide you with a link, or special access to their company server, to upload your files. If they don't, there are a number of large file transfer services available that you can use. The advantage of using a large file transfer service is that you can send a file of any size. Email accounts, on the other hand, often have 10–20MB attachment restrictions, so files larger than that are likely to be rejected. Popular large file transfer services that we recommend include: www.wetransfer.com, www.box.net, www.hightail.com, and www.dropbox.com. All of these services offer a free version, which should be more than adequate for your needs.

TIP Best practices for naming your electronic files

When sending files to other people, how you name your files is important. Firstly, naming files properly helps to prevent confusion – everyone in the publishing process knows exactly what the file is, for instance: Publish_Like_A_Pro_Cover_SA_Edition.pdf or Publish_Like_A_Pro_Inner_Revised_20180818.pdf. Secondly, some company's servers and online systems do not accept file names with special characters in them and will reject your files or prevent them from being uploaded. They may also reject files with very long file names. Here are some tips for naming your files before sending them off for production:

- Avoid using these special characters: ? ' ~ ! $ % @ # ^ & ` * ( ) ` < > , ; [ ] { } ' " ' "
- Special characters that are **safe** to use include:
  - Underscore, e.g. Publish_Like_A_Pro_Cover_SA_Edition.pdf
  - Hyphen, e.g. Publish-Like-A-Pro-Cover-SA-Edition.pdf
- Do not use spaces in your file name – some software will not recognise them; either use the safe characters above, or use camel case, e.g. PerfectBinding.tiff
- When using numbers to preface your filenames, use zeros in front of the numbers to ensure that your files sort in sequential order, for example: 001, 002, 003, ..., 009, 010, ..., 099, 100, ..., 999. This is especially helpful when numbering lots of images – inserting them into the document in the correct order becomes quick and easy.
- If you start your file name with a date, we recommend the YYYYMMDD format – this will ensure that all your files remain in chronological order.
- Choose a file naming convention and use that convention consistently.

DESIGN, TYPESETTING AND LAYOUT

The next stage of our publishing process involves the actual design and make-up of the book, such as formatting all the text, laying out the book, and providing PDF files that can be used for printing.

In a traditional publishing environment, book cover and book interior design are performed simultaneously after the designers have been briefed by the editorial team. The designers then present a few cover and interior design options that are assessed by the editorial, marketing and publishing teams. The author will usually be given an opportunity to offer his or her input before the final design is selected. The marketing team may also test covers among retailers to help them make a final choice.

With independent publishing, authors typically make these decisions on their own. A good independent publishing service may offer their input to make the job easier, but the author ultimately makes the final decision.

BOOK INTERIOR DESIGN AND STYLE SHEET SET-UP

Book design is where the interior look of the book is created; it gives each book its own unique character. Traditional publishers, particularly academic and educational publishers, frequently use a house style. This is a style that dictates design elements such as what fonts are used; the preferred layout style (e.g. shoulder or no shoulder, single column or multiple columns, and margin sizes); where the publisher's logo is positioned; the layout of the title page and copyright page; and so on.

It's much like a company's branding guidelines, ensuring visual consistency across all products in a range and reinforcing the publishing company's brand. The consumer unconsciously associates the consistent visual message with reliability and, of course, professionalism. It also makes the company's work, or range of products, immediately identifiable.

Designing a house or series style will be more applicable to an author who is publishing books that are part of a series.

Choosing your book size

Before you begin, you or your publisher will need to choose a book size, called a trim size. A custom publishing company will likely make this decision for you, or at the very least, recommend a suitable size. A vanity press may do the same. If you intend publishing through a print-on-demand platform, it's important to confirm their accepted range of book sizes so that when you prepare your print-ready PDF files, those files meet their criteria.

And finally, if you're going the true self-publishing route – doing everything yourself and having your local printer print the book – *you* will need to decide on the book size and then format your book to that size. We recommend that you stick to international book sizes so that if you swap over to an international print-on-demand platform, your PDF files will be compatible. The book size you choose should be typical of your genre of book.

Table 2 presents common international book sizes that are found on international print-on-demand platforms.

TABLE 2 Common international book sizes

International size in inches (w x h)	South African size in millimetres (h x w)	Name	Book genre
4.25 x 6.875	174.63 x 107.95	Pocket	Fiction, non-fiction
5 x 8	203.2 x 127	Digest	Fiction
5.25 x 8	203.2 x 133.3		Fiction
5.5 x 8.5	215.9 x 139.7		Fiction, non-fiction
6 x 9	228.6 x 152.4	US Trade	Fiction, non-fiction
7 x 10	254 x 177.8		Non-fiction
8.5 x 11	279.4 x 215.9	US Letter	Non-fiction, academic, educational, coffee-table
8.268 x 11.693	297 x 210	A4	Non-fiction, academic, educational, coffee-table

> **# TIP Local and international book sizes**
>
> International book sizes work on width x height; South African book sizes work on height x width. It's important to remember this when requesting a quote from a South African printer to eliminate the possibility of error.
> If in doubt, include the word 'portrait' or 'landscape' with the dimensions that you supply to your printer.
>
> Landscape orientation   Portrait orientation

Designing the interior

When your book interior is designed, special consideration is given to the following elements:
- The font styles (typefaces).
- Font sizes for text and headings.
- Margin widths, including inner margins for binding.
- Word, letter and line spacing.
- Graphic elements, if any.
- Formatting of tables, quotes, graphs and footnotes.
- The book's character, which is communicated using a combination of the elements mentioned above.

Your book interior designer should have considerable knowledge of printing and binding processes so that the design works for the process being used.

You and the publisher both want your book to look as good as possible, so the publisher will present an interior design option that can be further refined with your input.

Once the book interior has been designed, the designer sets up page templates and formatting styles to ensure that the formatting of the book remains consistent throughout.

Choosing fonts

A font is a set of text characters of a specific style; anyone who uses a computer is familiar with fonts. One of the tasks the book designer will perform is choosing fonts and font sizes (called point sizes) for your book based on the type of book, your target market, and the overall impression the book must make on the reader. For instance, academic books call for a serious font, whereas children's books require a font that is large and easy to read. Architectural books might call for a clean, contemporary-style font, whereas the character of an indigenous cookery book might be better reflected through a highly stylised font. So font styles not only have a practical purpose, they also help to convey the personality of the book.

For books featuring long tracts of text, such as fiction, a serif font is recommended. A serif is a slight projection finishing off a stroke of a letter, like a little foot. Well-known serif fonts include Times New Roman, Cambria and Book Antiqua. The opposite of a serif font is a sans serif font ('sans' meaning 'without'). Well-known sans serif fonts include Helvetica, Arial and Calibri.

This is a serif font and **This is a sans serif font**

Refer to the Glossary at the back of the book for printing and design terms.

So why are serif fonts used for large tracts of text? Because the serifs lead the eye easily and effortlessly from one letter to the next, forming a kind of bridge between them. This enables quick and easy reading. Sans serif text, on the other hand, is more difficult to read quickly and should be reserved for shorter sections of text. Sans serif fonts are good for headings, design features, quotes and captions. The exception is children's books. Sans serif fonts are recommended for children's books because young children are exposed to sans serif fonts when they're learning to read at school, so these fonts are familiar to them.

> **# TIP** Choosing your fonts
>
> **PRINT PUBLISHING:** If you're considering print-on-demand as your publishing solution and you're formatting the book yourself, avoid using Times New Roman as a body font. Publishing houses and graphic designers almost never use this font because it's uninspiring and overused. It's also a dead giveaway that a book has been self-published. Consider other fonts such as Minion, Palatino, Cambria, Garamond and Century. For headings, captions and special text boxes, you may want to steer clear of other overused, misused, and unprofessional fonts such as Comic Sans, Brush Script, Bradley Hand, Papyrus and Hobo. Also consider replacing Arial with a slicker sans serif font if you can. Finally, avoid using too many different fonts in your book – it looks unprofessional. Rather stick to no more than two or three font families for all your text and headings and use the variants of those families (italic, bold, bold italic, condensed) to create differentiation and interest.
>
> **EBOOK PUBLISHING:** It's perfectly acceptable to use Times New Roman for your reflowable Kindle or ePub fiction ebook. Firstly, most e-readers come standard with Times New Roman installed. Secondly, many e-reading devices allow users to change the fonts to suit their preferences, anyway.

TYPESETTING AND LAYOUT

Once the book template and style sheets have been set up, typesetting begins. Typesetting involves formatting all the text and laying out the book using the design specifications created in the previous step.

Your manuscript document is completely deformatted and then reformatted using professional publishing software. This ensures 100% style consistency throughout the document. It also means that if a style is changed at a later stage – for example, you decide you want all your captions in italic – editing the caption style will automatically change all captions in the document to the italicised font.

A typesetter cannot realistically work through a 300-page book and change font or heading styles manually. It's too time-consuming, introduces errors, and is not at all cost-effective – you would end up footing a costly bill. Reformatting all text using preset styles makes these kinds of changes quicker and easier to implement.

The typesetter also resizes images, converts them to the correct colour space for printing (greyscale or CMYK), redraws tables and graphs, and adds all the other bells and whistles you see in a book. Finally, the typesetter checks (preflights) the book to ensure that all files meet approved printing standards and that there will be no issues when the job goes to press.

The combination of book design and typesetting is what gives a book its professional look and feel inside. An industry professional can easily tell the difference between a professionally typeset book and one that has been put together by the author using software such as Microsoft Word.

ⓘ DID YOU KNOW?

Microsoft Word is never used for professional publishing as it does not offer the same control over the book content that professional publishing and design software does. Neither does it offer the technical control needed for professional file preparation for printing and binding.

So what software is used by publishing professionals, you may be wondering? Adobe InDesign and QuarkXpress are the most commonly used. Microsoft Publisher is sometimes used, but usually in a business environment where companies produce their own books and materials. It's rarely, if ever, used in a professional design or publishing environment. CorelDraw, while good design software for a commercial PC-based design and print environment, is not good for publishing as it lacks the speed, efficiency and control that professional publishing software provides.

YOUR COVER STORY

Unless you happen to be a professional graphic designer or book illustrator, we strongly advise you not to even attempt to design the cover of your book. You may have spent many hours dreaming about what the cover of your book will look like and how your name will shine in bright lights, but that's as far as you should go. By all means, share your thoughts and fantasies with your publisher – a good publisher will take these into account – but the ultimate look and feel of your front cover should be brought to life by a professional book cover designer.

People do judge a book by its cover. The front cover is a major deciding factor in the purchasing process. It can either persuade or repel. An excellent book cover design should convey the tone of the book and speak to the emotions of the reader. The cover should engage them on a deeper level than superficial judgement and subliminally convince them that the book and its message will rock their world. A brilliant, attractive, appealing book cover is not a luxury, it's essential.

The quality of the cover design is also a dead giveaway of whether a book has been professionally produced. As we've mentioned before, the book trade tends to steer clear of books that look self-published, so it's important to have a professional-looking cover for your book.

Traditional book publishers will consult you on your ideas for the book cover, but, ultimately, the final decision will be theirs, as they will want a book cover that has commercial appeal and has the approval of their sales and marketing team. Sometimes they will road-test a book cover with trusted bookstore managers before making the final decision.

When publishing independently, your input is essential as *you* will be selling your book. Your publishing service will discuss book covers with you and then, along with their graphic designer, translate your ideas into several versions to discuss and tweak, before a final book cover is selected. If budget is an issue, there are services available that offer pre-designed book covers. One such service is The Book Cover Designer[1]. They offer thousands of generic covers at excellent prices. They will change the title and author name for you at no extra cost and create a wraparound version of the cover for a small fee. All covers are unique: when you purchase a cover it is removed from the site and is no longer available for purchase. The main advantage of a pre-designed book cover – apart from the price – is that you can see exactly what you're paying for and it's quick and easy to order.

Similarly, the back cover is vital to the success of your book. When readers pick a book off a shelf, they do three things: look at the title of the book; examine the cover; and turn the book over to see what's written on the back. The latter is known as the **back cover blurb** and it comprises probably the most important 150 or so words of your book. Not only will it be used on the book itself, it will probably serve as an online sales description as well.

Consider the back cover blurb as an advertisement or sales pitch for your book. Your publisher may offer to assist you with this, but it pays to know what works. Above all else, the blurb should act as a hook for readers – it should catch their attention and reel them in. There are many good, online sources to help you write a winning blurb.

If you are writing **fiction**, your back cover should include a short description of your book, hinting at its plotlines, naming the main characters, mentioning any dilemmas they are facing and then creating intrigue that will leave readers wanting more.

Non-fiction authors need to be more specific, stating who their book is for and how it will help the reader. Bullet points are extremely useful and should be along the lines of: "In this book you will learn how to … bullet point, bullet point, bullet point" – no fewer than three bullets and no more than five. Don't forget your keywords for search engine optimisation.

---

1   http://www.thebookcoverdesigner.com

If you're stuck, it's probably best to let the person who has edited your book write the back cover blurb as well, as they will have an in-depth familiarity of your work and will know the benefits and sales points to highlight. You can then adjust the blurb as necessary. Other elements that should appear on the back cover of your book include:

- A brief author biography and recent photograph.
- Any especially good testimonials or endorsements.
- Barcode with ISBN (required for bookstore distribution).
- Publisher's name.
- Author's website address.

> Find out more about ISBNs and barcodes in the next chapter.

PAGE PROOFS AND FINAL SIGN-OFF

Once your typesetting is complete, you will receive first page proofs for checking, usually supplied as a PDF. This is one of the most exciting stages in book production. It's where you, the author, finally get to see your book in a professional format – where all your work for the past few months, or years, transforms into something that starts to look like a real book.

In a traditional publishing workflow, first page proofs are sent to a proofreader for checking and correcting. Your publishing service may automatically include this as part of your production workflow, but if not, then the responsibility for commissioning a proofreader will be up to you. This is also *your* opportunity to correct any errors that may have slipped through from editing and typesetting, and to make alternate layout recommendations if required.

It's advisable to let a few trusted friends or family members help you with the task of reading the proofs and highlighting the corrections that need to be made. This is the perfect time, for example, to have your newspaper editor brother-in-law step in and help. Corrections should be made **directly on to the PDF proof**, a copy of which should be kept for cross-checking later, or submitted in writing to your service provider, by email.

> To mark corrections directly on to a PDF proof, refer to the tip box titled "PDF proofs with 'Reader Extended' capabilities" on page 143.

You will then be given a second set of proofs to confirm that all corrections from the first set have been made. Sometimes a third set of proofs may be necessary if you've picked up additional errors on the second set of proofs. It's wise to find out, beforehand, how many sets of proofs you receive as part of the typesetting fee. Extra proofs could incur additional charges.

 # TIP Reader Extended PDF capabilities

Your publisher may provide you with a Reader Extended PDF file. This is a PDF that has extra functionality added to it, enabling you to make comments and corrections directly on to the PDF pages using Adobe Reader's Comment feature. This is easier and quicker than trying to explain what corrections to make in an email to your service provider. Many computers already have Adobe Reader installed, but if yours doesn't, it can be safely downloaded from the Adobe website (https://get.adobe.com/reader) at no cost. **So remember to ask your publishing service to supply you with a Reader Extended PDF file if they haven't done so.**

To make your corrections, first download the PDF on to your hard drive. Remember where you save it when you download it! Then launch Adobe Reader and open your file from *within* the open application. Click on the Comment tab and some editing tools will become visible. Don't forget to save your PDF before you exit the program or your changes will be lost. Return the corrected PDF to your service provider.

 # TIP The benefits of paper proofs for checking errors

It is much easier to pick up errors on paper than on screen. For this reason, and particularly if you will be printing your book in large quantities, leaving no further opportunity to fix mistakes until your next print run, it is highly recommended that you print your book at 100% scale (ensure that 'Fit to page' is not selected), and proofread the hard-copy. If you're worried about cutting down trees, refer to pages 166 and 167 in Chapter 12 – it will make you think differently about paper. Sustainably sourced and managed paper is good for the planet, far better than the computers and electronics that are needed to read our PDFs and ebooks. Paper is a renewable resource that gets recycled. It also has a low carbon footprint and forests cultivated for paper absorb CO_2, thus helping to counteract global warming.

If you're making corrections on to **hard-copy proofs** (printed proofs), you can use **proofreader's marks** to ensure that your corrections are easily understood by the typesetter. We have included some commonly used proofreader's marks on page 142, accompanied by an example on page 143 of how these should be inserted into your text. If your publishing company is a professional one, they will know what these marks mean. Use red or blue pen to make it easier for the typesetter to spot these instructions.

Signing off final proofs

Once you're happy with the proofs, you will be required to sign a proof sheet or send written approval to your publishing service giving them the go-ahead for the next stage, which is usually a digitally printed and bound sample book.

> **# TIP** The benefits of a printed and bound sample book
>
> Ensure that you receive a printed and bound sample book from your service provider before you sign off on the final print run. This is a valuable opportunity to carefully check the book and ensure that you are happy with the paper type and thickness, spine width, and print quality. If your book is hardcover, thread-sewn, uses spot colours, or has special finishes, a printed and bound sample book reflecting your book's specifications is not possible for practical and cost reasons. However, you can request a softcover, perfect-bound sample book that will at least give you an idea of what your book will look like. You may have to pay for an hour or two of design time to adapt your book cover for this purpose, but the extra expense is well worth it.

If your book is being litho printed, you should also receive an additional proof from the litho printer, which will typically be a set of unbound paper proofs or an online proof. This is your last chance to make corrections. There is no turning back after this point. If you spot anything after the book has been printed, it's too late for this print run.

Refer to Chapter 12 on pages 154 and 157 to find out more about litho and digital printing.

It is **never** a good idea to rush the production process. It is very difficult to pick up mistakes under pressure. Your book will require multiple reads, even during the production stage, and this needs to be factored into your timeline. Be honest: *must* your book be out on the date that you've decided? Rather readjust your thinking and be generous with your timeline and flexible with your expectations.

Proofreading and editing marks

∧	Insert something (the text to be inserted is normally provided in the margin)
ℓ	Delete
◡	Close up space
ℓ̃	Delete and close up
#	Add space
∼	Transpose
sp	Spell out
≡	Make uppercase
/	Make lowercase
stet	Let it stand (do not implement change)
eq#	Make equal space
∧,	Insert a comma
⊙	Insert a period
;/	Insert a semicolon
⊙	Insert colon
=	Insert hyphen
/N	Insert en dash
/m	Insert em dash
∨	Insert apostrophe
?	Insert question mark
!	Insert exclamation mark
(/)	Insert parentheses
[/]	Insert brackets
∨∨ or ∨∨	Insert quotation marks
bf	Set as bold
ital	Set as italics
wf	Wrong font
⌐	Move left
⌐	Move right
⊓	Move up
⊔	Move down
⌐⌐	Centre
¶	Begin paragraph

Reproduced with kind permission from Wordy.com – https://www.wordy.com/writers-workshop/proofreading-marks-symbols

This is an example of how to apply proofreader's marks to text. Every instruction features a mark in the margin and a mark in the text.

Instruction to typesetter	Mark made in the text	Mark made in the margin
Delete	She is not a lucky silver fish	⌒/ or ℯ
Close up	She is a lucv er fish	⌒
Delete and close up	She is a lucky fisɧh	⌒/
Insert in text	She is a lucky/fish	∧ silver
Insert space	She is a lucky/silver fish	#
Insert hyphen	She is a lucky silver/fish	/- or =
Insert dash	She is a/lucky silver fish	/—/ or ⊥/N or 1/M
Insert full stop, comma, semi-colon, colon, bracket	She is a/lucky silver fish/	∧: ∧⊙
Insert quotation marks	She is a/lucky silver fish/	∧" ∧"
Insert superior number	She is a lucky silver fish/	∧³
Transpose letters	She is a lukcy silver fish	trs
Change to bold type	She is a lucky silver fish	bold
Change to italic type	She is a lucky silver fish	ital
Change to roman type	(She is a lucky silver fish)	rom
Change to lower case	She is a LUCKY silver fish	l.c.
Change to capital letters	She is a lucky silver fish	caps
Insert new paragraph	[She is a lucky silver fish	[or NP
Run on (no new paragraph)	She is a ⌐ lucky silver fish	run on
Indent text	[She is a lucky silver fish	⌐
Align text with margin	⌊She is a lucky silver fish ⌋She is a lucky silver fish ⌊She is a lucky silver fish	∥
Leave text unchanged	She is a lucky silver fish	STET

Adapted from *How to Get Published in South Africa* by Basil van Rooyen, Southern Book Publishers (Pty) Ltd.

Fiction formatting tips to get you started

Follow these tips for a more professional book interior when using a print-on-demand service:

- **Font style:** Good serif fonts for main body text are Janson Text, Minion, Garamond, Century Schoolbook, Palatino, Caslon, Baskerville, Sabon and Utopia. Some of these fonts pair particularly well with certain genres, for instance: Sabon and romantic fiction; Garamond and thrillers; Baskerville and literary fiction; Caslon and academic non-fiction; Utopia and general-interest books. There are no hard-and-fast rules – whatever you choose, the font should be easy to read and should work for your genre.
- **Font size:** A good size for body text is 11 or 11.5pt with 15 or 16pt line spacing. The trend leans towards generous line spacing – from 4–6pt bigger than the font size. Try these sizes out by printing a formatted page at 100% scale and compare it to the font size and line spacing of a bestselling book of the same genre. Adjust your font size and spacing until it's similar or the same.
- **Margins:** Allow generous page margins of no less than 18mm all around. Preferably work with mirrored (two-sided) margins so that you can set the inside margin at least 5mm wider than the outside margin to compensate for the margin loss that occurs with perfect binding (see Chapter 12).
- **New paragraphs:** Create new paragraphs by indenting the first line of each paragraph by 5–6mm. First line indents should be created using your paragraph formatting palette. Do not TAB or spacebar to get your text to the required place. Non-fiction sometimes uses the space-before paragraph formatting option to create paragraph breaks, but space-before paragraph breaks are not normally used for fiction except to create scene breaks. If you are formatting non-fiction, pick one method or the other – do **not** use both methods together! After a scene break, which is typically indicated by asterisks * * * or a white line space, start your next scene with the first line of text flush left (no first line indent). The first line of a new chapter should also start flush left.
- **New chapters:** Look at other books for ideas on how to start your chapter. Allow generous spacing above and below your chapter heads or chapter numbers.
- **Page numbering:** Remember to add page numbering. Centre your page numbers if you don't know how to work with left and right pages in your document. Page numbers should be no closer than 10–13mm from the page edge.
- **Running heads:** A running head is a short descriptive title that appears at the top of each page. Include running heads to create a professional look, unless *not* having them is part of your design strategy. The left page will usually show the author's name and the right page will usually show the book title. With non-fiction, running heads aid navigation by helping the reader to identify the chapter or section they are in. The left page usually shows the book title or section number and name, and the right page shows the chapter number and name. There should be at least 10–13mm between the running head and the trim edge of the page – if not, your file may be rejected by the online publishing platform. You should also leave enough space between the running head and the body text – nothing less than 5mm, and usually no more than about 7–8mm.

- **Prelim pages (front matter):** These pages appear at the front of your book and should be included in your book document. There is an example of non-fiction prelim pages in Appendix C and on page 52. The prelim pages for fiction titles are a lot simpler. The first prelim page is page number 1 and it's the first right-hand page in the book after the inside front cover. The prelim pages must include your copyright page (see Appendix D on page 278). Prelim pages often use blind numbering (page numbers that cannot be seen) in roman numerals (i, ii, iii, iv) or Arabic numerals (1, 2, 3, 4). The first chapter normally starts on whatever page number comes after the last prelim page – typically the next right-hand page. It's quite acceptable to insert a blank page before the chapter start page if you need to force the chapter to start on a right-hand page. The page number is represented in visible Arabic numerals.

An example of prelim pages for a fiction title would be:

Page number	Page type	Details
i	Half-title page	Right-hand page; blind numbered
ii	Blank page	Left-hand page; blind numbered
iii	Title page	Right-hand page; blind numbered
iv	Imprint page	Left-hand page; blind numbered
v	Dedication	Right-hand page; blind numbered
vi	Blank page	Left-hand page; blind numbered
1	Chapter 1	Right-hand page; Arabic numeral

- **Endlim pages (end matter):** These pages are found at the back of a book. For fiction, they would include 'Other books from the author' and 'About the author'.
- **Last page:** Your book should always end on a left-hand page (even-numbered page) for printing purposes, even if it's a blank page.

When formatting your book, **consistency is key!** Apply your formatting consistently, throughout, using your word processor's paragraph and character styles. There are good online tutorials and videos that show you how to set up and work with paragraph and character styles. Once your paragraph and character styles have been set up, simply highlight the text you want to style, and then click on the paragraph or character style you want to change it to.

Also remember to let your content 'breathe'. This means allowing generous spacing for your margins, within your body of text, and above and below your headings and subheadings. One of the biggest mistakes self-publishing authors make is letting their text run too close to the edge of the page and using overly-tight line spacing for their main body text. Look at the layout of other, similar books to stimulate ideas about how to format your own book. See what you like and what you don't. There are also plenty of online resources available to help you create a more professional-looking book.

ISBN ASSIGNMENT, LEGAL DEPOSIT AND BARCODES

ISBN ASSIGNMENT

Books that are sold commercially should have an ISBN and a barcode. An ISBN (International Standard Book Number) is a unique numeric book identification number represented by a 13-digit number from which a 13-digit barcode is generated. Since books can share the same name, the ISBN is used to help retailers and consumers identify and purchase the correct book. It also helps them differentiate between different book formats (hardcover, softcover, ePub, Kindle, PDF) and different editions (1st, 2nd, 3rd edition). The barcode facilitates quick and easy retrieval of the book information at retail point of sale (POS) and distribution warehouses.

The ISBN is inserted on the imprint page, and both ISBN and barcode are inserted on the back cover of the book. Each new

You will find an example of an imprint page in Appendix D on page 278.

edition of the same book should receive a new ISBN, as should each format of that book.

Books published privately for distribution to clients, family, church groups or special interest clubs do not need an ISBN. Neither do they need a barcode. If, at a later stage, you choose to make your book commercially available, you can always apply for one then. Since most private publishing projects utilise short-run digital printing, files can be easily adapted to accommodate the addition of an ISBN number and barcode before the next print run. A barcode with the ISBN number can also be added to existing copies of your book by way of self-adhesive stickers.

If you are publishing commercially, most online publishing and distribution platforms, vanity presses and custom publishers will assign an ISBN to your book listing themselves as the publisher, unless you supply your own. Many self-publishing authors prefer to obtain their own. The advantage of doing so is that the ISBN is always linked to you, not a publishing service. So, the ISBN for each format and edition remains the same regardless of the number of platforms you distribute through, provided your book files have not changed. This eliminates potential confusion among customers and retailers regarding editions, book formats, and the publisher (you) if you change online publishing and distribution platforms.

The disadvantage of registering your own ISBN is that you may lack the credibility that comes with being part of a publishing imprint. In other words, you gain credibility when you're represented by a publisher, because the perception is that a publisher will produce a higher-quality product than a self-publishing author. Of course, this is only a consideration if you're using a reputable publishing service to begin with. If you're using an online ebook publishing or print-on-demand platform, or a vanity publisher, you're probably better served owning your ISBN.

Registering an ISBN in your name

To register an ISBN in your name, or the name of your organisation, you need to make application to the **national ISBN agency in *your* country of operation**. Your country of operation is the country in which you carry out your publishing business.

Examples:
- If you're South African and you publish your book in South Africa, you'd apply for your ISBN from the National Library of South Africa.
- If you're South African, but live and publish in the US, you'd apply for your ISBN from the US ISBN agency.
- If you're based in Zimbabwe and manage your book business in Zimbabwe, but use a South African author services company for your production and printing, you'd register your ISBN in Zimbabwe.

So, using a production and printing service in another country doesn't mean you must apply for an ISBN in that country – it's where you *operate* your publishing business from that determines where you apply.

To find the ISBN agency in your country or region, visit the International ISBN Agency[1] online.

Applying for an ISBN in South Africa

If you would like to obtain the ISBN yourself and be listed as the publisher, you can obtain it directly from the National Library of South Africa (NLSA)[2] in Pretoria. Visit their website for their contact details. ISBNs are issued by the NLSA free of charge.

---

1 http://www.isbn-international.org
2 http://www.nlsa.ac.za

To order your ISBN from the NLSA, you will need to provide the following information via email:
- Title of book (must be exactly the way you want it registered).
- Language (if not English).
- Author name or pseudonym.
- Contributors' names (e.g. author, co-authors, etc.).
- Publisher's name (this will be your name or your company name if your company is to be registered as the publisher).
- Book formats for which you require the ISBN (e.g. hardcover print edition, softcover print edition, Kindle, ePub, PDF).
- Your full postal address, including postal code.
- Your contact numbers and dialling code.
- Fax number (if you have one).
- Email address (double-check it to ensure accuracy as this is how you will receive future mailings and information from the NLSA).

Remember to notify the NLSA if there are any changes to your contact details so that they can update their records.

DID YOU KNOW?

DIFFERENT BOOK FORMATS AND EDITIONS REQUIRE DIFFERENT ISBNs

Book formats: A different ISBN is needed for each book format that you produce. In other words, your print edition must have a different ISBN to your Kindle edition, and your Kindle edition must have a different ISBN to your ePub edition. This enables consumers and retailers to search for and purchase the correct book format. Your hardcover edition should also have a different ISBN to your softcover edition.

Editions: Each new edition of your book must also have a different ISBN from the previous edition. Again, this is to help bookstores and customers purchase the correct edition of a book. When self-publishing, fixing minor errors in a book does not warrant a new edition. However, adding a new chapter, updating important information, major edits, and cover changes, does. In educational and academic publishing, all book updates are treated as revised editions. Very often lecturers will prescribe a particular edition of a book so that all students are working from the same edition with content on the same page of each book so it can be easily referred to.

> **ⓘ DID YOU KNOW?**
>
> Having a book registered with your national ISBN authority does not mean that retailers and the general public will be able to locate your book using an Internet search or by accessing some database. For this kind of discoverability, your book must be listed with an international bibiographic service, such as Nielsen BookData or South African Publications Network (SAPnet). SAPnet is the exclusive South African agent for Nielsen BookData. A book listing on SAPnet/Nielsen BookData provides important bibliographic information on your book such as book title and subtitle, authors, contributors, book description (long and short), ISBN, keywords, Book Industry Standards and Communications (BISAC) codes, book cover image, and more. Retailers and publishers around the world use this database to monitor sales trends and rankings, and to order books listed in their database. A vanity press and some custom publishers will list your book in this database, or at least offer you the option. If they don't, you can apply to be listed by contacting www.sapnet.co.za or www.nielsenbookdata.co.uk. There is a listing fee.

Find out more about BISAC codes on page 194.

LEGAL DEPOSIT IN SOUTH AFRICA

When applying for an ISBN in South Africa, it's a **legal requirement** to submit one book to each of the five places of legal deposit (national libraries) within 14 days of the book's public release date. You will need to put aside **five books** from your print run for this purpose. Failure to submit your books could result in a hefty fine and prevent you from obtaining further ISBNs until your previous obligations have been met.

The idea behind legal deposit is that your books are made available to library users and are preserved for the benefit of future generations – your book becomes your heritage to the nation. The NLSA provides full instructions on how to submit your books for legal deposit when you receive your ISBN.

If you are working through a custom publisher or vanity press in South Africa, they will usually handle legal deposit on your behalf. Print-on-demand companies in South Africa will seldom fulfil these obligations, so you will need to take responsibility for doing so. Legal deposit may not be applicable in other countries, but if it is, the ISBN agency in your country will inform you.

BARCODE GENERATION

A barcode is a rectangular image consisting of vertical lines of varying widths, which is read by a barcode scanner to enable quick and easy retrieval of product data, such as title name, product variant (hardcover or softcover), supplier, and price, among other things. Your book must have a barcode if you intend selling it through retail outlets, libraries, and when using a book distributor.

A barcode is generated from an ISBN, so you must apply for your ISBN *before* you approach a company to generate your barcode.

If you're working through a traditional publisher, custom publishing company, or vanity press, you will not need to worry about a barcode – they will generate one for you. Certain print-on-demand publishing platforms also provide you with a barcode, which you can download and insert on your cover artwork.

If you're using your own designer to create your book cover and your publishing platform does not supply you with a barcode, you will need to source a reputable company to assist with this. The barcode is usually provided in TIFF, BMP or PSD format; these formats are all suitable for printing and offer high quality, single-colour reproduction.

Barcodes should be used in **single colour black**, *not* RGB or CMYK. This is because you require sharp, black lines for reliable, problem-free scanning. RGB and CMYK are made up of multiple colours, and if the registration of the printing is out, even marginally, you will notice the other colours bleeding out from under the black, creating what appears to be a slight blur. A good example of the blur we speak of from poor registration can often be found in full-colour newspapers. The presses are running at such high speed that a paper shift of even a fraction of a millimetre throws the registration out.

> **# TIP** Placing the barcode on your cover
>
> - Always use the barcode at the size in which it has been provided – do **not** rescale it. Rescaling could compromise scanning at point of sale. If you need a smaller barcode, ask your service provider to generate a new one for you at your preferred size.
> - Ensure that there is adequate contrast between the bars of the barcode and the background of your book cover. A white background behind black bars is safest and therefore the recommended option.
> - **Never** place a barcode on a red background because the colour red appears black when scanned with a barcode scanner; your black barcode lines will not be visible.
> - Ideally, place the barcode at the bottom left-hand corner of your back cover where most barcodes are placed and where point of sale staff expect to find it. This makes for quicker, easier scanning at point of sale. If this is not possible because of your cover design, place the barcode bottom centre or at the bottom right-hand corner of your back cover.
> - To find out more about barcodes and best practices when using them, visit www.gs1.org.

ALL ABOUT PRINTING – LITHO OR DIGITAL?

Your cover has been designed, your book has been typeset, and final print-ready PDF files have been generated. Now you are ready to go to print. One of the decisions you will have to make as an author publishing independently is whether to print your books lithographically (also called litho or offset printing) or digitally. Fortunately, this is one of the easier decisions in publishing and will be based on a few considerations:

- The type of book you are printing.
- How many copies you are likely to sell.
- The financial resources you have available.
- How you intend to distribute your book.

Digital printing is used for small-run or print-on-demand publishing, while **litho printing** is used for larger print runs, or printing that requires custom finishes, book sizes and paper types. It's also the better option for colour printing.

LITHO PRINTING

Litho printing is a process that uses inks, metal plates and rubber rollers. The inked plate, which has an etched image of your page on it, presses the image on to a soft roller and the roller transfers the image on to the paper.

Litho printing is suited to larger print runs because the cost per unit *decreases* as the print quantity *increases*. The expensive costs of making the printing plates and setting up the machine are shared by a larger number of books. It is therefore the printing method chosen by trade publishers who print thousands of books at a time. In fact, most traditional publishers will not consider publishing a book if they are not assured of selling at least 5 000 copies, so this is normally the minimum print run they will consider. Smaller traditional publishers are willing to look at 3 000 books. Don't forget that if you've sold 3 500 to 4 000 books through bookstores in South Africa, you have a local bestseller on your hands! With these larger quantities, publishers benefit from low unit costs and can thus make a higher profit on each book.

If you choose litho printing, you will need to invest more. Very roughly, when printing 1 000 copies, you're looking at about R25 000+ for an average novel and R85 000–R150 000+ for a full-colour book.

Litho printing offers greater flexibility in terms of book size, paper choice and finishing options. You can cost-effectively add special touches to your book, such as a foiled or embossed cover, special inserts, spot varnishes and cover flaps, because the set-up costs of these added extras are amortised over a larger run. Litho printing also yields the best print quality.

Litho printing is done on presses using large sheets of paper. Multiple pages of the book are laid out on one sheet, known as a signature. A modern press has many upright units, each of which contains one of the four CMYK inks. Depending on the number of units available, spot colours and machine or spot varnishes can also be accommodated. The paper sheets pass systematically

> Find out more about budgets and costs in Chapter 15, and distribution in Chapter 16.

from one unit to the next picking up each new colour until the full sheet is printed. Once printed, the signature is folded multiple times and cut to form a stack of pages. Each sheet provides one stack of pages. These multiple stacks are then placed on top of one another, bound into the cover and trimmed to size.

Page counts for books that are being litho printed are based on multiples of 8, 16 or 32, depending on the book trim size and the size of the sheets that can be accommodated on the press. These multiples also allow for the thread-sewing binding method. This needs to be borne in mind when deciding on the page count of your book and your binding method. Multiples of 16 are the most common configuration and usually the most cost-effective. Multiples of 8 are used for larger books, such as A4 or US letter size. Multiples of 32 are suitable for smaller books printed on large presses, such as pocket books.

Find out more about binding methods on pages 162–165.

Litho printing is best suited to:
- Large print runs.
- Full-colour books.
- Books requiring specialised finishing and binding.
- Oversize books.
- Printing using spot colours.

FIGURE 2 **A full-colour lithographic press with eight colour units**

SECTION 3 | BOOK PRODUCTION PROCESSES – THE NUTS AND BOLTS

ⓘ DID YOU KNOW?

IMPOSITION is the name given to the process of arranging individual pages on a larger sheet so that when the sheet is printed, it can be folded and trimmed to give you a complete section of pages running sequentially. Figure 3 shows the imposition of a simple 8-page spiral-bound booklet. These particular sheets hold only four pages front and four pages back. Large printing presses can hold up to 32 pages front and 32 pages back. Imposition becomes very complex for larger books!

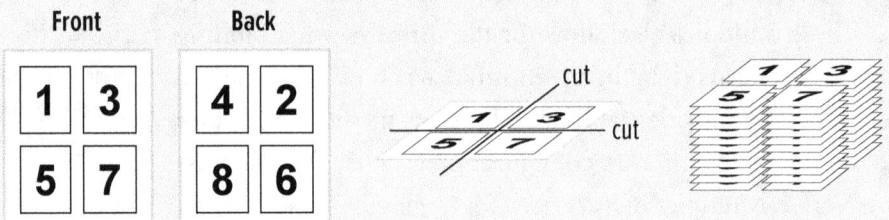

Above: Imposition of an 8-page booklet on one sheet of paper (four pages front, four pages back), cut twice. The loose pages are then spiral-bound or ring-bound.

Right: Imposition of an 8-page booklet, folded twice and cut once; the booklet is stapled on the vertical centre fold.

FIGURE 3 Imposition of a simple 8-page spiral-bound booklet

In printing, a **PAGE** is one side of a piece of paper. A **LEAF** or **SHEET** includes both sides of a piece of paper. So a book that is 64 pages in extent is actually made up of 32 leaves or sheets.

A **SIGNATURE** is the name given to a sheet of paper printed front and back with multiple pages imposed on both sides, making up one section of a book when the sheet has been folded and trimmed. Because a section of pages is contained on one sheet or signature, different sections of the book can be printed on different papers and in different colours. This is why you will find autobiographies with colour pages printed on white paper grouped into a section in the middle or at the back of the book, while the rest of the book is printed in black on off-white paper. This is the most cost-effective way of using colour in your book. If you don't group your colour pages together in a signature, and instead choose to spread them throughout the book, you will have to pay for full-colour printing plates for each and every signature on which a colour page appears.

> **# TIP** Obtain professional help for litho printing
>
> Due to the complexity and higher cost of litho printing, it's advisable to obtain the help of an experienced book designer or publishing consultant for the planning, production and management of your job. If things go wrong or there are quality issues (which happens), they will know how to deal with the printing company and ensure that the problem is rectified and the job is printed to your satisfaction.

> **ⓘ DID YOU KNOW?**
>
> CMYK is also known as 'process colour'. Process colours are printed as tiny dots of varying sizes at different angles. If you have a magnifying glass, look at some full-colour photographs in a magazine or coffee-table book to see just how these dots create perfect images in the full spectrum of colours. It's truly amazing!

DIGITAL PRINTING

With digital printing, an image is sent directly to a printer from a computer using digital files, such as PDFs. Instead of using inks, digital printers use powder toners in the four process colours – CMYK. This eliminates the need for printing plates and the kind of machine set-up required by litho printing, thus reducing costs and saving time.

Digital printing, therefore, has very low set-up costs, making it suitable for small print runs of up to 750 books. With smaller print runs comes lower cash outlay and therefore lower financial risk. Digital printing is cheaper and faster than litho printing at these smaller quantities.

Digital printing is best-suited to books with black-only text and greyscale images. Full-colour digital printing is still fairly costly and not a viable option for mainstream distribution through bookstores or other third-party resellers. Neither is it suitable for children's books if you want to keep your book competitively priced.

The beauty of digital printing is that you can print just one copy of your book, making it the printing method used by all print-on-demand companies.

Don't confuse digital book printers with your local copy shop, who claim to offer digital printing. Copy shops use high-end photocopy machines, a very different animal to a professional digital press. The print costs per page at a copy shop are typically more expensive than those of a digital book printer, whose pricing is optimised for higher page volumes.

Digital presses are smaller than litho presses and run smaller sheet sizes. This creates limitations in terms of the size of the books that can be printed, and the binding methods used. For instance, an A4 landscape children's book cannot be printed on a digital press because the sheet size is not long enough to accommodate an open spread if the book is being stapled at the spine or sewn into sections. A4 landscape children's books are therefore always printed on litho presses unless another binding method is used that allows for single sheet printing, trimming and binding.

> Find out more about bleed in the 'Did you know?' box opposite.

FIGURE 4 **A digital printing press**

All professional book printers use A4 and A3 oversize paper; this means that they can print A4 and A3 pages **with bleed**. Copy shops usually cannot print with bleed. They use sheet sizes that are exactly A4 or A3. This will be your clue to whether you are dealing with a professional book printing company.

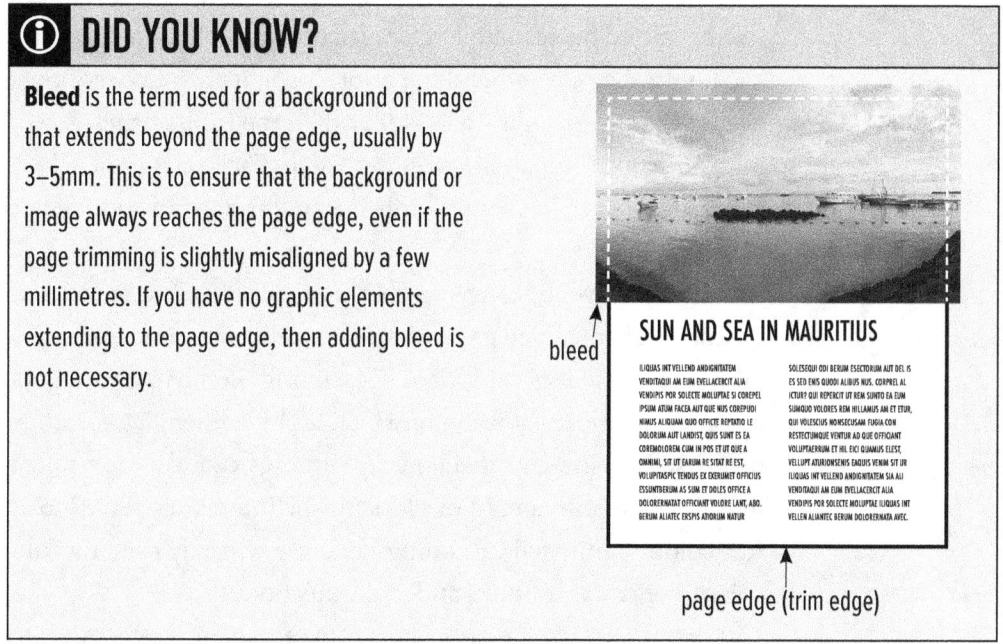

> ⓘ **DID YOU KNOW?**
>
> **Bleed** is the term used for a background or image that extends beyond the page edge, usually by 3–5mm. This is to ensure that the background or image always reaches the page edge, even if the page trimming is slightly misaligned by a few millimetres. If you have no graphic elements extending to the page edge, then adding bleed is not necessary.

CHOOSING YOUR PRINTING SPECIFICATIONS

Book covers

In the past, books were published first in hardcover and then, once sales of the hardcover version had slowed down, a softcover version (paperback) was produced. This was a costly tradition that has since died away and nowadays authors have a choice between the two. Here are some guidelines that may help you make the right decision when choosing your cover type.

Hardcover or softcover?

Hardcover

The cover of a hardcover book is about 3mm thick and does not bend. It's the type of cover usually found on full-colour coffee-table books, such as photographic, art, travel and cookery books. It's also found on academic reference books, such as medical and law books. If you can bend the book cover, it's a softcover book, even if the cover is quite a lot stiffer than the inside pages.

Hardcover books can be either squareback or roundback. A squareback has a flat spine, while a roundback has a rounded or curved spine.

All hardcover books have what is called a caselining, which is the material or printed paper that gets wrapped around and glued on to the raw, cover cardboard. Caselinings come in a variety of finishes, the most common of which include linen, faux leather, texturised plastic and metallic. Caselinings can also be printed in full colour with a matt or gloss finish. These are referred to as full-colour laminated caselinings, and are typically used for full-colour coffee-table books and children's books.

Then there are the endpapers. These papers are glued on to the inside of the front and back covers and form the first and last pages of the book. They may be plain white or printed.

Finally, your hardcover book may have top and tail bands. These are the thin, coloured fabric bands that line the top and bottom of the spine, giving the spine a finished look. Some books, such as diaries and planners, also have a ribbon attached to the top band that serves as a bookmark.

Choosing hardcover over softcover can add an extra R20 to R30 per book, assuming 1 000 books are printed. That's a hefty R20 000 to R30 000 extra on your printing bill! The more books you print, the lower the extra cost per book; the fewer books you print, the higher the extra cost per book.

Finally, your hardcover book may have a dust jacket. This is the loose wraparound sheet that includes your book title and cover artwork, book blurb, testimonials, as well as a short biography and photograph of you, the author. Books that have dust jackets usually have plain linen or mock-leather caselinings, with just the title and author name printed on to them, or hot-stamped using gold or silver foil.

Softcover

Softcover uses flexible board – typically a 230–240gsm sulphate board – to bind a wide variety of books, such as biographies, fiction, self-help, business, academic and educational books. It's much cheaper than hardcover and requires less binding time. Softcover is the main and sometimes only option offered by print-on-demand and digital printing companies.

Hi-bulk sulphate board has a smooth, coated surface on one side and an uncoated surface on the other. It's the coated side that gets printed and laminated on. Sulphate board is also used for postcards because the uncoated side supports smudge-free writing.

A great way to jazz up a softcover and take it to a new level is to include front and back cover flaps. This will add a few Rand to the cost of your book, but it's a great alternative if hardcover is out of your financial reach and you're looking for something smarter than a standard softcover. As always, the more books you print, the cheaper it will be, per book, to add the cover flaps.

> ### ⓘ DID YOU KNOW?
>
> Paper comes in different **weights** and is measured in grams per square metre (**gsm**), referred to as grammage. The gsm shows the weight of a sheet of paper 1 m × 1 m in size. The higher the gsm, the heavier the paper. But a higher gsm does not necessarily create a thicker paper. Paper thickness depends on how much the paper fibre has been compressed during manufacturing, so two types of paper with the same gsm may have different thicknesses. A 240gsm hi-bulk sulphate board feels thicker than a 350gsm art board, the latter being a highly compressed, very smooth board typically used for covers that are printed in full colour on both sides, such as those found on magazines and annual reports. Bear this in mind when comparing quotes from different printers.

Binding options

Book binding is the process of assembling or securing the pages of a book within a book cover. The three most commonly used binding methods in book publishing are perfect/PUR binding, thread-sewing and saddle-stitching. The method you choose for your book depends on:
- The number of pages in the book.
- The page size.
- How the book is being printed (litho or digital).
- What the book will be used for.
- What visual impression you want the book to make.

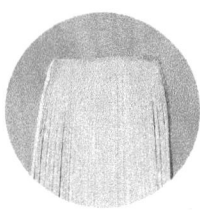

Perfect/PUR binding

Perfect binding and PUR binding are basically the same thing, except that a strong, more durable glue is used in PUR binding (the name comes from Polyurethane Reactive Adhesive). PUR binding is used by litho printers. Many digital printers don't have the machines to PUR bind, so they use perfect binding instead.

Perfect/PUR binding is the cheapest form of binding and is used on most paperbacks you find in bookstores. The printed book pages are trimmed and stacked together into what is called a book block. One edge of this block is glued and the entire block is then inserted into the book cover. The glue holds the pages together *and* affixes the book block to the spine of the cover. So, perfect binding essentially consists of a lot of loose pages all glued together at one end.

This binding method is the least durable, as the glue can become brittle over time and the pages may come loose, particularly when perfect binding. There is also a limit to the number of pages that can be successfully bound without compromising the strength of the binding. Perfect/PUR binding is not recommended for books with a spine width of less than 3mm (64 pages). It also works best with uncoated paper, which offers better grip due to its fibrous quality.

Thread-sewing

This involves folding the printed sheets into sections of 8 or 16 pages and then stitching each section down the middle along the fold. Page imposition is needed to work out the sections. Don't worry, your printer or publisher will work out the imposition for you! All the folded and sewn sections are then placed on top of one another, and the folded ends are glued into the spine of the book.

Thread-sewing is recommended for books that need to remain flat when open, such as cookery books. It's also recommended for books that need to be durable, such as children's books, and books that are used frequently, such as educational, academic, and reference books. With thread-sewing, pages cannot fall out because they are sewn together. Thread-sewing can be used on books with both high and low page counts, provided they meet the page multiple requirements.

Thread-sewing takes longer – you can expect to add an extra three days to your printing lead time. It is also more expensive. It is most cost-effective when used with litho printing where the binding set-up costs can be shared by a larger number of units. It is expensive when you're printing digitally due to the smaller runs. Most digital printers also have to outsource the thread-sewing to larger printers or specialist binderies, which adds to the cost and the delivery time.

Saddle-stitching

A saddle-stitched book is folded and wire-stapled at the spine. This binding method is suited to books with a page count of less than 64 pages if an 80gsm bond is being used, or 80 pages if a 70gsm bond or 115gsm art paper is being used.

Saddle-stitching is a good option if you are wanting to produce a durable, yet competitively priced range of children's books, pocket books, and teachers' guides. Your final page count must be a multiple of 4.

> **# TIP Saddle-stitched books and bookstores**
>
> Many large-chain bookstores don't accept saddle-stitched books as they have no spine, and the cover must therefore face the customer for the title name to be visible. This takes more space on the shelf, and shelf space costs money. If you are marketing and selling directly to your customers, saddle-stitched books won't be an issue and will provide a durable, cost-effective binding option for your book.

TABLE 3 A feature comparison between perfect/PUR binding, thread-sewing and saddle-stitching

Feature	Perfect/PUR binding	Thread-sewing	Saddle-stitching
Cost	A relatively cheap binding option because it's simple and quick to do.	A more expensive binding option because more work is involved: pages are folded and sewn into sections before they are glued into the cover.	A relatively cheap binding option because it's simple and quick to do.
Source	Is usually offered inhouse by the printer.	Is usually outsourced to specialist binderies; sometimes done inhouse by litho printers.	Is usually offered inhouse by the printer.
Page count	Page counts in multiples of 2 if printing digitally; always follow the page count rules when litho printing.	Page counts in multiples of 8 or 16 are required; for smaller-sized books, multiples of 32 may be more economical.	Page counts in multiples of 4 are required; always follow the page count rules when litho printing.
Printing method	Suitable for digital and litho printing.	More economical with litho printing.	Suitable for digital and litho printing.
Cover type	Used for softcover books.	Used for softcover and hardcover books.	Used only for softcover books.
Lay of the book	Suitable for books that don't need to open up flat.	Recommended for books that must open up flat.	Recommended for books that must open up flat.
Spine width	Spine width must be at least 3mm thick, preferably more.	Can be used for books with as few as 8 pages; in reality, an 8-page book would normally be saddle-stitched.	Can be used on any book where the book block is less than 4–5mm thick – usually no more than 80 pages.
Paper coating	Best suited to books using uncoated papers for better grip with the glue.	Suitable for any book, regardless of paper coating.	Suitable for any book, regardless of paper coating.

Feature	Perfect/PUR binding	Thread-sewing	Saddle-stitching
Durability	Best suited to books that won't be handled roughly or frequently.	Best suited to books that will be handled roughly or frequently – it's a durable binding method.	Suitable for books that will be handled roughly or frequently – it's a durable binding method.
Type of book	Used on most paperbacks found in bookstores.	Better suited to non-fiction; more frequently used on educational, academic, reference, coffee-table and children's books.	Often used for pocketbooks, guides, workbooks and children's books.
Distribution options	Suitable for bookstore distribution.	Suitable for bookstore distribution.	Usually not suitable for bookstore distribution within the larger chains.

Choosing paper for your book interior

Fortunately, most book printing tends to be fairly straightforward, so unless you are creating something special or unique – such as a design-driven or specialist art book – your paper requirements will fall into one of four categories:

- Creamy hi-bulk
- White book bond
- Cartridge
- Art paper

Within each paper type, you have a choice of brands that are manufactured by different paper mills. So while one printer may quote you on a 150gsm Magno Art, another may quote you on a 150gsm Galerie Art because they obtain their paper from different paper merchants or mills. There may be subtle differences between the two: one may be slightly whiter than the other, or slightly more compressed and therefore thinner in feel, despite the same grammage. It is wise to see samples of the paper first before making a final choice.

If you are approaching a printer directly, you will need to choose your own paper weight, remembering that the same grammage does not necessarily equate to the same thickness. Most vanity publishers and print-on-demand platforms make choosing paper very easy by providing only one or two options. Custom publishers will usually make recommendations based on the page count, book thickness, ink coverage and quality requirements.

Finally, when choosing your paper, consider using paper sourced from sustainable forests rather than paper sourced from elsewhere. By using a sustainably sourced paper, you can be sure that for every tree that is cut down for paper, another one is planted to replace it. It's a sad fact that in some parts of the world, countless natural forests are being destroyed. Not only does deforestation displace the wildlife that live there; it upsets the ecosystem and negatively impacts climate change. Sustainable forestry, on the other hand, involves *creating* forests for wood products, leaving natural forests untouched. Ask your printer about sustainably sourced paper brands. Paper from mills that have received the chain of custody (CoC) certification will carry the following logo:

ⓘ DID YOU KNOW?

FSC labels assure you that the product is made of wood from responsible sources.

FSC 100%: All the wood comes from FSC-certified forests.

FSC Recycled: All the wood or paper comes from reclaimed (re-used) material.

FSC Mixed: The wood is from FSC-certified material, recycled material, or controlled wood.

> ### ⓘ DID YOU KNOW?
>
> - To address climate change, we must use more wood, not less. Using wood sends signals to the marketplace to grow more trees.[1]
> - Over 51 million tons of paper were recovered from recycling in 2015 – enough to fill the Empire State building 124 times.[2]
> - Only 17% of cut forest trees are used by the paper industry.[3]
> - The myth of print not being environmentally friendly has been unjustly promoted. The print industry is not only environmentally friendly, it is one of the most sustainable industries around.[4] The industry makes a tremendous investment in applying renewable energy sources and creating environmentally friendly supplies.[5]
> - Direct mail in the US saved 110 million shopping trips, cutting CO_2 emissions by 35 000 tons.[6]
> - There are 20% more trees in the US today than on Earth Day 40 years ago.[7] The North American paper industry plants 1.7 million trees per day, which is more than it cuts.[8]
> - Reading a newspaper instead of 30 minutes of online news produces 20% less CO.[9]
> - An average person wastes 2.4 times more electricity powering a single computer than the energy used to produce the paper they use in a year.[10]
> - Forestry is the most sustainable of the primary energy and materials industries.[11]
> - Print represents 80% of 2015 book sales worldwide.[12]
>
> Reprinted from www.printisbig.com, with kind permission.
>
> ---
>
> 1 Dr. Patrick Moore, Co-founder, Greenpeace; 2 American Forest & Paper Association; 3 TAPPI; 4 DMA; 5 American Forest & Paper Association; 6 DMA; 7 DMA; 8 DMA; 9 Swedish Royal Institute for Technology; 10 www.printisbig.com; 11 Dr. Patrick Moore, Co-founder, Greenpeace; 12 Deloitte

Creamy hi-bulk

Creamy hi-bulk, creamy bulky or creamy book bond is an off-white paper typically used in fiction, biographies, self-help and some business books. Its colour makes reading easy on the eye, hence its popularity in these genres.

It's an uncoated paper that offers hi-bulk properties at a low grammage. This means that your book will look thicker, yet be remarkably light. This helps to keep down delivery costs, which are based on weight.

It is manufactured by paper mills outside of South Africa, so all our creamy hi-bulk paper is imported. It used to be a fairly expensive paper but, due to its popularity in recent years among independent publishers, prices have come down as digital printers have started ordering in bulk.

Any good digital or litho book printer should be familiar with this paper and have no problem obtaining it. If your printer does not know about or frequently use creamy bulky, it is likely they will charge more for it as they cannot offer you the cost benefits of bulk buying. Since paper makes up a good percentage of the printing cost, it may be more cost-effective to find another printer.

The most popular and readily available weight for creamy bulky in South Africa is 70gsm, but it is also available in 60, 80 and 90gsm. You can rest assured that the 70gsm creamy hi-bulk paper your printer is quoting you on is thicker than a 90gsm bond – so guard against turning your nose up at it for fear that it's an inferior or thinner paper. It's not.

White book bond

This is a well-known and popular paper in South Africa that is used mostly in non-fiction publishing. It is commonly associated with educational and academic publishing, but is also used for business and reference books, as well as workbooks and handbooks. You will be most familiar with it as the paper you use in your home printer or photocopy machine.

Bond is an uncoated paper. The most common weights are 70, 80 and 90gsm, with 80gsm being the most widely used trade publishing weight. The 70gsm is typically used for diaries and school textbooks, as well as books with a high page count. Because it is slightly thinner and cheaper than 80gsm, using this paper helps to reduce printing costs and the thickness of the book. By contrast, the 90gsm is preferred if the page count is low and the book needs bulking up.

Manufactured locally, bond is the cheapest of all the papers and the most readily available.

> **# TIP** Avoiding the year-end bond shortage
>
> Towards year-end, from November through December, 70–80gsm bond is often in short supply because of educational and academic publishing for the following year. If your book requires this paper, best get your project on the press beforehand to avoid unnecessary delays and paper shortages. If you're not ready, you can pay your printer or publishing service a deposit to purchase and secure your paper in advance so that the printer has the paper ready when you go to press.

Cartridge

Cartridge is a white paper that has a slightly better look and feel than bond, and offers a little extra bulk; so a 90gsm cartridge will feel slightly thicker than a 90gsm bond. If your page count is low and you feel that your book is a bit thin and needs some bulking up, choose cartridge over bond to provide thickness without adding to the weight. It's a bit like creamy bulky in that respect. Still, creamy bulky remains the lightest and bulkiest of all the papers covered here.

Cartridge gives full-colour printing a slightly rustic feel. The international award-winning recipe book *Mila's Meals*, by Catherine Barnhoorn, was printed in full colour on 105gsm cartridge, and it looks fabulous. The book is about wholesome, 'free-from' eating and food preparation for kiddies, so the slightly rustic feel of the paper supports the subject matter well.

Cartridge comes in a variety of weights, the most popular and readily available being 90, 105, 120 and 135gsm. It is more expensive than bond.

Art paper

Art paper is a high-quality, fine-grained, coated paper that is typically used for full-colour or photographic printing as it holds ink well and retains the brightness of the colours. It is especially suited to full-colour coffee-table books and cookery books, but is also used for other books where high-quality printing and a smooth paper finish are required.

It comes in a gloss, matt or satin (silk) finish, and in a variety of weights. The most common weights for book printing are 115gsm and 130gsm. The 115gsm is often used for books with a higher page count, while the 130gsm is preferred for books that have a lower page count, or that are image-rich and have dense ink coverage. The thicker paper prevents images on one side of the paper from showing through to the other side.

An even thicker option is 150gsm, which is suited to high-end coffee-table and art books, and some children's books. Photobook printing, for instance, is mostly done on 150gsm art paper to bulk up the books and give them a quality feel. If you're familiar with photobooks, then you'll be reasonably familiar with art paper and the weights discussed here.

Art paper is highly compressed, so a 115gsm art paper feels slightly thinner than an 80 or 90gsm bond. Your final choice of art paper thickness will depend on your ink coverage, quality requirements, and the number of pages in your book.

Thicker paper compensates for low page counts and creates the perception of quality and value. Thinner paper prevents books with a high page count from becoming too thick and heavy. For instance, it is impractical to use 150gsm paper in a book that has a few hundred pages. Not only will it be very expensive to print, but the book will be extremely heavy to hold, and the weight would also impact substantially on the delivery costs.

And finally, the higher the paper grammage, the more expensive it is. There is usually no difference in price between matt and gloss art paper – your choice would be a matter of preference and what works best for the content and type of book you are publishing. What you choose will also be influenced by your budget and what you can realistically afford.

> **# TIP** Seeking paper and printing advice from a professional
>
> When publishing a book that requires art paper, it is advisable to seek the services of a professional graphic or book designer. They are familiar with different paper weights and the suitability of various paper types to the particular purpose and consumer market you have in mind. They understand colour and how inks perform on different papers. They also have a good working knowledge of other finishes that may be required during printing to ensure a high-quality product.

OBTAINING A PRINT QUOTE

Now that you have an idea of your book size, cover, binding and paper options, it's time to obtain your printing quote. Assuming you have opted to go the solo route and are not using a publishing service to assist you, there are two ways to go about doing this. You can approach a printer directly or you can use an independent print consultant with publishing experience.

Approaching a printer directly

Printers know their trade; they know about the physical task of printing products and delivering an end product that meets industry print-quality standards. However, they don't know the ins and outs of publishing or the book trade. Nor are they designers, so it's unlikely that you will get the advice and support you need when it comes to choosing suitable papers, book sizes and binding methods for your book genre and the distribution channels you are using. Unfortunately, even some self-publishing service providers are not strong on the technicalities of printing and production and may advise the wrong option for your book. For example, if you have been incorrectly advised to use PUR binding rather than thread-sewing for your cookery book, your book will not lie flat because PUR binding naturally pulls a book closed.

If you are going to approach a printer directly, it's best to approach one who specialises in book printing. They are more likely to use or recommend suitable papers and binding options, and are generally competitively priced as their machines and systems are optimised for book printing. Book printers also have their own sales consultants who can offer very basic printing advice, present you with paper samples, and show you copies of books they've printed. Viewing these samples helps tremendously when choosing your own specifications as you can see exactly how your choices will translate into a physical product.

The downside to working directly with a printer is that there are economics involved in book publishing, so all production decisions, including printing, should be made holistically, bearing overall budget, target market and economic viability in mind. This becomes more important when publishing independently because budgets are generally very tight and sales volumes are much lower than those of traditional publishers. It is likely that you will have to tweak your printing specifications to fit your budget, without compromising on quality. A printer is not going to be able to assist you in a holistic manner, nor make recommendations.

Using a publishing print consultant

A publishing print consultant has partnerships with a number of printers and will choose the printer best suited to your book and budget. They will also be able to advise you on your paper options and suitable binding methods, highlighting the pros and cons of each and recommending the best option for your book. A good consultant will also tell you which page sizes and orientations are more economical to print.

You may end up paying a little more going through a print consultant, but they do all the legwork for you, including sourcing comparative pricing on the correct specifications; supplying the info to the printer in print jargon; ensuring that there are no misunderstandings and that the correct things are being asked for and quoted on; and, most importantly, ensuring that a quality product is delivered to you.

Should anything not be up to scratch, the print consultant will liaise with the printer on your behalf and ensure that the printer corrects any printing and binding errors. Their job is to look after your best interests, and they know how to do that because they know what you *should* be getting from the printer; they also know what will be accepted or rejected by the book trade.

A publishing print consultant also has a better idea of the economics involved in publishing and is likely to offer more appropriate, cost-saving advice on your printing choices.

Finding a knowledgeable publishing print consultant may prove challenging, so you could try book production specialists or professional book designers who handle both production and printing processes on behalf of their clients. If you are using a custom publisher, you don't have to worry about any of this – they automatically handle the printing for you and they do all of the legwork on your behalf, keeping you in the loop and advising you each step of the way. Vanity publishers and online print-on-demand services offer a limited range of print options, thus eliminating many of the decisions you would otherwise have to make.

Working out your page count

Unlike editing costs, which are based on your word count, **production and printing services are based on your page count.** You need to know the page count of your book to obtain an accurate production or printing quote. If you have not yet started production, this will have to be an **estimate**.

To work out your page count, take the total word count of your manuscript and divide that by the number of words you expect to fit on a page. The easiest way to work out your words per page is to use an existing book similar to the one you will be publishing and make your calculation according to the following example:

1. Open the book to a random page.
2. Count the number of words in each line for three consecutive lines.
3. Add the number of words for the three lines together, and divide the total by 3 to get the average number of words per line.
4. Now count the number of lines on one page.
5. Multiply the number of lines by the average number of words per line.

Example

Find the average number of words per line:
- Line 1 has 12 words
- Line 2 has 10 words
- Line 3 has 11 words

The total number of words is 12 + 10 + 11 = 33, divided by 3 gives you 11. So the average number of words per line is 11.

Assuming there are 30 lines on the page, multiply 11 words by 30 lines to get 330. There are 330 words per page.

You are now ready to calculate the number of pages in the book. Assuming your manuscript has a total of 49 500 words, you have 49 500 words ÷ 330 words per page = 150 pages in the book.

Your book will be roughly 150 pages, excluding front matter. Now add extra pages for your front matter and your photographs and artwork. Blank pages must also be included – these form part of your page count. Assuming you have no artwork, and for the purpose of this exercise, add an extra eight pages for your front matter. That brings you to 158 pages. You need a multiple of two for digital printing – you're all good there – and a multiple of eight or 16 for litho printing. Your page count for litho printing will therefore be 160 – it's easy to add an extra two pages, even if those pages are blank pages at the back of the book. You can say that 160 pages is an excellent page count for litho printing because it is divisible by 16, allowing the entire job to be run on a 16-page imposition scheme.

> An example of front matter can be found on page 52 and in Appendix C on page 276.

With book publishing, there is always a juggle between quality and cost. The challenge is to produce a good-quality product at a cost that does not annihilate the financial viability of your project. Remember, the customer has to perceive enough value in your product to put their hand in their pocket and pay what you're asking. By the same token, one cannot be short-sighted and skimp in places where adding that extra touch or choosing a better paper could make a positive difference to the quality of your book and the customer's perception of value.

After all is said and done, the following rule holds true: no matter what you do or don't do at the printing stage, *everything hinges on your content* – do you have solid, well-edited content? Without solid content, no fancy paper or binding method is going to give your book the traction it needs for sustainable success.

ⓘ DID YOU KNOW?

Traditional publishers decide on a page count *before* production begins. They work out the publishing and printing costs based on that page count and then work out a suitable retail price. The more pages there are in a book, the more expensive it becomes to produce and print. They are therefore very strict about adhering to the set page count. Designers and typesetters have to design and typeset the book with the page count in mind, and editors will trim the content down, if necessary, to meet the allocated page count.

TIP Your page count and the cost implications

Two extra pages in a book will change a digital printing price by only a few cents per unit, but it could change a litho printing price by a few Rand per unit, especially if those extra two pages tip the total page count over a multiple of 8, 16 or 32 pages, forcing an extra set of printing plates and machine set-up time.

It's important to bear this in mind and stick to your planned page count, particularly if you are litho printing. The extra cost will chip into your profits or force you to increase your selling price.

Sending off your printing enquiry

When requesting a printing quote, you will need to provide the following information:

- **Book title** (or working title).
- **Size of book** (height × width) and whether it is portrait or landscape.
- **Number of pages.**
- **The paper stock and weight, in gsm, for the inner.**
- **What colour the inner should be printed.**
- **The paper stock and weight, in gsm, for the cover.** If it's a standard paperback, 230–240gsm sulphate board is typically used; if it's a hardcover book, it is good enough simply to say squareback hardcover or roundback hardcover, and include the type of caselining (e.g. full-colour laminated caselining). Also, specify the endpapers you want – choose between art paper and cartridge, printed or plain.
- **The binding method to be used**
- **The quantity of books required.** You can give a few options, e.g. 100 / 200 / 300 (digital printing), or 750 / 1000 / 1250 / 2000 (litho printing).

> A list of international book sizes can be found on page 133.

> Review hardcover binding on page 160.

PREPARING YOUR BOOK FOR PRINTING

These guidelines are useful to authors who are doing the book formatting and layout themselves and will be approaching a printer or print-on-demand service directly.

Setting up and formatting your book inner

- Set the page size of your document to the size at which you want the final book to be printed. In other words, if you want a 5 × 8 book (127mm wide × 203.2mm deep), you must change the page size of your word-processing document to the required measurement. If you're using a print-on-

- demand service, visit their website and choose a book size from their list or refer to the list of international book sizes on page 133.
- Format your book the way you want it to look when it is printed. What you give to your printer or print-on-demand service is *exactly* what they will print.
- Remember to include your front matter – this includes your copyright page.
- Include a table of contents if your book is non-fiction. Remember to include page numbers with your table of contents entries otherwise the table of contents is of little value. If you have inserted the table of contents manually, ensure that the page numbering in the table of contents matches the relevant pages in the book.
- Include page numbering in your document – all even-numbered pages are left-hand (verso) pages and odd-numbered pages are right-hand (recto) pages; pages up to and including the table of contents do not need to be numbered. The first page of your book always starts on a right-hand page. The last page of your book should be an even-numbered, left-hand page. If your book ends on an odd number (right-hand page) add an extra blank page. Centre the page numbering on all pages if you don't know how to work with left- and right-hand page numbering.
- Include reasonable margins between your main body of text and the edge of the page – anything from 18mm to 20mm is adequate. If you know how to set inside and outside margins, make your inside margin 5mm wider than your outside margin. This will compensate for the few millimetres taken up at the spine by the perfect binding and will ensure that text close to the spine can be easily read. If your book is being saddle-stitched or thread-sewn, you don't need to worry about extra margin space at the spine.
- Minimum page margin requirements for print-on-demand services must be checked beforehand. Generally, they insist on margins of no less than 13mm from the trim edge on

> See Appendix C on page 276 for an example of front matter and Appendix D on page 278 for a sample copyright page.

all sides. This means that all page content, including page numbers, running heads, and non-bleeding art, must not extend beyond this margin. Text too close to the trim edge could be cut off during binding and trimming.

> Review saddle-stitching and thread-sewing on page 163.

- For the best black and white print quality, use tints (shading) judiciously and preferably only to highlight specific blocks of information, such as special feature boxes. Digital printing does not handle tints as gracefully as litho printing.
- If printing in black and white, use shades of grey rather than colours for headings, design features, tables and graphs when formatting your book. It is difficult to know how colours will turn out when automatically converted into shades of grey by the printing system. For instance, the colour red becomes black and light yellow text tends to fall away completely, so a yellow heading will disappear when printed. Pie charts and graphs using colours to distinguish segments or values may also become illegible as certain colours become too similar in tone and shade.

  Convert all your text and images to black and white, or greyscale; if you can distinguish between shades of grey on your screen, chances are you will see them in print. When in doubt, check those pages by printing them out in black and white on your printer at home or at a nearby copy shop.
- Follow the image quality and resolution guidelines provided in Chapter 8, and use the formatting tips in Chapter 10.

Creating your book inner PDF files

Printers don't print from word-processing documents, so you will need to supply your printer with a print-ready PDF file of your book inner. Some print services require that your files meet PDF/X-1a standards. PDF/X-1a ensures that all fonts have been embedded and all colours have been converted to CMYK or spot colours. Litho presses can print using spot colours, but digital presses can't, so if you are printing digitally, all spot colours must be converted to CMYK.

When using an online print-on-demand service, be sure to download and follow their specific file set-up and PDF guidelines. Their guidelines are formulated for their particular presses and production processes.

The guidelines provided here will get you started and help you with PDF file creation for local printing.

- The book inner should be supplied in PDF format as **one complete file**, including front matter, end matter and blank pages. The final page should be blank.
- Do not supply your book inner as spreads when making the PDF – leave the inner to flow as single pages.
- The book inner must be supplied separately to the cover.
- If you have images or backgrounds that run off the page, include a 3mm bleed to your document.
- Do not include crop, registration or printer marks for international print-on-demand. When printing with a local printer, we recommend *including* them for improved cross-compatibility across different systems and printing methods (litho and digital).
- If you're not using the PDF/X-1a profile to create your PDFs, always choose the Print Quality option in your PDF-maker to ensure the highest resolution. Most PDF-makers offer print-quality PDF file creation.
- All fonts must be embedded.
- Do not include spot colours unless you are litho printing.

Setting up your book cover and creating a PDF

- The cover must be supplied as one flat piece of artwork consisting of back cover, spine and front cover.
- Allow a no-text margin on your cover of at least 6.5mm from the page edges. Anything less than that becomes a trim hazard and your type might get cut off or end up too close

- to the page edge during binding. Some print-on-demand platforms will generate an error message or reject your file if this requirement is not met.
- Request the correct spine width from your printer. If you are using a print-on-demand service, a spine-width calculator will be available on their website.
- Include 3mm bleed on all four sides of the cover artwork.
- Centre the text on the spine at least 2mm or more from both spine folds. For thin spines, ensure a margin of at least 1mm from both spine folds. Also, make sure that the spine text is the right way up when the book lies flat on it's back on a table.
- File resolution should be 300 dpi or 180 lpi with a CMYK colour space.
- Convert all spot colours to CMYK.

TIP Cover preparation and MS Word

If you are using MS Word, you will need to enlist the help of a professional production, DTP or design service for your cover file preparation, as MS Word does not offer the functionality required for this. Also, PDFs created using MS Word's print-to-PDF function are not supported.

TIP General file preparation

For print-on-demand publishing, visit the website of the service provider you will be using and follow their guidelines on how to prepare your files. Alternatively, consider engaging a professional DTP or design service. International services may cost more than local ones due to the Rand-Dollar exchange rate, so consider using someone closer to home. Besides, it's great to support local!

FIGURE 4 An example of a book cover, supplied as one piece of artwork

Note the direction of the spine text (which is correct) and the ample margins between the text and the page edge. The page bleed measures 3mm and trim (crop) marks have been provided.

13

EBOOKS IN A NUTSHELL

WHAT IS AN EBOOK?

In this digital age, most authors make their books available as an ebook. This is an electronic version of a printed book that can be read on a computer, smartphone and tablet by way of downloadable e-reading software called apps. Ebooks can also be read on specifically-designed devices that come complete with their own software, such as the popular Kindle, Kobo and Nook Readers.

Ebooks offer interactive functionality, such as click-through cross-references; active links to websites and other pages within the ebook; links from the table of contents to the relevant sections of text; and so on. Some ebook formats also offer embedded video and sound, making for a fully interactive experience.

The advantages of ebooks

- Ebooks can be purchased online and downloaded immediately on to your device; there is no waiting and there are no delivery costs.
- Ebooks can be read on multiple devices owned by you.
- You can change the font style and text size for easier reading.
- Certain ebook formats offer full interactivity, such as active links, audio and video.
- Ebooks are cheaper to publish than printed books and are easily distributed globally.
- Ebooks are usually cheaper to buy than printed books.
- Most major stores offer digital rights management (DRM), which limits the free distribution and copying of your ebook.
- You can travel easily with ebooks because you can fit thousands of ebooks on an e-reader, smartphone or tablet.
- Ebooks can be easily and instantly delivered to hard-to-reach areas, provided there's an Internet or mobile connection.
- Some e-readers and ebook apps feature built-in dictionaries, bookmarks, and other handy tools.
- Ebook readers are light and easy to hold, saving bookworms from wrist-cramp during extended reading periods.
- Some e-readers are backlit, enabling easy reading in the dark.

> More about ebook formats and their features can be found on page 184.

The disadvantages of ebooks

- Many people still prefer the feel of a paper book.
- Ebooks have been slow to take off in South Africa; fortunately, this is starting to change.
- Reflowable ebooks offer limited formatting capabilities, which could impact on the reader experience, especially with non-fiction.
- Books that are design or layout-heavy are expensive to convert and their distribution platforms are limited; so are the devices on which they can be read.

- Ebook quality is often substandard due to the low barriers of entry into the self-publishing market and the lack of adequate editorial and design control.
- As an electronic file, an ebook can be easily shared if no DRM is applied, and even if there is DRM, people can find a way to remove it.
- To be read, ebooks require some form of device and a power source. Printed books on the other hand require nothing.
- Book buyers must register an account with the online retailer selling your ebook and own a credit card to pay for the purchase. They must also be somewhat comfortable with technology and online shopping. This excludes certain sectors of the market.

EBOOK FORMATS

Ebooks come in different formats. We will look at the four major formats currently sold by online retailers: ePub, fixed layout ebook, Kindle and PDF.

ePub

An ePub is a reflowable ebook format in which the book content reflows according to the screen size of the device on which it is being read. The reader can change the font size of the ebook text for easier reading, and can also choose whether they want to read the book in a horizontal or vertical format.

Due to the reflowable nature of the content, publishers have very little control over how their book content will be displayed on different devices. Therefore, books using multiple columns, inset text and margin text need to be reformatted into a single column format and all images and design elements need to be embedded into that single column. ePub is therefore best suited to fiction, as well as non-fiction books that have simple or flexible formatting requirements.

ePub also offers a fixed layout option with ePub2 and ePub3. The ePub format is sold in most online stores except Amazon.

Fixed layout ebook

This format looks just like the print edition of a book in that the integrity of the layout is maintained. Users cannot change the font size and the content does not reflow.

Fixed layout ebooks come in different formats, such as ePub2, ePub3, Apple iBooks, Amazon KF8, and PDF. They include full interactivity and multimedia capabilities, including voice, video and flash animation. They are typically used for full-colour children's books, art books, magazines, cookery and travel books, or any other book in which design, layout and interactivity are important.

Due to the extra work needed for a slick and fully functional fixed layout ebook, this is the most expensive ebook format. It is also only suitable for devices with larger screens, such as tablets and computers. Unfortunately, distribution for fixed layout ebooks is still somewhat limited, although major online retailers such as Apple, Amazon, Kobo, Barnes & Noble and Google Play Books sell them.

Kindle

This is Amazon's proprietary format and the largest selling format globally; Amazon sells at least 60% or more of all ebooks. Kindle uses three file types: KF8, MOBI and AZW.

Mobi and AZW are reflowable formats in which the user can change the font and font size, device orientation, and so on. They offer no real layout capabilities, although images, tables and some design elements can be embedded in the text.

The KF8 file format supports reflowable and fixed layout ebooks. It also offers colour, HTML5 and CSS3 support, and many other formatting features such as drop caps, numbered lists, nested tables, scalable vector graphics, sidebars, and more.

PDF

Many book buyers still automatically assume that ebooks are PDFs, and PDF remains the preferred format in which to read an ebook. A PDF ebook preserves the integrity of your layout and is usually generated from the original design document, so a PDF ebook looks exactly the same as your print edition (as such, it technically falls into the fixed layout category, but we feel it deserves a mention of its own).

Interactivity can also be included, such as click-through links, video and sound. Unfortunately, distribution for PDF ebooks is limited, and major online retailers such as Amazon, Apple, and Barnes & Noble don't sell them.

File protection and digital rights management are also difficult. While there are platforms that offer various measures to protect PDFs from being copied or circulated, these measures are cumbersome and very annoying for book buyers. Also, PDF protection can be removed using software created for this purpose. PDFs are therefore often sold directly from authors' websites and smaller online retailers without any protection, but with certain limitations in place, such as the disabling of editing, printing, and copying text from the document.

> Find out more about digital rights management on page 189.

TABLE 4 A comparison of the different ebook formats

ePub	Kindle	Fixed layout ebooks	PDF
A reflowable format that adjusts to the screen size of the device.	A reflowable format that adjusts to the screen size of the device.	A fixed layout format that remains the same regardless of the device on which it is being read.	A fixed layout format that remains the same regardless of the device on which it is being read.
Fonts can be resized for easier reading.	Fonts can be resized for easier reading.	Fonts cannot be resized for easier reading but a zoom function is available.	Fonts cannot be resized for easier reading but a zoom function is available.
Suitable for all screen sizes.	Suitable for all screen sizes.	Requires larger screens, so best read on tablets and computers.	Requires larger screens, so best read on tablets and computers.
Distribution through most global retailers, except Amazon.	Distribution through Amazon and some global retailers.	Limited distribution; available mostly from the major retailers.	Limited distribution; usually sold directly by authors and independent publishing companies.
DRM available.	DRM available.	DRM available.	Limited DRM.
Suited to text-based books with few formatting requirements.	Suited to text-based books with few formatting requirements.	Suited to image-based books with specific formatting and layout requirements.	Suited to image-based books with specific formatting and layout requirements.
Created using professional software as well as from MS Word*.	Created using professional software as well as from MS Word*.	Created using professional software; requires specialist input.	Created using professional software as well as from MS Word*.
Inexpensive	Inexpensive	Costly due to the specialist input required.	Inexpensive; it is generated from the formatted book.
Formats: ePub, ePub2, ePub3.	Formats: MOBI, AZW, KF8.	Formats: ePub2, ePub3, KF8, iBooks, PDF.	Formats: PDF.

> ### ⓘ DID YOU KNOW?
>
> When purchasing an ebook from an online store, you download the free proprietary store app that enables you to automatically receive and read the ebook on your mobile device or tablet when the app is opened. If the app has been downloaded on to multiple devices that you own, then each device will receive the purchased book when the app on the respective device is opened, provided each device is linked to your online store profile. These apps are available in your device-specific store, such as Google Play and Apple App store. Simply click on your phone or tablet's app store icon, search for the e-reading app you want, and click 'Download'.
>
> All the apps for handheld devices are also available as free downloadable apps for desktop and laptop computers:
> - The Kindle reader is available from Amazon.
> - The Nook reader is available from Barnes & Noble.
> - The Kobo reader is available from Kobo Books.
> - The Google Play reader is available from Google Play.
> - The iBooks app is available on all Apple devices.
>
> Other popular e-readers include Adobe Digital Editions, which is freely available from Adobe.com and reads ePub and PDF format from any platform; and Calibre, which reads all formats and can be downloaded from www.calibre-ebook.com.
>
> Note: No apps are required if you are using a dedicated e-reading device such as a Kindle or Nook Reader, as these devices come with pre-installed software on them.

TABLE 5 **File formats accepted by online publishers for ebook conversion and distribution***

Publisher	Original file formats accepted for ebook conversion
Smashwords	MS Word doc, ePub
Amazon KDP	MS Word doc, HTML (ZIP, HTM, HTML), MOBI, ePub, Rich Text Format (RTF), Plain Text (TXT), Adobe PDF (PDF), Kindle Package Format
Apple	ePub2, ePub3, iBooks
Barnes & Noble	MS Word doc, Text (TXT), Rich Text Format (RTF), HTML, ePub
Kobo	MS Word doc, OPF, ePub, MOBI
Lulu	MS Word doc, ePub, ePub2, ePub3, Rich Text Format (RTF),
IngramSpark	MS Word doc, ePub2, ePub3 (reflowable and fixed)

*Correct at the time of going to press

DIGITAL RIGHTS MANAGEMENT (DRM)

Digital rights management (DRM) is an access control technology that adds copyright protection to digital media and is applied at the distribution level. Because an ebook file is a digital file, without DRM it would be very easy to forward the ebook to others without those recipients having to pay for it. DRM therefore restricts the ways in which consumers can read and share the ebook files they've purchased, thus protecting your intellectual property.

However, there is much debate around DRM and whether it really helps to prevent copyright infringement. In the one camp are those who believe that it simply inconveniences legitimate customers. Others add that DRM makes it difficult for customers to legitimately back up their files or copy files to other devices they own that are not linked to the platform from which the ebook was bought. It's difficult to lend files out through a library; or use copyrighted materials for research and education under the fair use policy.

In the other camp are those who are less concerned about DRM because they believe that anyone who wants to copy and share a file can easily do so by using software that removes the file protection. Furthermore, they say that we have always lent books to others – be it family members, friends, or book club members. Circulating books has been an effective way for book lovers to discover new authors. It's common for people who borrow a book to enjoy it so much that they end up buying a copy for themselves or as a gift for someone else. They are also more likely to buy the next book the author releases. They might never have done so had they not been introduced to the author by reading someone else's copy in the first place.

There will always be people who buy, and people who borrow; this has not damaged the book industry thus far, and it's unlikely to damage it in the future. Amazon understands this psychology and they now allow customers who have purchased a book to lend that book to another person for a limited period of time, provided lending is enabled for that title.

What one definitely does *not* want, however, is some unscrupulous entity copying books and distributing them en masse or reselling them to others without giving the authors their due royalties. Unfortunately, this happens in the ebook space and it is difficult to stop because, even with DRM applied, these entities remove the file protection and upload the book in their own stores. Very often, books are sold for substantially less than their normal price – and this should set off the first alarm bell. These websites also fail to provide proper contact and customer service details, which should set off alarm bell number two.

When purchasing ebooks, it's best to stick to legitimate outlets – that way you know the author is receiving their due share of the sale and you are not supporting ebook piracy. And when you have the option, always try to buy directly from the author or author's representative. Fair, ethical practice starts with us. We need to buy wisely.

CREATING YOUR OWN EBOOK – THE DANGER OF AUTOMATIC FILE CONVERTERS

You might think it's easy to publish your own ebook and there are certainly services that enable you to do so at no cost. But, let a very loud warning bell sound here. Publishing an ebook is not just about taking your MS Word document and converting it into ePub or Kindle format using an online auto-converter.

Just as a print edition requires professional formatting and styling, ebooks also require file preparation beforehand to ensure accurate and reliable conversion; consistent treatment of design and text elements throughout; and a user-friendly experience for the reader.

Some ebooks also require post-conversion HTML tweaking to meet the requirements of the platform through which they're being distributed. As with print publishing, this level of input sets the difference between a poorly self-published product and

More about ebook publishing platforms can be found in Chapter 17.

a professional product that reflects well on the author, engages the author's audience – the reader – and makes for a pleasurable reading experience across a range of devices. A professional ebook that is easy to read and displays well helps to build consumer trust in the books that you publish.

Unfortunately, auto-converters cannot be relied on to convert your file to look the same as your MS Word document. When using an auto-converter, a computer algorithm makes decisions about how to treat certain elements in your book without understanding the content. You may find elements landing up in the wrong place or in a sequence that doesn't make sense.

MS Word is also notorious for embedding weird formatting into ebooks in odd, and often indiscernible, ways. Therefore, most MS Word documents need to be deformatted completely and reformatted again using the guidelines provided by the online conversion service you are using.

Additionally, reading an ebook is very different to reading a printed book. Ebooks need to be structured in a way that accommodates the reflowing of content. An added challenge is that different consumers use different devices, so the way your ebook looks on one device will be different to the way it looks on another. This lack of control over how your ebook will display on different e-readers must be accommodated in the layout of the ebook, including the treatment of design elements and certain types of information. For instance, large tables, or images with a lot of detail or embedded text, become small and illegible when viewed on smaller devices.

There is so much in a printed book that impacts our reading experience that we take for granted; this becomes apparent when we buy and read ebooks. Book layout is an art and makes subtle psychological impressions of which we, as readers, are not even aware. If you are considering converting your book into an ebook and have never actually downloaded and read an ebook on an e-reader, smartphone or tablet, then we encourage you to do so. You'll have a new appreciation for books that are properly formatted and adapted for the e-reading space.

Finally, never forget that a poor experience will put your customers off ever buying another ebook from you. Respect your customers. Respect their time. And respect the good money they are paying to download your book and read it. If they feel that they have received good value for money for a well-edited book that renders properly on their devices, they are sure to come back and buy from you again.

PREPARING FOR EBOOK PUBLISHING

Many authors turn to a self-help ebook publishing and distribution service to upload their MS Word documents for automatic online conversion into an ebook. If you are such an author, this next section is for you.

Automatic MS Word document conversions are only recommended for simple books that require little to no formatting, such as fiction and narrative non-fiction. All other ebook conversions should be handled professionally.

Choose your publishing service

First, explore the list of good ebook publishing services provided in Chapter 17. You'll need to sign up for an author account using your email address and a password that you create when you register. All platforms offer free registration. Some platforms send a confirmation email with an activation link. You need to click on the link to verify and activate the account. In the case of Amazon KDP, you don't have to sign up if you already have a customer account with the Amazon store – you simply use your existing customer email address and password. If you've ever bought anything from Amazon, you already have an Amazon customer account.

It is important to read the publishing service's Terms and Conditions, or Membership Agreement, which can be found on their website. This document forms the basis of your relationship with the publisher and tells you everything you need to know about doing business with them, including what you'll earn; when you'll get paid; how you'll be paid; if there are restrictions in terms of publishing elsewhere; pricing rules that must be followed, and so on. This document is the leg you have to stand on should they fail to fulfil their obligations. It also provides the vital information you need to conduct an apples-for-apples comparison between different service providers. It is the fine print of your contract with them.

When you've found your publishing service, you're ready for the next step.

Prepare your document for publishing

Before your MS Word doc can be converted into an ebook, it needs to be properly formatted and prepared. An excellent guide that will help you with this is *The Smashwords Style Guide* by Mark Coker, which is available as a free download from the Smashwords website[1].

Although created primarily to assist authors with distribution through the Smashwords platform using their notoriously fussy online ebook converter called Meatgrinder, formatting your book using these guidelines will ensure acceptance of your ebook file by all the other major retailers that Smashwords distributes to. But be warned, it's not easy getting it right and you may experience a few file rejections before your file is eventually given the green light.

Amazon also offers a free guide called *Building Your Book for Kindle*, which helps you prepare your file for Kindle conversion on their KDP publishing platform[2].

---

1   http://www.smashwords.com
2   https://kdp.amazon.com

What you need for the upload

Before you can upload your book files for publishing, you need to ensure that a few basics are in place.

1. You have a **prepared and formatted book** in MS Word doc format, which *must* include the following:
   - A title page – usually the first page in your book.
   - A copyright page – usually the second page in your book.
   - An interactive table of contents if your book is non-fiction or needs one. This comes after your copyright page.
   - The main body of your book.

   If your book was professionally converted into ePub or Kindle format and you are handling the publishing and distribution yourself, you should have your ebook file/s ready.

2. You have a well-designed, full-size front-cover image at 300 dpi in JPEG format.

3. You have a recent author image and a short biography for the author page on the publisher's website.

4. You have a well-written, detailed description of your book for the book information page.

5. You have a short, succinct description of your book for the search results page. This description must be engaging enough to prompt readers to find out more about your book.

6. You have a list of five relevant keywords for your book for online customer searches. One keyword can usually be made up of two or three words to form a keyword group.

7. You have two BISAC codes for your book. BISAC codes are book category codes used by retailers and libraries to accurately identify the subject area of your book. Some publishing platforms offer a handy drop-down list of BISAC categories, but it's easier to know your options and choose your categories beforehand. A list of BISAC categories and codes can be found by visiting the Book Industry Study Group[3] website.

> A standard copyright statement can be found in Appendix D on page 278.

---

3 https://bisg.org

> **# TIP** Add important keywords to your book description
>
> Research and follow some of the online tips for writing a good book description. Use pertinent keywords to increase your chances of being found when readers search for a book in your genre, or themes similar to those contained in your book.

Complete your book information and upload your files

All self-help publishing platforms offer a guided publishing process that systematically leads you from one information screen to the next, prompting you, eventually, to upload your book files. Since each platform differs in their processes, we will not go into detail here. Suffice it to say that most platforms are very user-friendly and have good help guides.

Once your files have been uploaded, they are checked and the platform either flags any errors or gives your files the green light, indicating that they have been accepted. Some flags result in outright file rejection, while others simply alert you to potential issues in the book, such as spelling errors. If it's the latter, you normally have the choice to override the warning or fix the file and upload it again.

Most platforms offer you the option to preview your ebook online or to download the ebook file to check it on your own devices before going live. This is your opportunity to see what your ebook will look like from a customer's perspective. You can fix formatting issues and upload your file again, if necessary.

Assuming you're happy with the ebook, you can now press PUBLISH! Depending on the platform, your book will go live immediately or within 24–48 hours. Certain retailers have a vetting process to ensure that your book meets their technical requirements and is of sufficiently good quality to be sold in their stores. If this is the case, your book will take longer.

Finally, you should complete your author profile page. While this is not mandatory, it's highly recommended. This page is more than just a biography – it helps people find you when they search for you online. This is not the time to disappear into the shadows. You need to be visible and out there, even more so if you're a subject specialist and your book is about something you know. This is your opportunity to establish your credibility and convince readers that they can trust what you've written.

Non-fiction relies heavily on credentials, so include them. An author biography for fiction, on the other hand, does better if it's more personal in nature. Include where you live, information about a partner and children, what you love doing, what you're passionate about, and what's important to you. The idea is to engender a personal connection with your readers.

Also, if you've published before, mention your other books as well as any writing or book awards you've received. Use some of the good online resources available to help you structure a compelling and effective author biography.

Lastly, take the time to browse your publisher's website. Many offer excellent tutorials and videos aimed at familiarising you with your author account features, and helping you succeed.

Monitor your account

It's important to keep abreast of how your book is performing, and ensure that key information, such as selling price, contact details, and payment information, are up to date. This can be done from within your customer account on the publishing platform. Here you can see what you've earned; generate sales reports; run promotions; tweak your book description to be more SEO-friendly; see which of your marketing initiatives are paying off; adjust your campaign; upload revised book files; and even unpublish your book.

With online publishing, you're in the driver's seat. You're only limited by the capabilities of the platform you're using. So when shopping around for a suitable ebook publisher or distributor, bear these things in mind:

- Can the platform support your marketing initiatives?

- Can you offer discounted pricing – or even free ebooks – to your customers during promotional campaigns?
- Can you generate special coupon codes with redeemable discounts that give you the opportunity to effectively boost and track sales generated by specific advertising campaigns and social media channels?
- Are there other marketing, sales and reporting tools that you can make use of?

> **# TIP** Preparing your ebook file for publishing
>
> **THE GOLDEN SECRET TO CREATING AN EBOOK IS TO KEEP IT SIMPLE!**
> - Format your document using an A5 page size for a more realistic idea of a tablet screen and how your content is likely to flow when converted into an ebook.
> - Don't complicate your design; limit the number of font and heading styles used.
> - Use web and device-compatible fonts such as Times, Times New Roman, Georgia, Cambria, Verdana, Arial, Courier New and Trebuchet.
> - Modify and use MS Word's pre-existing Normal, Heading 1, Heading 2, Heading 3 formatting styles. Create new styles from these styles, if needed.
> - Some e-reader screen sizes are small, so bear this in mind when preparing your ebook content. Rework your content, if necessary, to fit smaller screens.
> - Embed all images.
> - Refer to Mark Coker's *The Smashwords Style Guide* or Amazon's *Building your Book for Kindle* for MS Word document formatting guidelines.
> - If your book is anything other than straightforward fiction or very simple non-fiction, we urge you to seriously consider using a professional service for your conversion – your readers will thank you!

> **# TIP** ePub file validation
>
> **EPUB files should be validated** before they are uploaded to ensure that they meet ePub technical requirements. You can do this using **IDPF's free ePub Validator**. An online search will help you find it.

Now that you have a better understanding of the full range of production processes, what they involve, and how everything fits together, it's time to look briefly at the production timeline and how to create one for your project.

THE PRODUCTION TIMELINE: PLANNING AHEAD

If you are using a traditional publisher, they will set up a production timeline for your book, which is likely to be based on a commercial decision. The publishing process can easily take one year from the signing of the contract to delivery of a final product, but some books can take up to two years to produce. It all depends on the book.

If you are publishing independently, this process is much quicker, and one of the attractions of self-publishing. Remember, however, that producing a good-quality product takes time. Design, typesetting and printing may be quick, but the editorial process and author revisions are often slow and can take a few months to complete.

Many variables need to be factored into your timeline, including the fact that you will most likely not have the luxury of working on your book full-time. Like everyone else, you probably have a job and personal life – both of which require your attention. This means that once you begin the publishing process, all publishing queries, revisions, and the checking of proofs will have to be done in whatever spare time you have.

If you still have to commission artwork or photography, and apply for permissions, this will need to be factored in, too. And don't forget to include enough time to review and correct artwork, if necessary. Building in some generous padding at each stage of the production process will help you remain on schedule, even if one of the stages takes a bit longer than expected.

We have provided a rough timeline on page 201 to give you a basic idea of what you can expect, and when. You should confirm the timeline with your service provider when you're ready to start publishing; it may change depending on how busy your service provider is and the resources they have available at the time.

> **# TIP** Avoid publishing at year-end
>
> Many authors decide, towards year end, to rush the production process to catch the festive season spend. From our experience, releasing towards year-end does not impact significantly enough on authors' book sales to warrant the stress and potential compromise in quality that results from rushing the job. If the book has good sales potential, it will sell no matter what time of year it is released. The exception is when the book is highly topical or the subject matter is seasonal; in these instances, timing is important, sometimes even critical.
>
> YEAR-END IS NOT A GOOD TIME TO START PUBLISHING A BOOK. This is in capital letters because it's really important to pay attention to what we're about to say next. The publishing and printing industry usually closes down from mid-December to the second week in January. Towards the end of the year, things become chaotic and overly busy, and from November onwards, jobs take longer to get out and things start bottle-necking at the printers. Few service providers take on new work. Production focuses mainly on finishing jobs that entered the production pipeline in August and September. People are trying to get ready to go on leave.
>
> Furthermore, suppliers of paper and printing materials also start closing down at the end of the year, which makes ordering supplies and consumables difficult. The South African school year starts in January, so presses are chockablock with school book printing. This results in paper shortages and presses being tied up for days or even weeks.
>
> **Expect delays on everything,** including quotes and enquiry response times. There is generally too much work at this time of year and not enough people to do it. If you are looking for a good company to do justice to your project, it is well worth waiting until the new year when things are back to normal and you can have the service provider's full attention.

> Use our handy production timeline template in Appendix H on pages 284–285 to plan your own project.

The production time for a typical independent publishing project can be as long as four to six months, sometimes longer, from initial manuscript evaluation through to delivery of the final printed product. Some production processes can be expedited, but this must be arranged with your service provider in advance. They will secure the necessary resources and prioritise your job in their production queue. Vanity publishers usually have quicker turnaround times, but your manuscript must be fully edited and good to go.

The timeline shown here includes two full editorial passes and proofreading of the first set of page proofs provided by the typesetter. Proofreading, and the checking of page proofs by the author, normally happen concurrently. A book with hundreds of footnotes, an index, tables and graphs, and a lot of technical detail may take longer to proofread than the 7–10 days allocated here.

Your printing and ebook conversion will probably also happen at the same time. When your book goes to print, this is the perfect time to have your ebook conversion done.

And finally, don't forget to add the time needed for the delivery of your proof copy sample book, and your main consignment of printed and bound books.

 # TIP The impact of changes to your production schedule

Most service providers have multiple projects on the go. In order to meet the deadline requirements of their authors – some of which may be non-negotiable – they draw up their own internal production schedules. This helps them allocate the appropriate resources at the necessary times to keep their projects rolling smoothly and on track. Most publishing and production processes take days or weeks to complete, so a delay on your part could result in resources being redirected to other projects in the meantime. If that is the case, you may have to wait until those resources are available again for your project. While some delays cannot be helped, it is best to bear this in mind when planning your project.

FIGURE 6 **A typical production timeline**

The timeline below allows for two proper edits, but excludes additional extras, such as commissioning artwork and photography, obtaining permissions, reviewing your book, checking additional sets of proofs, delays in production or printing, and delivery times.

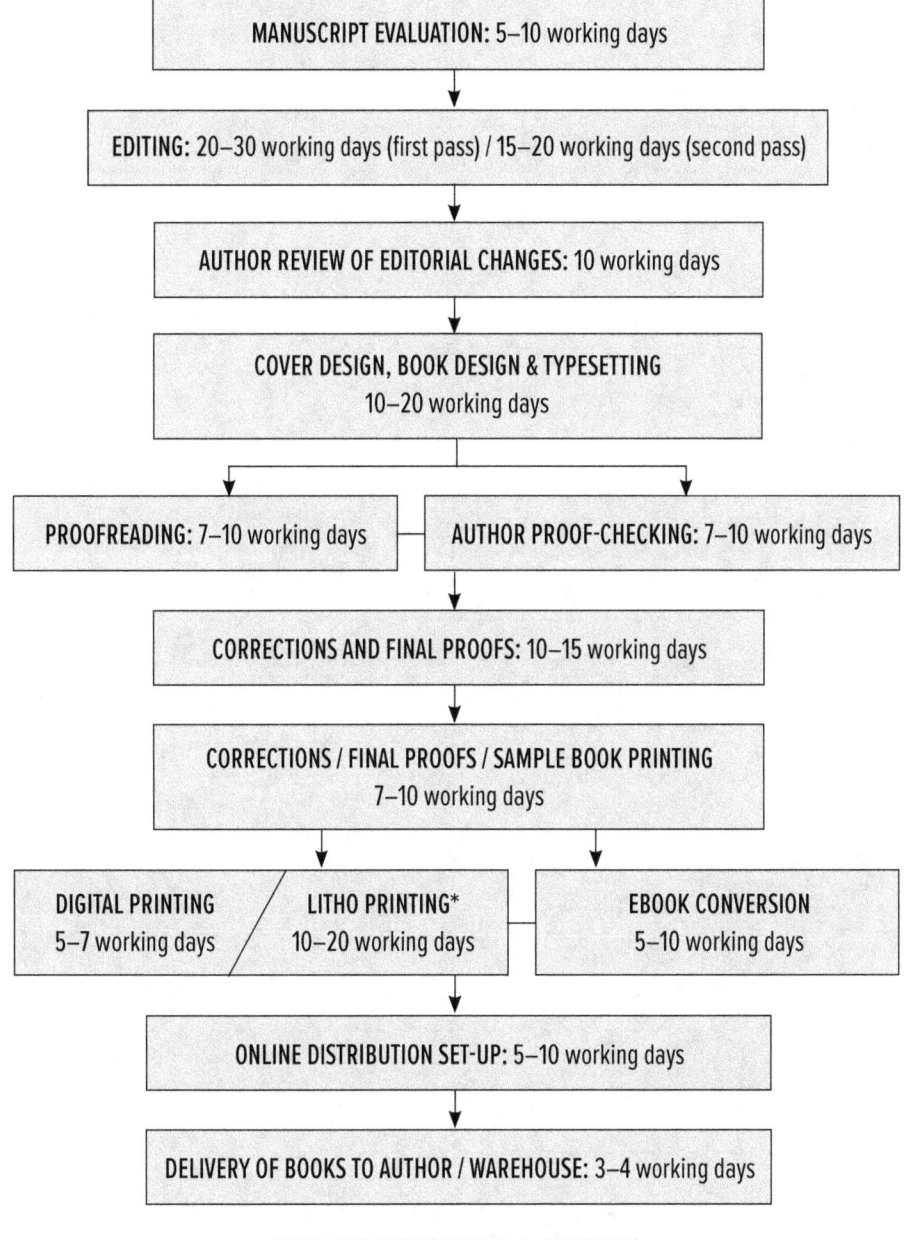

TOTAL PRODUCTION TIME: 4–6 MONTHS

*Softcover book printing: ±10–12 working days; hardcover book printing: ±15–20 working days

SECTION

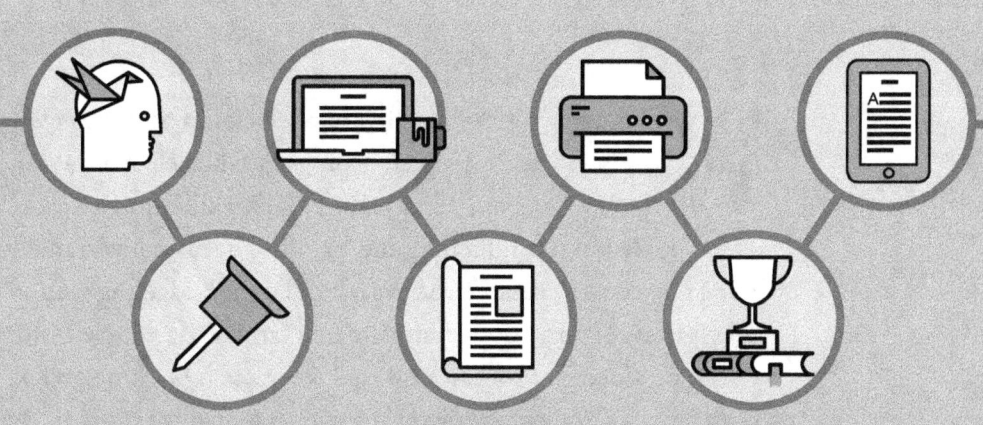

TAKING CARE OF
THE PENNIES

15

BUDGETING AND BOOK PRICING

Working out your publishing budget should be done *before* you begin your project. Doing so will help you assess whether your project is viable, and it will influence some of the publishing, production and printing decisions you make along the way. The reason we have included the budgeting section here is to give you an opportunity to first familiarise yourself with all the production processes needed to create a book or ebook. With a better understanding of the processes, you're more likely to compile an accurate budget.

To assess the viability of your project, you need to consider:
- The publishing cost per book.
- The sales price per book to cover costs.
- Whether customers would be willing to pay that price.
- The number of books that must be sold to cover costs and whether it is feasible to sell that number of books.

If your figures look positive and you believe that the sales volumes are achievable – understanding also that *you* will be driving the bulk of your sales – excellent! If not, you will need to go back to the drawing board and assess other publishing options, or look at ways to adapt your project to make it viable. Remember, **always publish responsibly and never get into debt to publish**, especially if you have no prior experience in publishing. Books take much longer to sell than most authors think, particularly in South Africa.

Although one's budget may be tight, there is definitely such a thing as being penny-wise, pound-foolish when publishing independently. This is because standards of production can differ markedly from one service provider to the next. If this is a serious publishing project, or your professional reputation is linked to your book, it is important to invest in expert production with experienced service providers.

At the same time, you need to be smart and plan ahead. It is amazing the number of authors who publish first and only *then* work out the financial viability of the project and how many copies they need to sell to make their money back. They have often not thought of a retail price until the book is on the press and they realise that they need to get their marketing ducks in a row. By then it is usually too late: authors come to us seeking advice after having spent a small fortune, only to realise that in order to recover their costs, they need to sell their books at an unreasonably high price.

While they may believe their book to be unique and therefore worth the price – a book's true worth ultimately lies in whether readers believe the same and are willing to part with their money.

When it comes to traditional publishing, working out the budget is the very *first* step taken by the publisher, not the last. If a traditional publisher believes a book will sell, they will formulate a publishing budget before production begins, and will usually have an idea of the retail price. Service providers are contracted with that budget in mind and are expected to honour the pricing agreed upon unless the job specifications change.

Organising different service providers yourself could end up being disadvantageous and, instead of saving you money, could cost you more, for the following reasons:

- Inexperience on your part and the inability to know whether a particular service is worth the money or is of good enough quality. If it's not, you may need another professional to step in and fix the problem.
- Lack of proper management of your production resources – again, usually because of inexperience and not knowing what can or should be expected of your team.
- It's easy to overlook an expense if you're not familiar with all the different processes involved and their related costs – this can blow your budget.
- Skipping the manuscript evaluation stage at the beginning of your project can result in unexpected editorial expenses as issues with the manuscript start coming to light.
- Freelance editors and commercial graphic designers may make costly recommendations that do not support the financial viability of your project; or they won't be shy about billing if something takes longer; or they may charge corporate rates for their services, which are often higher than the rates charged in the publishing industry.

Sometimes, it is easier and cheaper to approach a custom publisher who will do everything for you at a precalculated cost. At least you'll know what you're in for and you won't receive any nasty surprises. They will manage the production team and will usually have editors and designers who work at pre-agreed rates. If anything is not up to scratch, the service provider will sort it out and absorb the cost, since they are responsible for their own resources.

One caveat: Your publishing costs will change if your word count is vastly different from the one on which you were quoted.

If you fail to meet the agreed deadlines but demand the same delivery date, your service provider might yield to your demands, but may also add to the quoted price to cover turning away other work, or paying their staff overtime rates to meet the deadline. You should clarify these implications before you begin the project.

Once the budget has been set, you need to ensure that you stick to it. If you request an additional change that falls outside the scope of your agreement, obtain a quote up front. Each cost must be logged and added to your total project cost, otherwise you will quickly lose a handle on your expenses and wonder why you're battling to recover your investment.

YOUR PUBLISHING BUDGET

If you approach a custom publisher or vanity press, you will know what the bulk of your budget is up front as you will have received a quotation or prospectus detailing their pricing options. A custom publisher will normally include editorial services in your quote, whereas a vanity press won't. As a result, a vanity press package may look much more attractive. **Editing usually forms the single largest production expense**, so any quote without it is a very distorted reflection of your costs!

It's crucial to know your publishing costs so that you can work out a retail price for your book, and identify the channels of distribution that will result in profits rather than losses. Jotting down rough figures is not enough. Very often, authors start off with the intention of selling directly to their customers and their rough figures look really good. Very profitable, in fact!

At some point, usually after they see their magnificent first copy in print, or when they decide that their own direct-to-customer sales are too slow, they decide to open up their sales channels to include bookstores. However, they've failed to factor in the 70% of the retail price that goes to the distribution chain for this small luxury. They realise, much too late, that they will make a substantial loss!

If you require bookstore distribution, you **must** do the homework of completing your publishing budget and working out your cost price per book, your distribution costs, and

> See Appendix F on pages 280–281 for a template to help you record your publishing costs. Appendix G on page 282 provides a simpler template for private or personal publishing projects.

whether a market-related retail price will be sufficient to cover your costs and make you a profit. You should also bear in mind that self-published authors generally don't make money selling through stores – most of their money (and profit) comes from direct-to-customer sales and corporate or business deals. Stores simply provide added exposure and purchasing convenience for the customer.

We've provided handy templates in Appendices F and G on pages 280–282 detailing possible costs you may encounter so that nothing is forgotten. Ignore the items that are not applicable to your project. Use the remaining blank rows to include extra items, such as additional services you require that are specific to the type of book you are publishing. Once you have a final figure on hand – known as your publishing cost – you can start doing the calculations that follow.

WORKING OUT YOUR COST PRICE PER BOOK

First, you must know how much each book will cost to produce. In a traditional publishing environment, this is relatively easy: publishers print a large number of books, say 5 000 copies. They simply add up all their publishing and printing costs, and divide the total by the number of copies to get a cost price per book. Let's have a look at this calculation.

Assume you are publishing a 6 × 9, 160-page self-help book and have the following information to calculate the price per book:

- Total publishing cost (excluding printing): R125 000
- Printing cost of 5 000 books @ R15 per book: R75 000
- Number of copies printed: 5 000

Example 1
(publishing cost + printing cost) ÷ print quantity = cost price
= (R125 000 + R75 000) ÷ 5 000 copies = cost price
= R200 000 ÷ 5 000
= R40 per copy

Each book costs a traditional publisher R40 to produce, excluding distribution costs.

Now, let's look at this scenario for an author publishing independently who has one print run of 1 000 books with the same publishing costs. The printing cost per book will be higher because fewer units are being printed:
- Total publishing cost (excluding printing): R125 000
- Printing cost of 1 000 books @ R25 per book: R25 000
- Number of copies printed: 1 000

> Remember that the smaller the print run, the higher the print cost per book. The larger the run, the lower the cost per book.

Example 2
(publishing cost + printing cost) ÷ print quantity = cost price
= (R125 000 + R25 000) ÷ 1 000 copies = cost price
= R150 000 ÷ 1 000
= R150 per copy

In this example, each book costs a self-publishing author R150 to produce, and *only* because the author has a small print run of 1 000 books as opposed to 5 000 books. In our example, the author is investing the same amount for production, marketing and publicity. This shows us how changing the number of books printed changes the unit cost. This is the advantage traditional publishers have over self-publishing authors – it's why traditional publishers are able to make a profit selling through bookstores.

In reality, the self-publishing author's costs for a self-help book would be closer to R65 000. That excludes printing and it assumes that the author will be handling all their own marketing and publicity. The author is also able to save on operational costs.

Let's now look at an example using the lower publishing cost of R65 000.

Example 3
(publishing cost + printing cost) ÷ print quantity = cost price
= (R65 000 + R25 000) ÷ 1 000 copies = cost price
= R90 000 ÷ 1 000
= R90 per copy

Most authors don't have the cash available for a litho print run and tend to print only 200 books at a time. This is usually the optimum quantity if you are printing *digitally*. The cost per book when printing 200 books is much cheaper than when printing 100 books, but often *not* much cheaper than when printing 300 or more books. So, unless you can afford to have your capital tied up in a large digital run, saving only a couple of Rand per book for the pleasure, 200 books offers the best value for money and we will base our next calculation on that quantity.

So, let's look at an example taking *digital* costs per book into account with a more realistic self-publishing budget of R65 000.

But wait, what about the publishing cost per book? Surely you can't divide R65 000 by 200? That would leave you with a publishing cost of R325 per book, before you've even taken your printing costs into account! Using 200 books clearly won't work. Instead, you need to figure out how many books you can realistically sell over the next, say, year or two, and divide your publishing and printing costs by that number, even if it means engaging a few digital runs of 200 books per run over that period. Assuming you're driven, have good access to your target market, and believe you can sell 1 000 books in total, the calculation now looks like this:

- Total publishing cost (excluding printing): R65 000
- Printing cost of 1 000 books (five runs of 200 books per run) @ R40 per book: R40 000
- Number of copies printed in total: 1 000

Example 4
(publishing cost + printing cost) ÷ print quantity = cost price
= (R65 000 + R40 000) ÷ 1 000 copies = cost price
= R105 000 ÷ 1 000
= R105 per copy

It takes only a quick calculation to see that your cost per book in examples 2, 3 and 4 is fine for direct-to-customer sales – you will still make a decent profit. Assuming customers are willing to pay

R240 for the book, this is the profit you will make in each of the examples:

- Example 2: R240 less R150 = R90 per book × 1 000
  = R90 000 profit
- Example 3: R240 less R90 = R150 per book × 1 000
  = R150 000 profit
- Example 4: R240 less R105 = R135 per book × 1 000
  = R135 000 profit

This is considered an excellent return on investment of 37.5%, 66% and 56% respectively! Most traditional publishers don't make that much because the bulk of their sales are made through bookstores and are subject to high distribution costs. Author royalties must also be deducted.

Now, let's consider another stark reality...

The majority of self-published authors rarely sell 1 000 books unless those books have solid content and are backed by good marketing and publicity, or are constantly promoted by the author. It also helps if the book is released at the right time.

Through the Eyes of an African Chef, the international award-winning cookery book by Chef Nompumelelo Mqwebu, is a good example. It elegantly and powerfully positions African cuisine in the local and international food scene, while at the same time placing strong emphasis on sourcing local produce and encouraging sustainable farming practices. But it also celebrates South African food culture at a time when South Africa finds itself heaving toward a spirit of greater inclusivity and pride – where African culture is being reclaimed and celebrated, not just locally, but also abroad. With multiple topical themes emphasised in the book, the timing of its release couldn't have been better. The media were clamouring to have a bite, and just couldn't get enough.

Despite the media attention and accolades, the best sales have not been through bookstores, but through Mpume's own efforts in successfully landing corporate orders for the book.

Most authors are lucky to sell between 350 and 500 copies. And some manage to sell only 100 books, if that. If you think you are a 50 to 200-book author, then a high-end professional publishing option is not for you. You will be better served using a self-help ebook and print-on-demand platform, or a low-cost, vanity publishing package for your project – unless you're happy to spend money on a top quality product with no expectation of financial recovery.

If you're brave, motivated and still reading, let's do one last cost-price calculation using a realistic and achievable sales volume of 600 books.

Assume you print 200 books at a time, your costs are:
- Total publishing cost (excluding printing): R65 000
- Printing cost of 600 books @ R40 per book: R24 000
- Number of copies printed in total: 600

Example 5
(publishing cost + printing cost) ÷ print quantity = cost price
= (R65 000 + R24 000) ÷ 600 copies = cost price
= R89 000 ÷ 600
= R148.33 per copy

Selling directly to your customers will give you:
R240 less R148.33 = R91.67 per book × 600 = R55 002 net profit

This works out to a return on investment of 61.8%. Very good.

Now put this into practice and work out your own cost price. Guestimate your print quantity based on the number of books you think you can realistically sell over the next year or two. Whatever you decide, commit yourself to selling that quantity.

Calculating your cost price per book:
- Total publishing cost: _____
- Printing cost: _____
- Number of copies printed: _____

(publishing cost + printing cost) ÷ print quantity = cost price

= (R_____ + R_____) ÷ _____ copies = cost price

= R_____ ÷ _____

= R_____ per copy

Now that you know how much each book is costing you, let's move on to distribution options and setting a retail price.

SETTING A RETAIL PRICE

How much should I sell my book for? This is the question that plagues most authors. The answer lies in a combination of factors:

1. How much does each book cost to produce?
2. What channels of distribution will you be using?
3. How much are similar books selling for and what are customers willing to pay?
4. How much profit do you want to make?
5. What is your long-term marketing strategy – maximum reach or maximum profit?

> Find out more about distribution channels in Chapters 16 and 17.

Traditional publishers price their books for sale through retail stores, such as bookstores, as this is where they make the bulk of their sales. However, your book price will likely be based on where *you* expect to make the bulk of your sales. Will that be through bookstores or through your own customers and business-to-business (B2B) contacts? The latter allows for more flexible pricing and good discounts to encourage volume sales, while still allowing you to make a decent profit because there are no middlemen taking a cut.

1. How much does each book cost you to produce?

It goes without saying that you need to sell the book for more than it costs you to make. So your production costs will influence your price and your channels of distribution.

2. What channels of distribution will you be using?

Where and how you sell your book will influence your selling price and resulting profits. Each channel carries a cost that must be deducted from your selling price and leave you with a profit.

Selling large volumes directly to corporates allows for the greatest pricing flexibility and yields the highest profits because there are no middlemen taking a cut. Selling through bookstores, on the other hand, will yield the lowest profit and require you to think carefully about your pricing – you may be forced to sell your book at a higher price.

Your earnings through each channel

Let's look at some of your distribution options and **what you will receive for sales** through these channels. Your earnings are given as a percentage of the selling price:

- Bookstores: 30%
- Independent or specialist stores that you approach directly: ±60%
- Libraries: ±60% when using a library supplier
- Publisher.co.za: 70%
- School and academic book distributors: 60–70%
- Amazon KDP: 70% on ebooks priced up to $9.99; 35% on ebooks priced at $10 or higher; 60% on paperbacks, less the printing cost (Amazon distribution only); 40% on paperbacks less the printing cost when selecting Expanded Distribution to libraries and other retailers.
- Takealot: 60–70%; there is also a monthly subscription fee and a warehousing fee if not enough books are sold in a month.
- IngramSpark (ebook and print): 40% on ebooks; variable % on paperbacks based on selling price less printing cost less the retail discount set by you.

Your selling price must take these percentages into account to ensure that your costs are covered and you're making a profit.

3. How much are similar books selling for, and what are customers willing to pay?

Finding a market-related price for your type of book is a relatively easy exercise. Simply visit a bookstore and look at the prices of books similar to yours. To compare apples with apples, you should look at books that match yours in terms of:
- Genre
- Size (dimensions)
- Binding type (e.g. softcover or hardcover)
- Number of pages

Deciding what customers would be willing to pay for your book is a bit more challenging to pin down. Ask yourself if your book is specialised in any way or fills a neglected niche and is thus capable of commanding a higher price.

Some caution is needed here: the average book buyer will pay more if *they* perceive additional value in the book, not if *you* believe that value exists. Many self-publishing authors make the mistake of over-valuing their work and the demand for it in the marketplace.

What customers are willing to pay also depends on how you are selling your books. When selling through bookstores, for instance, you are competing against other high-quality books produced by major global publishers who print high volumes and can keep their retail prices down. The average book buyer in South Africa still considers books to be expensive; the fact that VAT is charged on books and that many books are imported, doesn't help.

Customers have become more discerning about how they spend their money, especially when faced with competing titles from bestselling authors. So when selling through stores, it's best to stick to a price that matches or is near that of other similar books.

Direct-to-customer and B2B (business-to-business) pricing has a slightly different psychology behind it, as your own clients and corporate supporters will probably be far less concerned about the price of the book and more invested in the value the book has to offer them. Having said this, the world is struggling economically and businesses continue to feel the pinch, so they are always weighing up the best value for their money: buy 500 copies of your book for clients, or 500 corporate gifts that may be considerably cheaper?

A mistake many authors make is a refusal to drop their price because they believe that, in doing so, it sends a message that they are devaluing their content and themselves. This is self-sabotaging. Companies and customers care about the bottom line – the Rands and cents in the balance column. Customers like to think that they're getting good value for their money.

Since you are cutting out the distribution chain with direct-to-customer sales, you can be flexible with your pricing. It's better to sell 300 books in one go at a cheaper price, than stubbornly hang on to your normal retail price and lose the sale altogether. Working from cost price upwards (your unit cost per book plus a mark-up) might better serve this situation to ensure a more competitive price, particularly if volume sales are likely. You will also know, in advance, what your minimum acceptable price is, leaving you good room to negotiate.

There is one last factor to consider that affects what customers are willing to pay – it's a psychological one. The theory is that certain prices have a psychological impact on consumers. For instance, retail prices are often not rounded off but expressed as odd prices, such as $9.99 or £3.65. Once you have determined your retail price by performing all the calculations in the previous section, you may wish to tweak your final price slightly to appeal to consumers. For this, you need to know your consumer and what *motivates* them to buy.

Here are a couple of interesting angles regarding psychological pricing:

- **Charm pricing**: This involves converting numbers ending in zero to numbers ending in 9. The brain processes R50.00 and R49.99 as different values; your brain perceives R49.99

as being closer to R40.00 than to R50.00. Consumers need to use more mental resources to process non-rounded numbers, so non-rounded prices are better for *rational purchases*. This strategy relies on cognition.
- **Prestige pricing**: This is the opposite of charm pricing; it involves turning numerical values into rounded figures, for instance R49.99 becomes R50.00. Rounded numbers are processed more fluently and quickly, and therefore feel right to consumers, thus driving the buying process by feelings rather than cognition. This pricing option works better for *emotional purchases*.

Considering the two strategies, experts recommend that you avoid rounded price intervals, like R200, R300, and R1 500, because customers feel they are artificial and randomly arrived at. You should also remove cents from emotional purchases and add cents to rational purchases.

Since books are very often *emotional* purchases, the prestige pricing technique would better apply.

For example, to apply the pricing strategies on a R300 book:
- R290 would encourage an emotional purchase.
- R295.50 would encourage a rational purchase.

A quick browse around your local bookstore will reveal mostly rounded pricing. Very often, bookstores round down or up to the nearest R5 or R10, but you may also find books priced at R249. It still looks better than R250, because it's seen as R240. It also appeals to emotions as it is easier and quicker to process – it has no cents – offering the best of both worlds.

4. How much profit do you want to make?

In an ideal world, we all want to make a lot of money from our published book. In reality, we may have to settle for a lot less. Traditional publishers make small profit margins on print editions, and larger margins on ebooks.

a. If you will be selling mostly through bricks-and-mortar bookstores, then you should use the simple formula provided in the 'Selling through bookstores' section to arrive at a retail price that will cover your publishing and distribution costs, and leave you with a profit.

b. If most of your sales will be to your own customers, you can decide on a market-related retail price. To calculate your profit per book, calculate what customers currently pay for books like yours and deduct your publishing costs. Adjust your retail price until you're happy with your profit. This is the most lucrative option and will yield the greatest profit.

c. If you will be selling through other third-party retailers, such as online stores, affiliates, and specialist stores, you will make more profit than when selling through mainstream bookstores, but less profit than if you sold books directly to your clients and customers.

Find out more about bookstore distribution in Chapter 16.

In reality, you will most likely be selling through all three channels. Since bookstores yield the least profit due to high distribution costs, let's start there to see what your minimum retail price should be. You may decide that the minimum retail price is too high and scrap bookstore distribution altogether, or you may decide to recoup only your printing costs with your bookstore sales and rely on direct-to-customer sales to cover all your other publishing costs and make a profit.

Selling through bookstores

When selling through bookstores, you need to factor in the costs of the entire distribution chain. The distribution chain takes **70% of the retail price**, leaving you with only 30%.

So, assuming you make 30% of the retail price, the simplest calculation is to take your cost price per book, add your mark-up to give you what you need to make from the deal, and then multiply that figure by **3.35**. This will give you a final retail price that will cover the costs of the distribution chain and leave you with your desired earnings per book.

> *Mark-up formula for 30% of retail:*
> (cost price per book + mark-up) × 3.35 = retail price

Occasionally, authors may be offered 35% of the retail price, but this usually happens only if your book distributor expects the book to do really well, or the book carries a much higher retail price. If you are lucky enough to strike a **35% deal**, then multiply your cost price plus what you need to make by **2.86** instead of 3.35.

> *Mark-up formula for 35% of retail:*
> (cost price per book + mark-up) × 2.86 = retail price

Since the standard author percentage is 30%, we suggest you base your calculations on 30%.

 # TIP The difference between mark-up and profit margin

In the average business, a 30% profit margin is considered very good, but when selling through bookstores, you are unlikely to make a 30% profit margin if your print quantity is lower than a few thousand units.

Profit margin and mark-up are not the same thing. Mark-up is the amount you add to your cost price to make a total selling price. Profit margin is the profit you make as a percentage of your selling price.

Let's assume you have a cost price of R100 and you add a 30% mark-up to that. You will now have R100 + R30 = R130.

To calculate your **profit margin**, divide your mark-up by your selling price. In this case, it's R30 ÷ R130 = 23%. Your mark-up is 30% but your profit margin is only 23%. To make a 30% profit margin, you would need to mark up your book by R43 (which is **43%** of R100): R43 ÷ R143 = 30%.

Let's now look at a pricing example. Using the self-publishing unit cost of R105, and armed with a formula, you can now calculate the retail price for your self-help book. Assuming your profit margin is 30%, you can see from the Tip box on page 219 that to achieve a 30% profit margin, you need to add a 43% markup.

Example 6
(cost price per book + mark-up) × 3.35 = retail price
= (R105 per book + 43% mark-up) × 3.35
= (R105 + R45.15) × 3.35
= R150.15 × 3.35
= R503.00

At the time of going to press, R503.00 would be considered a *very* expensive book! Self-help books currently retail for around R250 to R300, maybe R340 at a push. So, you have a problem and you need to find a solution. There are a few possible options:
1. You decide not to sell through bookstores at all; or
2. You print a larger volume of books to reduce the unit cost; or
3. You cover at least the printing cost of each book with a small mark-up added on, and then rely on your own direct-to-customer sales to recoup the rest of your investment.

Most self-publishing authors settle on option 3, and this would be our recommendation *unless* you are entirely reliant on bookstore sales *and* you believe you will sell a large volume of books through bookstores to justify a larger print run. So, let's look at option 3 above, assuming you want to make a 30% profit margin on printing.

Example 7
(printing cost per book + mark-up) × 3.35 = retail price
= (R40 per book + 43% mark-up) × 3.35
= (R40 + R17.20) × 3.35
= R57.20 × 3.35
= R191.62

This is perfect! Your printing costs have been covered and you make a profit, so any price the same as or higher than R191.62 is safe, and workable.

Selling directly to your customers

With direct-to-customer or B2B sales, you can work **retail price downward** or **cost price upward** – whichever works best for you.

Retail price downward: Look at the selling price of similar books, deduct your unit cost per book from that, and see if you're happy with the profit that's left. Without distribution costs, you have the flexibility to do this. You also have the freedom to offer attractive discounts to encourage sales while still making a decent profit.

Cost price upward: Work out the unit cost per book and then add a suitable mark-up, using a lower mark-up for high volume sales or books with a high unit cost, and a higher mark-up for low volume sales or books with a low unit cost. You can then balance your final selling price against what you think your clients will pay, adjusting your price accordingly.

CALCULATING YOUR BREAKEVEN POINT

Breakeven is the point at which your publishing costs are covered by your earnings – at this stage you are making neither a profit nor a loss. Sales above this point will put profit in your pocket.

So, how many books must you sell directly to customers to breakeven? This is the simplest of all the calculations, but you need to know your retail price and your full publishing cost. You then divide your publishing cost by your retail price.

Let's assume you sell your book for R240 and you use the publishing cost of R89 000 in *Example 5* earlier in this chapter.

Example 8

R89 000 ÷ R240 = 370.83 books (round up to 371)

You need to sell 371 books directly to your customers to cover all your publishing costs.

If you sell all 600 books, your profit can be calculated as follows:

600 − 370 = 230 books remaining
230 books × R240 per book = R55 200 profit

Note: If you are selling through other channels, the cost of distribution through those channels must first be deducted from the selling price before you do your calculations.

5) Maximum reach or maximum profit?

Your marketing strategy will also influence your selling price. Are you going for maximum reach or maximum profit?

Maximum profit requires you to make the most from each sale, which does not allow for much discounting and may even require that you set a higher retail price.

This strategy is most often used by authors who have books that are unlikely to sell in large volumes or cost a great deal to publish. Academic books and books of a specialised nature, usually with a niche market, typically fall into this category. This strategy might also be used by authors who have only one book in them and want to make the most that they can from that one book.

Maximum reach is aimed at having as many customers as possible buy your book. This is usually achieved using deeply-discounted pricing. This strategy is often seen in the ebook space where you can purchase books for just $2.99. Using this strategy, you can establish a large and loyal reader base in your particular genre by hooking them in with a super-low, 'no-brainer' price, and then cross-selling them other books you've written at a higher price. If readers enjoyed your book, they're likely to support future books you publish. With this option, it's all about getting your name out there and building a reputation and loyal following. The money and profits follow later.

Conclusion

Pricing decisions can be fairly complex and depend on a number of different factors – the most important of which is how much you need to charge for your book to cover publishing costs *and* make a profit that is attractive enough to make all the hard work worth it.

Clearly, it's possible to make good money from independent publishing *provided* you sell a good portion of your books directly to your target market, even if it takes a couple of years to do so.

It's now time to turn our attention to a topic that is pivotal to the success of your publishing venture: marketing and selling your book.

SECTION

5

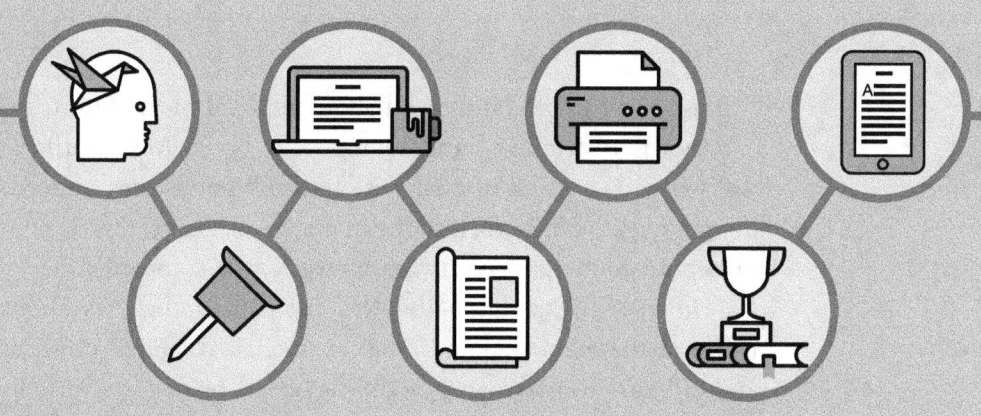

DISTRIBUTING, MARKETING AND SELLING YOUR BOOK

16

DISTRIBUTION – CUTTING THROUGH THE CLUTTER

Just as writing a book is all about survival of the fittest, so, too, is distributing and selling your book. Most authors, when they think of distribution, think bookstores. Indeed, if you can get your book into the major book chains, this usually presents a good opportunity for exposure, and some sales.

However, distribution involves more than that: it's about using all the wholesale and retail channels available – physical and online – to make your book easily and readily available to customers. Selling books on your own website or directly to your customers is therefore also a form of distribution.

But it doesn't stop there. For distribution to be effective, potential customers need to *know* about your book. Simply having your book in bricks-and-mortar bookstores and listed on Amazon or in the Ingram global catalogue that reaches tens of thousands of retailers, libraries and educational institutions does not, by itself, create sales.

Traditional publishers, for instance, have dedicated marketing and sales teams. The publishers' sales reps build long-term relationships with bookstore buyers and important retailers, and encourage them to push new or big titles in their stores. Their marketing teams let consumers know about their books.

Author and owner of The Book Designer blog, Joel Friedlander, puts it well when he says: "What the big publisher is able to do is both push books into the thousands of retailers where book buyers will find them, and pull the buyers into the store with coordinated advertising and promotion."[1]

This illustrates how distribution – the process of making your book readily available for purchase – works hand-in-hand with marketing – the process of driving sales by letting consumers know about your book and motivating them to buy.

Most authors publishing independently tend to miss this vital link. Still, you can't begin to market a book if consumers have nowhere to buy it, so let's start our journey with every author's dream – the bookstores.

THE STATE OF BOOKSTORES

At the time of going to press, The South African Booksellers Association[2] lists just more than 400 general trade bookstores throughout the country: a tiny number given the country's current population of almost 55 million people[3] and rising.

Consider, also, that most of these stores belong to larger conglomerates, some of which operate on a central buying basis rather than relying on the purchasing wisdom of individual store managers.

Sadly, with a few brave exceptions, the days of the mom-and-pop bookstores are long gone, and most book retailers now combine their book offerings with other products such as stationery, toys and novelty items, which further compromises the book selection process.

---

1 https://www.thebookdesigner.com/2010/07/what-does-distribution-really-mean-for-self-publishers
2 http://www.sabooksellers.com
3 http://www.worldometers.info/world-population/south-africa-population

Current statistics are difficult to obtain but, according to the 2014 Publishing Industry Annual Report[4] by PASA, almost 1 500 trade books were published locally that year with national chain stores representing 29% of purchasing. The report does not cite how many general trade books were imported, but one only has to visit a bookstore to witness how imported titles, particularly fiction, outnumber locally produced books.

In other words, bookstores are generally offered a huge number of new titles and they have to choose stock according to what they think will yield significant income in the form of sales and profit. This is often referred to as the blockbuster mentality. It's an easy choice when faced with the latest title from a well-known South African fiction author such as Deon Meyer, but many good-quality local books written by lesser-known names can fall by the wayside.

Shelf space is limited, so bookstores no longer keep large stocks of books, buying only what they think they can move, re-ordering as necessary, and quickly replacing what does not sell with the next best thing. The situation is exacerbated by bookstores' sale-or-return policy, which poses a huge financial risk to the independent author. Unsold books are simply returned to the distributor, often in a less than pristine condition, which leads to pulping rather than reselling.

Getting your book into the stores

The major chains

Major book chains, such as Exclusive Books, don't order directly from authors anymore due to their complex ordering, billing, and returns systems. If you are determined to get your book on the shelves, you will need to use an approved distributor. To find one, ask your local bookstore for their list of suppliers. If you are using a custom publisher, the company likely has existing

---

4 http://www.publishsa.co.za/documents/industry-statistics

partnerships with approved vendors and can recommend a few for your consideration.

A **book distributor** is a wholesaler who represents a publisher by selling their books to the trade, such as bookstores and libraries. Some also sell to schools, tertiary institutions, and niche markets, such as the medical and legal industries.

Distributors have a team of reps who visit each store with their latest stock lists, Advance Information (AI) sheets, and copies of new titles for the store buyers to look at. Stores don't always purchase immediately – sometimes it takes a few days before they place an order. And sometimes they only order when demand becomes apparent, such as when customers walk into the store and actually ask for the book.

> Find out more about the Advance Information (AI) sheet and how to create one for your book in Appendix I on pages 286 and 287.

So handing your book over to a distributor does not mean your book will reach the shelves. And if a book is not available, it's not always the distributor's fault. Bookstores are not obliged to stock or sell your book. Also bear in mind that it's much easier for bookstore staff to say that a product is out of stock or that they don't know about the book, than honestly tell a customer or, worse, the book's author glaring at them over the counter, that they *chose* not to stock it.

Appointments with store buyers are set in advance – reps have their allotted days every month to meet with each buyer. Bargain Books and CNA offer central buying, which makes the job easier, but Exclusive Books doesn't. Each Exclusive Books store is approached independently. It can also take up to one-and-a-half months for your book to be presented to all bookstores countrywide, depending on the distributor you use, the start of their sales cycle, and the number of reps they have. You must take this into account when planning your marketing and publicity. You want books in the stores *before* your publicity breaks or, at the very least, on their system and in a few of the major branches. Should a customer walk into a store and ask for your book, branches that don't keep stock can always request a copy from branches that do.

Sometimes only the smaller distributors will represent self-published books. These distributors are up against the giants in the industry who have a lot of muscle and tend to receive special favours from the stores, but who also, partly in their defence, strongly promote the stores in return as this is their primary sales channel. Because the self-publishing model does not financially favour bookstore distribution, authors are forced to prioritise and push direct-to-customer sales. Sales of self-published books in bookstores are therefore not consistent or high enough to attract the loyal and ready support of the buyers. Space is money and buyers need to make each square centimetre of retail space pay to remain in business – and profitable. It's a difficult space for the self-publishing author to compete in.

If we haven't frightened you off and you're keen on bookstore distribution, interview prospective distributors to find the best fit for your book. Also consider the main genres they represent – a distributor with a strong and successful list of titles in your genre might prove more beneficial to your book.

The ideal distributor has good representation in most of the stores and shows a keen interest in representing your title. You'll need to provide them with sample copies of your book and an Advance Information (AI) sheet. Remember, also, to keep them in the loop regarding all upcoming publicity. Expect to earn 30% of the retail price – 35% if you're lucky – on books sold.

And yes, the distributor will be assessing *you*, the potential client. They will look at the quality of your book; your planned marketing and publicity; what you'll be bringing to the table in terms of actively promoting your book through author appearances and social media; and whether they feel your book will sell well enough to warrant their time and effort.

> Find out more about the Advance Information (AI) sheet and how to create one for your book in Appendix I on pages 286 and 287.

Independent bookstores

Independent bookstores are more willing to order directly from authors, and if you're able to supply these stores yourself, you'll make approximately 60% of the retail price, less the cost of getting your stock to them. If you're already using a book distributor, your distribution agreement will probably preclude you from supplying independent stores yourself. Some authors opt to forego distribution through the major chains altogether and to rather sell through independent stores only. It then makes sense to focus on pushing sales through these stores because you'll be making a decent return.

Some independent stores are still willing to accept books on a **consignment stock** basis – you provide them with books and they pay you as they sell them. The advantage of consignment stock is that there is less risk to the store if they don't sell the stock, so they can order larger quantities. This increases your chances of a sale as a pile of books are more easily noticed than just one or two tucked among a bunch of others. The disadvantage is that stock can become shop-soiled and not suitable for resale. The author must also keep good stock and delivery records, so supplying books on consignment involves more work.

In a **sale-or-return** agreement, there is more risk for the store because they are paying in advance for a product that will take up valuable space on their shelves. They tend, therefore, to order very low quantities, such as one or two books per store, unless they really see the book moving. If they're not sure about a book, they may take nothing.

TIP Managing consignment stock

DELIVERY OF STOCK: When working on a consignment stock basis, get yourself a carbon copy delivery book and write in the date, title of the book, ISBN, number of books dropped off, and price of the book. Ensure that the store manager or assistant on duty signs for the delivery – your proof that they have the books. Remember to check your stock levels once or twice a month and bill for the books that have sold. Don't leave your follow-up for too long – certainly not more than two months. Also, don't pester the store staff by checking your stock every other day. They're likely to become irritated and possibly uncooperative if you do.

BILLING: You will have to give the store an invoice for books sold. Buy a carbon copy invoice book and make out an invoice that includes the store name and details; your name and details; invoice date; title of book; number of books sold; unit cost per book; and, total cost owing (unit cost x number of books sold).

Better still, try **free online accounting software**, such as Freshbooks or Wave, to generate your delivery notes, invoices and statements. Your terms and conditions, as well as your bank details, can be included on these documents. Retailers will take you more seriously, and you'll be able to track your book sales at the click of a button. This software also alerts you to monies owing for books sold and invoiced.

SELLING TO LIBRARIES

Libraries can be a fairly lucrative sales channel; however, your book must meet professional publishing standards.

In South Africa, Afrikaans and local African languages are in high demand and any well-published book will spark the interest of provincial and local libraries. Securing a library deal can help you sell a larger quantity of books – anything from 100 to 500 or more, depending on the book.

Most book distributors supply the libraries, but you will usually make only 30% of the retail price with this option. If you have no existing distribution agreement in place and would like to sell to the libraries, you will require the help of your publisher or a library supplier. Libraries don't buy directly from authors, but many seem willing to review books that authors present to them.

When showing your book to a library, be sure to leave them your publisher's contact details. Your publisher will take a percentage of the selling price for handling the order on your behalf, but you will still make good money on the sale. Also approach provincial rather than municipal libraries if you can. Provincial libraries order for all the municipal libraries in their jurisdiction and this could save you a ton of work.

If you use a library supplier, they will handle everything for you – they present your book to the library buyers and take care of the orders, billing and delivery. They normally take 40% of the retail price for this service, but it is well worth it. You will need to make anything from 5 to 15 books available for this purpose, depending on the number of reps they have in each province, and the number of provinces they service. The smaller suppliers often service only one or two provinces – in this case, you'd need to source additional suppliers for the others.

Often, and rather shortsightedly, authors turn to libraries only as a last resort, when they're desperate for sales. However, library members are just as keen to read the latest bestseller as you are. Libraries, therefore, only want books that have recently been released. As soon as your book is off the press, get your library supply wheels in motion, too.

SELLING TO SCHOOLS AND TERTIARY INSTITUTIONS

If you have published a book aimed at the school or academic markets, you can try approaching these institutions directly, or you can use a company that specialises in educational book distribution. These distributors have established relationships with decision-makers in schools, colleges and universities; they also handle all sales, order fulfilment and billing on your behalf. An Internet search for school or academic book suppliers in South Africa will bring up a list of distributors and retailers specialising in these markets. Also visit the PASA[5] website and view their directory of members.

School and academic book distributors take anything from 30–40% of the retail price on books sold. You will need to supply sample books along with an AI sheet, and deliver your stock to the distributor's warehouse on a consignment basis once initial order quantities have been confirmed.

> **# TIP** The hidden costs of distribution
>
> Remember to factor in the hidden costs of distribution. These include book delivery charges to and from your distributor's warehouse. Some distributors also charge a small fee when you uplift stock from their warehouse for your own use. This fee covers the administration involved and the costs of picking and packing the quantity you require. You must also factor in the cost of digital sample books if your books are not yet off the press, and the delivery costs for getting these books to your distributor.
>
> You normally get paid 30 days after the distributor has been paid, which could be up to 60 days after the sale has been made by the bookstore, library or educational institution – a total wait of up to 90 days, assuming all parties pay on time. This will have an impact on your cash flow.

---

5   Publishing Association of South Africa – http://www.publishsa.co.za

OTHER CHANNELS OF DISTRIBUTION

Unfortunately, finding representatives to help distribute and sell your book to markets other than bookstores, libraries, schools and academic institutions are difficult to find. Online local platforms such as Publisher.co.za, Takealot, Loot, and Facebook with Shopify store integration may help to get you going. There are also many online, international print-on-demand and ebook platforms that you can consider. These channels have been explored in the next chapter.

Consider collaborating with others who sell products that complement or are similar to yours, and then appeal to their customer databases, offering them a percentage of your sales in return. Also, piggy-back off existing initiatives; for example, don't rent a costly stand at a market yourself – ask someone who already has a stand if they would represent your book in exchange for a fee or a percentage of sales.

Selling directly to the reader is the key for all independent authors, so you need to find and create sales opportunities – whether it's making printed copies available at events, supplying books via your own or affiliated websites, giving free copies away as prizes, or putting copies of your book in the boot of your car and taking them directly to potential buyers. The more outlets your book is registered on or selling through, the better. As a self-publishing author, there is no limit to the number of sales platforms through which you can sell your book. Strike while the iron is hot, as they say, by making it as quick and effortless as possible for interested customers to make a purchase when they hear about your book and feel motivated to buy.

ⓘ DID YOU KNOW?

If you're looking for a good South African online store through which to sell your books without the hassle and cost of working through a major retailer, try **www.publisher.co.za**, a dedicated store for all self-published books. Specially set up and operated with the self-publishing author in mind, you receive **70% of the retail price** on each book sold. You can also use coupon codes to help boost sales during special promotions.

ONLINE DISTRIBUTION PLATFORMS

In this chapter, we turn our attention to online channels for ebook and print-on-demand distribution.

Ebook publishing is the most profitable form of publishing because you can achieve high sales volumes with very low distribution costs. Print-on-demand publishing yields much lower profits than bulk printing, but there is no financial risk. Most online publishing platforms handle both print-on-demand and ebook distribution, so we are going to cover both types of distribution through online channels in this chapter.

There are many ebook publishing and print-on-demand distribution platforms that you can use to make your book available to readers globally. Since we cannot cover them all, we are going to look briefly at some of the most well-known ones. Each will require further research and due diligence on your part. They are constantly improving their services and changing their publishing terms and conditions to keep up with advances in technology and market demands – becoming more competitive and author-orientated in the process. We admit that it can be difficult assessing a company in terms of whether you're getting a good deal and will receive what the company is promising.

Jay Artale from The Alliance of Independent Authors (ALLi), says[1]: "Any time that you are evaluating a vendor or a service company, look at what their intent is". Does the company you're considering focus on upselling other services, or do they focus on delivering what they profess to be experts at? Always ask the all-important question: how can this company help me achieve my goals?

Publishing and distribution platforms are divided into two groups: 1) single-channel distributors, and 2) multi-channel distributors (also called aggregators).

1. **Single-channel distributors** offer distribution through their retail channels only. They include:
   - Barnes & Noble (print-on-demand and ebooks)
   - Apple iBooks Store (ebooks)

2. **Multi-channel distributors** offer distribution through a variety of retail channels. They include:
   - Amazon KDP (print-on-demand and ebooks)
   - Smashwords (ebooks)
   - IngramSpark (print-on-demand and ebooks)
   - Kobo Writing Life (ebooks and audiobooks)
   - Blurb (print-on-demand and ebooks)
   - Lulu (print-on-demand and ebooks)
   - BookBaby (print-on-demand and ebooks)

Working through **single-channel distributors** involves more work on your part because you will have to open accounts with each distributor and complete their steps for online publishing.

---

1   Jay Artale, June 21, 2016: https://selfpublishingadvice.org/whats-the-best-print-on-demand-service-for-self-published-paperbacks

However, you are usually assured of higher earnings since they take only their portion of the retail price for books sold. Some single-channel distributors deal with authors from certain regions (countries) only, so you will need to check if your region is included.

Multi-channel distributors – aggregators – deal with authors from most regions. They conveniently feed your book through to all the other distribution and sales platforms, making for much less work on your part as you need only upload your book files and complete your account and book information once. However, they generally pay you less because they take their cut for distributing to the other platforms and they deduct the retail discounts demanded by those other platforms.

Many of the distributors mentioned offer similar services, royalties and distribution terms – all of which are constantly changing to help them keep abreast of new technologies and their competition, and to meet the increasing demands of self-publishing authors. We will cover the services of the four major online distributors, and leave you to research the others in your own time. The four we have chosen are Amazon Kindle Direct Publishing (KDP), Apple's iBooks Store, Smashwords and IngramSpark. They are different enough to make comparison worthy, and they cater to most authors' needs.

Amazon Kindle Direct Publishing (KDP)

https://kdp.amazon.com

Amazon currently holds the largest US market share for ebook sales and is the most important store through which to sell your ebook. If you are thinking of ebook publishing, distributing through Amazon is a must!

Kindle Direct Publishing (KDP) is Amazon's free publishing platform that previously offered only ebook publishing, but now also offers print-on-demand publishing in an easy one-stop solution.

Books published on the KDP platform are fed through to Amazon's online stores worldwide, or to regions that you specify when you set up your title. Print-on-demand titles are also distributed to other retailers if you choose the Expanded Distribution option for your title.

Ebooks purchased via Amazon stores are wirelessly delivered to Amazon's proprietary Kindle e-readers, and to other devices you own using the free Kindle app.

To get started with KDP, simply open an account on the KDP site and upload your ready-to-go KF8 (Kindle Format 8), Mobi or AZW ebook files. Alternatively, you can upload an MS Word doc or ePub file for automatic conversion into Kindle format by Amazon's online converters. Epub file conversions work well.

Authors can access their publishing account by logging on to the KDP site. Here they have full control over their promotions, pricing, book information, metadata, and print-on-demand and ebook file updates. They can also access their sales and royalty reports. The author account area of the website is user-friendly and offers a guided publishing process from start to finish.

Once complete, in-store availability of the title is quick: English language ebooks are usually available for sale within 12 hours and other languages are available within 48 hours. In-store availability of print-on-demand titles is approximately 3–5 days.

When updating book files with revised versions, KDP keeps your book available for sale in Amazon stores until the new files have passed the review process, thus ensuring no downtime or interruptions in the sales process.

> You can find out more about DRM on page 189.

You can specify, when loading your ebook on to the platform, whether you want to apply DRM. Once your ebook has been published, however, this cannot be changed.

Amazon offers various programmes to help authors sell books and to stimulate book readers to buy. You have the option of taking part in the KDP Select and Kindle MatchBook programmes.

KDP Select is a promotional programme that offers you the opportunity to reach more readers but requires three months' exclusivity in which your ebooks may not be published or sold elsewhere during that period.

Kindle MatchBook gives customers who buy a print edition from Amazon.com the option to purchase the Kindle version of the same title for $2.99 or less.

Then there's the Kindle Book Lending feature, which allows book buyers the option to lend ebooks they have purchased through the Kindle store to their friends and family. Each book may be lent once for a duration of 14 days. All KDP titles are enrolled in lending by default, except when pricing your book higher than $9.99 or when choosing the 35% royalty option.

Amazon offers authors a 70% royalty on ebooks priced from $2.99 to $9.99, and a 35% royalty on ebooks priced from $10 upwards. You can also choose the 35% option if your ebook is less than $10 to receive other benefits, such as greater control over how and where your book is distributed.

If you are also selling your book through other retailers, your Amazon list price may be no higher than the list price of your book sold elsewhere.

Royalty payments to authors who have US bank accounts are made via EFT; non-US bank account holders can use an international service such as Payoneer to receive their payments. Royalty payments are made every 60 days.

> Find out more about the Payoneer payment service in the Tip box on page 245.

Apple iBooks Store

www.itunes.com/sellyourbooks

This is an Apple-based ebook publishing platform through which you can open a free account and upload your ePub2, ePub3, and fixed layout ebook files for publishing. Beautiful image-rich ebooks can also be created using Apple's proprietary software, iBooks Author. Books created in iBooks Author are only available for sale via iTunes.

Ebooks can be accessed and read using the iBooks app on iPhone, iPad and iPod devices.

For uploading both ePub and iBooks files, you must have an Apple computer and the iTunes Producer software, which is Apple's tool to upload the ebook to iTunes Connect. Once you've set up iTunes Connect for iBooks, your ebook publishing is managed automatically.

The author account area is user-friendly and beautifully designed, with a clean and functional interface, as can be expected from Apple. However, getting set up with Apple ebook publishing is a lot more complicated than the other platforms.

When signing up for iTunes Connect, be sure to provide a **physical address**, not a postal address, as the physical address is the one that is used on the US Tax Interview form and is *automatically* inserted on the form by iTunes Connect. Unfortunately, this is not easily corrected if your physical address is wrong or you used a postal address by mistake. You will have to contact Apple to have it changed.

> Find out more about the US Tax Interview form on page 244.

Authors receive a 70% royalty on sales when loading their books directly on to the iBooks platform, and approximately 40–60% when using multi-channel distributors that distribute to Apple.

Once files have been uploaded directly through the Apple platform, in-store availability can be as quick as a few days or as slow as a few weeks, depending on the complexity of the ebook. When using multi-channel distributors to sell through the iBooks Store, ebooks can take anything from two to four weeks to become available for sale.

Payments are made via bank transfer once a minimum royalty threshold of $10 has been reached. Apple pays directly into South African bank accounts, but you can also use a Payoneer account.

 # TIP How to check whether your book is available in the Apple store

You can search for your book through the Apple iBooks app on iPhone, iPad or iPod Touch. You can also Google search for your book using your book title, author name and itunes in the search field. Note that the iTunes store is where you *purchase* the book, and the iBooks app is where you *read* the book. All books purchased in the iTunes store become available in the iBooks app as soon as the app is opened.

Smashwords

www.smashwords.com

This is a popular ebook publishing platform that enables you to open an account and upload either an ePub file or an MS Word doc file. The MS Word doc file is converted into various ebook formats by the Smashwords automatic ebook converter. But beware! Your book needs to meet the very strict formatting requirements laid out in *The Smashwords Style Guide* in order to prevent errors and file rejection. For this reason, Smashwords is better suited to fiction and simple text-only books if you're using the auto-converter.

When uploading ePubs, your files must pass validation to be included in the Premium Catalogue that reaches all other retailers, including Apple's iBooks Store, to ensure that your book is available for sale in their stores.

After your book has successfully passed the Smashwords file check, it is immediately available in the Smashwords store. It takes approximately 2 to 4 weeks to reach the other retailers.

Smashwords offers broad distribution and the highest royalties of up to 80% through their own store, 70.5% through their affiliates, and around 60% through major retailers such as Apple, Kobo, and Barnes & Noble. Their publishing system is simple and their website is easy to navigate. Their help guides are also good. They don't offer DRM on ebooks sold through their own store.

Payments are made by cheque within the US, or using PayPal. Cheque payments are only made when a minimum royalty threshold of $75 has been reached. Payments are generally made every 30 days, even though their terms of service say within 40 days of the close of each calendar month.

IngramSpark

www.ingramspark.com

IngramSpark is a division of Ingrams, the world's largest distributor for major publishers globally. It is the most professional option used by smaller publishing presses and authors who require high-quality products and global bookstore and library distribution.

The IngramSpark website is user-friendly and functional, and offers a ton of excellent author resources and tutorials to help you get your files ready for publishing. It also has an online auto-converter to transform your MS Word document into an ebook.

There is an initial set-up cost of $49 US per book if you upload both your print and ebook editions at the same time; or $49 for the print edition only, and $25 for the ebook edition only. Your set-up costs are refunded if you place an initial print order of 50+ copies of your book within 60 days of set-up. Unlike the other services, IngramSpark charges $25 per upload to update your ebook and print files once they have gone live, so it is very important to ensure that your ebook and print files are correct before publishing.

IngramSpark offers Market Access – a wholesale distribution service through all their distribution channels – at no additional cost. They also have a Global Connect Programme (GCP) in which they've established agreements with printers in countries not served by them, to provide print and distribution capabilities in those markets. This means that retailers and customers ordering books in those markets save on international shipping costs and receive their books fairly quickly.

IngramSpark offers enhanced print customisation and a far greater variety of page sizes and paper options than other print-on-demand services. Their printing quality is also better than any other platform, particularly their full-colour printing.

You earn 40% of the retail price for ebooks sold. For your print edition, you receive the retail price less the print charge less the wholesale discount that you set for your book.

Payments are made via direct deposit, PayPal or Payoneer, 90 days from the end of the month in which the sales take place. A minimum threshold of $25 is applicable for electronic payments made in AUD, EUR and CAD.

> Find out more about the Payoneer payment service in the Tip box on page 245.

Oh, how the industry changes!

Authors who have been around the publishing block will notice a conspicuous omission from our list of multi-channel distributors – CreateSpace. Due to CreateSpace's immense contribution to the self-publishing community and the role they have played in many authors' lives, we feel they deserve a special mention, and a thank you!

Founded in 2002 as CustomFlix Labs, a DVD on-demand company, they were acquired by Amazon and their name was subsequently changed to CreateSpace. CreateSpace offered a variety of book production services, as well as print-on-demand distribution primarily through Amazon, but also through other retailers via their Expanded Distribution programme.

In 2018, Amazon announced that its Kindle Direct Publishing (KDP) and CreateSpace print-on-demand platforms were merging. But what exactly does this mean for authors? For one, authors can no longer distribute their books through CreateSpace. This is not a problem because CreateSpace was feeding books through to the Amazon stores, and Amazon now does this directly through its own KDP platform. Frankly, it makes more sense for authors to distribute both their print and ebook editions through one platform, anyway. Not only is it more convenient, but it means that earnings from both ebook and print-on-demand sales are paid together.

But what about books already published through CreateSpace? Fortunately, authors need not worry. All books will be seamlessly migrated over to the KDP platform. At the time of going to press (August 2018), this was already underway.

While we are sad to see CreateSpace go, and despite the fact that we resist mega-corporations and monopolies – hence our passion for independent publishing – Amazon's KDP platform is undeniably efficient and works well for authors.

And so we say *adieu*. As a major player in independent publishing, CreateSpace leaves an indelible mark on our global, self-publishing history.

US TAX WITHHOLDING

Before you receive your royalties, the service providers are obliged to deduct US tax of 30% from your earnings unless you are a US citizen, a registered US business, or a tax payer in a country that has a special treaty with the US.

South Africa has a special treaty with the US, which means that South African authors do not have to pay the withholding tax, provided they have a valid South African tax number. If you reside outside the US, you will need to see if your country has such a treaty in place, and if so, what your tax withholding rate will be (it differs from country to country).

To apply for reduced tax withholding, assuming you qualify, you must complete the Claim of Treaty Benefits section on the online US Tax Interview form. The form is usually presented to you when you set up your payment options in your author account on the publishing platform. Some platforms won't allow you to complete the publishing process until this is done.

If you are a US citizen or own a US registered tax-paying entity, such as a business, tax will not be deducted from your earnings. You will simply declare your earnings and pay the relevant taxes when you file your tax returns.

If you don't qualify for reduced tax withholding and would like to apply for an ITIN or EIN to receive the same tax benefits as a US citizen, you can do so directly with the United States

Internal Revenue Service (IRS). You must provide the IRS with a letter from your online publishing platform stating your reason for requesting an ITIN. Most publishing platforms offer guidelines on how to go about doing this, as well as forms that you can download for this purpose.

> **# TIP** Payoneer – an easier way to get paid
>
> Some distributors apply **minimum royalty thresholds** when making payments by cheque or in certain currencies. These thresholds need to be met before you get paid. To receive your payments quicker, a handy service that you can try is Payoneer (www.payoneer.com). Payoneer provides you with three bank accounts that are compatible with most international distributors (certainly the ones we've covered here): Wirecard (EUR), Barclays (GBP) and First Century Bank (USA). Use the bank and account number that matches your distribution platform's country of operation. Whenever you get paid, Payoneer sends you a notification that funds have been deposited into your account. You have the option of transferring the funds into your local bank account or withdrawing them at an ATM using a bank card that they supply. Easy as that! If you are sceptical about whether it works and can be trusted – we have successfully used them without any problem. Signing up was also easy and free.

EXPANDING YOUR MARKET BY EXPLORING OTHER BOOK FORMATS

Audiobooks

As the fastest growing segment of the digital publishing industry, audiobooks are an avenue worth exploring when publishing.

In a nutshell, audiobooks are voice-recorded versions of books read by professional voice artists. The reasons for the sustained climb in audiobooks' popularity boil down to one common factor: convenience.

Firstly, the convenience of being able to multitask. Sixty-eight percent of frequent listeners do housework while listening to audiobooks, 65% listen while baking, 56% while exercising and 36% while crafting. Driving is another popular activity, with 32% of listeners preferring to listen to an audiobook in the car.

Secondly, the convenience of having all your books with you wherever you go has contributed to the rise in popularity. While ebooks and e-readers have revolutionised the way we carry books, audiobooks have taken this a step further and eliminated the need for a specialised device, since a cellphone is all you need.

While currently more of an international phenomenon, with $2.5 billion dollars in sales in 2017 in the United States alone[2], audiobooks are starting to experience an increase in market share in South Africa, too, with publishing powerhouses such as Penguin Random House now investing in them.

For independent authors who want to enter this booming market, there are a few options to explore. The main players in the international audiobook production and distribution industry are Audiobook Creation Exchange (ACX) – a division of Amazon – and Findaway Voices, who have partnered up with ebook aggregator sites Smashwords and Draft2Digital.

In South Africa, Audioshelf is currently the pioneer in the audiobook space. They offer production services and international distribution, and they pay your royalties directly into your local bank account. They recently launched an app for local audiobook buyers, making South African audiobooks more accessible and affordable.

The costs involved and the royalties offered by these companies vary, but owing to the expensive nature of the production of audiobooks, which involves voice artists, sound engineers and professional recording equipment, the costs are, as a rule, far greater than those of ebooks. Authors may be tempted to cut costs by narrating the book themselves or skipping professional production. However, this is strongly discouraged by all retailers. If the audio files don't meet the strict submission guidelines, the audiobook will be rejected. Even if the files meet all the technical requirements and are accepted by retailers, voice acting is an

---

2   https://www.statista.com/statistics/249854/audiobook-industry-size-in-the-us/

art, and listening to an audiobook involves a substantial time commitment. A narrator's voice that is even slightly off-putting in the sample excerpts that all retailers offer will deter buyers from making the purchase.

The higher production costs have led to the distribution agreements of audiobooks being far more binding than those of ebooks. As with any binding financial agreement, we encourage interested authors to familiarise themselves with the fine print of all these companies before signing an agreement or commencing production. The ever-evolving nature of digital publishing also means that any information you encounter, online or elsewhere, might already be outdated. The safest way to ensure that there are no nasty surprises when publishing your audiobook is to go straight to the terms and conditions of each company. If you're unsure about anything, reach out to their customer service or support team for clarity.

Large-print and Braille books

Additional formats to explore in the spirit of inclusivity are large-print books and Braille books. According to the national Census of 2011, 9.3% of South Africans reported mild difficulties with their eyesight, while 1.7% reported severe difficulties. This means that there is a sizable and severely under catered-for market for large-print and Braille books.

Large-print books

Producing a large-print edition of your book will follow much the same course as the production of a standard print edition, except that you will use a larger font size for your text, and the page count will be higher.

You will also need a unique ISBN for the large-print edition so that buyers can easily distinguish it from the standard print edition.

Large-print books are available at most public libraries in South Africa, so if you choose to publish a large-print edition, make sure that library distribution is one of the distribution channels you will be focusing on.

> **# TIP** Formatting large-print books
>
> Large-print books, by convention, use a 16- or 18-point font for the main body text. If you are converting a standard print edition into a large-print edition, the text will have to be typeset and laid out again to accommodate the difference in font size and the reflowing of text that will happen as a result.
>
> A larger book size is also recommended so that you can fit a reasonable number of words on each line. It will also help to limit the increase in both page count and printing cost. A good, print-on-demand book size is 152.4mm wide x 228.6mm deep, which is the US Trade size of 6 x 9.
>
> You should use a straightforward layout with minimal distracting elements. It is best to use simple fonts that are easy to read. Avoid fancy or ornate fonts. Italics should also be avoided – words or phrases that would typically be italicised can be made bold, instead – and the text should preferably not be justified.

Braille books

When it comes to Braille books, several South African companies can assist you with this highly-specialised process, including BlindSA[3], The South African Library for the Blind[4], and Pioneer Printers[5] in Worcester.

Publishing a Braille book is divided into two stages: production and duplication. The production stage involves translation into Braille, file editing, Braille layout, and proofreading. Duplication entails the Braille embossing – the process whereby the raised dots that make up Braille characters and words are punched on to the paper – binding, and finishing.

Unlike your print edition, your control over how the final product will look is very limited, as Braille books need to be

---

3   http://blindsa.org.za
4   http://salb.org.za
5   https://pioneerprinters.org.za

produced with specific paper, at a specific size, and Wiro bound to allow the book to lie completely flat when open. There is also no economy of scale – whether one copy of your book is created or one hundred, the unit price for each copy remains stable and does not get cheaper with higher quantities.

If your motivation for producing a Braille edition of your book is not to make any money but to make your book accessible to the visually-impaired, it might be worth approaching one of the organisations mentioned above for an assessment of your print edition. If they see value in your book for the sight-impaired community, they might produce the book in Braille at their own cost and make it available on their booklist to schools, organisations and individuals. If this is the case, you will not benefit financially from its distribution, but you can be sure that your book will reach the right places.

18

PROMOTE, PROMOTE, PROMOTE!

Many new authors find the idea of marketing and promoting their own book daunting. There's no doubt that it's a steep learning curve, but it's one that you have to learn to navigate if you want your book to be a success. Even if you are using a traditional publisher with a huge marketing department, you will still be expected to do your bit.

Obviously, there are experts out there who can do it for you. A good, independent publisher will be able to recommend a quality marketing/PR company that will do its level best to professionally promote and publicise your book on your behalf. Of course, this service does not come for free, but there are many ways to get publicity and the companies will tailor their efforts to suit your budget.

Few authors going the independent route have the financial resources to pay for extensive marketing campaigns, so sometimes you need to gird your loins and be prepared to either go it alone or to subsidise your PR company's campaign by getting involved in promotional projects. It helps that you believe in what you're selling. There is nothing like having confidence in a product – and relying on it for income – to give your efforts a bit of va-va-voom!

Here are some ideas you can use to promote your book:
- Create a media kit.
- Develop your book pitch.
- Hold a launch party.
- Plan an author roadshow.
- Network.
- Make your worth known.
- Create a website.
- Use social media to promote your book.
- Join forums of readers who enjoy your genre of book.
- Enter your book in publishing competitions.
- Share the costs of a stand with other authors at your local book fair or expo.
- Offer free talks to the public or special interest groups on the subject matter of your book and have books available for sale.

CREATE A MEDIA KIT

This is vital collateral designed to inform others about your book. It should include the following:

1. **Professionally printed business cards**. Business cards may seem like an old-fashioned concept, but they are still an effective marketing tool. One side of the card should contain your book cover and the other your contact information. Don't even think about producing these yourself and printing them on your home printer. This is a time to invest in your product and yourself, not save money. Your business cards must represent your brand.
2. **A head shot of yourself** taken by a professional photographer. This is the image you want the media to use, so think about how you want to portray yourself. We advise authors to go for the professional-but-approachable look.

3. **A 100–150 word biography.** The main purpose of the biography is to tell a reader why you are uniquely qualified to have written this particular book. Remember, no more than 150 words or you will lose their interest.
4. **A one-page press release** about your book, accompanied by the front cover artwork, preferably full size at 300dpi. No more than one page.
5. **An Advance Information (AI) sheet** that your book distributor will require for marketing to bookstores. This sheet can also be used for marketing to libraries.

    The typical AI sheet includes a book cover image; title and author name; a brief overview of the book; a very short author biography; and some testimonials if you have any. It should also include technical data such as ISBN; retail price; book format; publishing date; contact and ordering details.

> Find out more about the Advance Information (AI) sheet and how to create one for your book in Appendix I on pages 286–287.

What makes a good press release?

The media still rely on press releases for information they can publish. If you can write your own professional press release, you stand to save yourself a lot of money. The release should not be a long, boring description of your book. Journalists won't read it and they won't use it, therefore potential readers will not see it. Think of it, rather, as a news report. Give it a catchy headline; 8 out of 10 people will read a headline, but only 2 out of 10 will read the rest of your content, so think of your headline as your first impression. The website copyblogger.com[1] offers some useful tips.

Then think of a unique angle for your story. Don't say why you wrote the book; rather tell readers why they should read it and what they will get out of it.

---

1   http://www.copyblogger.com/how-to-write-headlines-that-work

Choose information rather than over-promotion. Journalists will take note of why you are qualified to write the book, but they won't be impressed by self-aggrandisement.

> **# TIP   The press release**
>
> Avoid using clichés. You want your press release to make an impression, so shun empty, over-used words or phrases that show a lack of imagination. Don't claim that your book will "transform readers' lives" or give them a "world-class reading experience". Other examples of words to avoid include: best; largest; most; unique; revolutionary; breakthrough; unparalleled; and unrivalled.

Thoroughly research the specific media contacts you want to reach and personally address your communication to each of them. Most press releases are distributed by email these days, so be specific; a press release sent to an 'info' or 'admin' email address will be ignored. Similarly, a magazine promoting new engineering techniques will not publish a press release about a book dealing with women's health issues, so choose your media wisely. There are many good online resources about how to write a winning press release – use them!

Previews and reviews

A **preview** of a book is when your book is covered by the media *before* it is actually published. This is a rare media favour that is usually granted only to well-known or repeat authors whose next book is eagerly awaited by its audience, and prepublicity is likely to generate considerable excitement.

A **review** is when your book is written about *after* it has been published. A good review can boost sales of your book whereas a bad review can condemn it to obscurity.

Previews are excellent for creating interest, and reviews are brilliant for driving sales. Be willing to offer giveaway copies to readers. This is more likely to secure a review because media space is limited and competition for that space is great. The media love to give away free products to their readers and it could mean the difference between them choosing your book over another. It's best to set 15–30 books aside for review and giveaway purposes. Also remember that some media, such as magazines, have lead times of three months or more per issue. This means that the issue they are working on now will only be available in three or more months. If they choose to feature your review in a later issue, it will mean an additional wait. So don't expect immediate exposure – it's nice if it happens, but it rarely does. Obviously, daily newspapers and online media are an exception to this rule.

> **# TIP** Feeding promotional information to the bookstores
>
> If you are using the services of book distributors, it is essential to keep them updated on reviews that have been secured, and the publications that will be featuring them, before publication. The book distributors can then let the bookstores know. Bookstores tend to order more books when higher sales are anticipated. You should also do this when you have radio or TV interviews. Every bit of publicity helps to get the stores on board, but they rely on the distributor's reps to let them know, and the distributors rely on you to keep them in the loop.

DEVELOP YOUR BOOK PITCH

This is different from your press release, as it is something you are going to *say* rather than write. Think of how you would verbally describe your book to someone who is a prospective reader; in other words, a sales pitch. Then create pitches of 10 seconds, 30 seconds and 60 seconds. Use the 10-second-pitch initially and, if the other person shows interest, elaborate accordingly. A pitch is required if you are addressing a workshop or conference, for example, or if you are speaking to corporate clients or a potential bookseller of any kind. It is also useful for media interviews.

Your pitch must contain a unique hook (what's compelling about your book) and what's-in-it-for-them (why people should buy and read your book). Practise your pitches on friends and family until you get it right. Avoid verbal overload.

HOLD A LAUNCH PARTY

This often seems like an unnecessary expense to an author, but it provides an excellent opportunity to get people excited about your book, especially the media, who may want to attend after reading your fabulous press release! Apart from media representatives, invite friends and family as it's always good to have supporters cheering you on; business and industry acquaintances; people of influence within your particular industry or network; social media followers; community members; and potential booksellers and distributors.

It doesn't have to be a lavish affair. Sometimes, the more limited your budget, the more imaginative and appealing the event. You don't need to hire the city hall; just be clever with your location and make sure it's easy to find and physically accessible. If your book is of generic interest, you may be able to convince a bookstore or library to host the event. If the bookstore is located in a shopping mall, all the better to attract a crowd.

Think of a launch party as an investment. The books sold at the event may well cover the cost of organising it and, even if you don't manage to sell any books, the fanfare is bound to generate interest – provided you have chosen your guests wisely.

Remember, if you host your launch in a bookstore, the bookstore will require their standard retail discount on all sales made.

WORK YOUR NETWORK

Having an established contact network in place is particularly important for authors who write non-fiction. As an industry professional, niche expert, or entrepreneur who has chosen to write a book, you should have a network of people who are interested in the subject matter of your book. If you don't, then acquire one fast by joining an organisation that is pertinent to your industry or topic and provides a forum for you to meet and network with similarly-minded people.

Many networking forums provide members with an opportunity to speak to, or otherwise inform, other associates about what you are doing, providing you can offer something of worth to fellow members.

Nowadays, networking is intricately linked with **social media** so don't miss out on the abundant opportunities offered by sites such as LinkedIn and Facebook to get people excited about your book. Social media is covered in more depth later in this chapter.

MAKE YOUR WORTH KNOWN

This concept goes hand-in-hand with networking. No-one is going to know about you and your book unless you tell them. Many authors are under the illusion that people who know about their book will simply tell other people about it. This is just not true. Most people are too busy looking after their own interests to promote yours.

Making your worth known should not be confused with bragging. Nobody likes a braggart. What people do like are individuals who can offer information, suggestions or solutions that are of value to them. As an author, you should be able to offer at least one of the three, so get out there and tell people about it.

The words 'public speaking' may strike fear into your heart, but speaking about your book at an event designed to attract like-minded people is one of the best ways of making your worth, and the worth of your book, known to others. If you develop an anxiety attack just thinking about speaking in public, there are coaches who can help you with techniques and building confidence. This could be a worthwhile investment as many knowledgeable authors go on to earn money as professional speakers.

Contribute to appropriate media by writing interesting articles; start a blog or contribute to other people's; approach radio stations and contribute to shows (local radio, in particular, is always looking for variety that will appeal to its listeners); seek out suitable television programmes, contact the producer and offer your services as an expert author.

There are two factors to consider when making your worth known to others: identify your audience and create your hook. Whether you are writing or speaking, you need a hook to generate interest in what you have to say. It's often a good idea to start by asking a question – that way, you get your audience thinking about the topic and you prep them for wanting to read or hear more. You could also use a quotation, but only if it's pertinent to your topic.

Another idea is to use a little-known statistic or fact about your topic. A "Did you know…", followed by a fact or statistic covers the opening question gambit as well. You could even try to create conflict in your opening statement by issuing a statement of challenge that gets people's attention quickly. The hook is all about grabbing attention!

EVENTS ARE AN EVENT

To boost your networking prowess and establish yourself as an author, you should seriously consider creating your own events. Ensure that these do not just promote you and your book, but offer something of value and interest to attendees. These could take the form of free talks and mini-seminars, or events in which attendees pay an entrance fee. Invite co-presenters, if appropriate.

Don't miss out on the opportunity to sell your book at your events and talks, but make sure you create sufficient interest to encourage people to part with their cash. It is also recommended that you let attendees know in advance that your book will be available for sale so that they arrive with money on hand. Despite attendees' best intentions while at the event, once they've left the venue, life takes over and the initial excitement fades, very often resulting in a lost sale. In this age of instant gratification, people want what's easy and requires the least effort.

To encourage people to buy on the day, you can:
- Organise an eye-catching display of your books at the venue.
- Offer a one-off discount for the event.
- Hold a lucky draw or competition and offer a copy of your book as a prize.
- Offer signed copies for sale on the day.
- If you are hosting a seminar for which delegates must pay to attend, you could charge a bit more to cover the cost of the book and include the book as part of the seminar package.

Make sure you get the contact details of each and every attendee and follow up with an email requesting their permission to add their names to your network.

For free venues, try local libraries in your city. Some local libraries have basic catering and presentation facilities, which they offer free of charge, provided you are not charging people to attend. They don't seem to have a problem with book sales, however, and almost expect authors to arrive armed with piles of books. Libraries also allow you to advertise your event by putting up posters and leaving flyers at their help counters. It's best to have your promotional material up and visible at least two weeks to one month prior to the event.

> **# TIP** Making book purchase payments easier at your events
>
> Consider offering other payment options at your events to make it easier for attendees to buy your book. There are a few good mobile phone services that make point of sale payments easy and affordable. Some South African services include Snap Scan, FlickPay, Zapper, MasterPass and VCPay. An Internet search will provide more information on each one. For authors in other countries, do an Internet search using the keywords 'pay by phone services' and add your country to the keywords to turn up results of mobile phone payment options in your country. These apps allow people to pay using their cellphones. The apps must be installed on their phones but they're usually quick to download and set up.
>
> Yoco is a service that enables you to accept credit card payments using a small, mobile machine. There are no monthly fees and no contracts. Simply buy the machine, set it up and start transacting. This eliminates the need for customers to have software on their cellphones. Let attendees know ahead of time, through your marketing material, about your accepted payment methods so that they arrive prepared.

Finally, don't forget to let people know about your event by listing it in the What's On section of the community newspaper for the area in which your event or free talk is taking place. An event listing in this section of the newspaper usually costs nothing. Also consider a road show in which you visit various libraries around your city. If you don't have to pay for the venue or for advertising in community newspapers, you have nothing to lose!

ENGAGE SOCIAL MEDIA

With more than one billion users, **Facebook** is a no-brainer part of your marketing strategy. A personal Facebook profile is not enough; you should opt for a public page for yourself as an author, or even a page just for your book. This page must be interesting so that people will Like and Follow.

Available options to explore include video introductions; quality images reflecting what's going on in your life; interviews; invitations to events; webinars; giveaways and competitions; book reviews; opinion polls and surveys; and a link to your website, blog and online shop. Try not to make your Facebook page all about the sale as this will cost you followers. Rather engage your followers by informing and involving them and including posts on topics of interest that relate to the subject matter of your book.

These days you can put Facebook to good work by selling your book directly from your Facebook page using Shopify[2]. Shopify offers a fully integrated Facebook store and has been designed with mobile users in mind, making it easy for customers to buy your book using a smartphone or tablet. The Shopify Lite package should be more than adequate for your needs. It also allows you to add a store option to your website, if you have one, and you can accept credit card payments from anywhere. An added bonus is that Shopify comes with a point of sale app, making it easy to accept payments with your iOS or Android device wherever you are. This is just one such service; an Internet search will turn up others.

Use **YouTube** to promote your book. Get a friend to videotape you at your book launch or other events; film yourself speaking about your topic; have someone interview you on film about your book; produce a video book trailer. Keep videos short and don't forget to link your Facebook page and website to YouTube. Creating your own YouTube channel is also quite simple.[3]

As an author, you should already have a business profile on **LinkedIn**. This network is a great way to find reviewers, publicists and organisations that may want to use your book. You can also share information on your launch and other events, conferences, book signings and webinars. Participate actively in any relevant groups, sharing and posting content through updates. Be a Thought Leader and form your own group with like-minded

---

2   http://www.shopify.co.za
3   For help on creating your own YouTube channel, go to https://support.google.com/youtube/answer/1646861?hl=en

people. Go to LinkedIn.com to learn more about the site and to create your own page and profile.

Many authors use **Twitter** as a promotional tool as it allows them to actively engage with potential readers. Twitter is an extremely popular instant messaging system using short messages called tweets. Authors can use the forum to post tweets about their books, their writing, events and interests. Use hashtags to make your content more searchable. For example, if you are posting a writing tip, mark it #writingtip so that people interested in this topic can find it easily. You can also follow other authors and book marketers; you might even pick up a few pointers along the way. Go to twitter.com to sign up and create your account.

Most people understand that social media is a must-have promotional tool, but many shy away from it, believing it to be time-consuming and somewhat daunting. But it doesn't have to be difficult. Rather than attempting to have a presence everywhere, it's better to start with two or three platforms and experiment to find out which site gives you most return for your effort. If you bear in mind that people generally don't visit social media sites to be sold something, they visit them to connect with others and learn about topics that interest them, then you're good to go.

One final caveat: **be careful about what content you share on your social media sites.** Steer clear of political or religious statements, and avoid undue criticism of others. Your goal is to build relationships, not destroy them, so avoid any topic that is likely to offend readers who might not share the same views.

It's also a good idea to join online **book forums** to promote your book and even find early reviewers. These forums bring like-minded people together and offer the opportunity to focus on specific genres. One of the most popular is Goodreads[4], which

---

4   http://www.goodreads.com

offers genre groups such as romance, fantasy, humour and self-help. Other similar book forums include Booktalk[5]; Wattpad[6], and Library Thing[7]. These forums boast hundreds of members and thousands of site views and offer links to conversations about books, specialised discussion groups, book reviews, and so on.

CREATE A WEBSITE

In these days of social media, where people are active on various forums, creating a website for your book might seem like a slightly out-dated idea. But ignore this notion; a book website is an excellent way of promoting, and more importantly, selling your book online. Just like your launch event, the website does not have to be fancy, but it should be well-designed and easy to navigate. Must-haves include the following:

- A clear brand for you and your book.
- A sign-up option for your blog or newsletter.
- An 'About the author' page.
- Information about your book and services.
- Social media icons that take users to your other information pages on Facebook, LinkedIn, etc.
- A 'buy' button and connected link to where people can buy your book.
- A CALL TO ACTION: Tell people what you want them to do (buy your book) and then make it easy for them to do so.

You can use a professional web designer, which will require a financial investment, but these days it is relatively easy to build your own simple website using free website builders, such as Wix.com, Weebly.com, Wordpress.com, Sitebuilder.com or

---

5   http://www.booktalk.org
6   http://wattpad.com
7   http://librarything.com

Web.com. You then include links to online retailers where your books can be purchased.

If you would prefer to handle book sales yourself, you can consider Shopify, a subscription-based online store builder that also integrates easily with Facebook. Using Shopify eliminates the need to set up your own website as it is a fully functional, e-commerce website. The web builders mentioned above also offer easy integration with the PayPal online payment system.

To maximise the effectiveness of your website, install a site analytics tool. Google Analytics is free and available to anyone with a Google account. Once you install it, you'll immediately collect data on your website traffic and visitors, your most popular content, and how people navigate or use the site. This information will be invaluable in shaping marketing and promotion ideas; data garnered may even help shape a new, updated edition of your book (give people what they need!) or generate ideas for a new book.

It's also important to keep your website updated with the latest information – a blog is a very effective way of doing this.

For an example of a good author website, check out Bob de la Motte's website[8] for his book *Runaway Comrade*.

ENTER PUBLISHING COMPETITIONS

One way to get exposure for your newly published book is to enter it into competitions. There are many literary awards in South Africa, spanning all genres and languages, so do a bit of research into the competitions that would best suit your book. A good place to start is The South African Literary Awards (SALA), which comprises a variety of categories, recognising nearly all literary forms in any of the official languages. For cookery books, The Gourmand World Cookbook Awards

---

8   http://www.runawaycomrade.com

presents an excellent opportunity to create a buzz for your book, and this respected award includes a category for self-published authors.

All competitions have their own rules and submission requirements, so make sure that your book is eligible for entry and familiarise yourself with the rules and deadlines in order to make the most of the opportunity. There are some lucrative cash prizes to be won – but even if you don't win, the publicity your book will receive from being short- or longlisted for an award will be invaluable in generating future sales and creating interest in your work. The opportunity to meet and mingle with authors and other figures in these circles will also assist you in getting your name out there and help you establish yourself as part of the literary community.

ATTEND BOOK FAIRS AND EXPOS

A tried-and-tested way to promote your book is to take part in exhibitions or events, either internationally (depending on the geographic appeal of your book) or locally. Some of these can be prohibitively expensive, but you might get around this by joining forces with your publisher or other authors to share the cost and effort involved.

For South African traditional publishers, the most important international book expos are the London Book Fair in England, usually held in April every year, and the Frankfurt Book Fair in Germany, which is the world's largest trade fair for books and takes place in October every year. Publishers participate in these events to showcase their books with the aim of attracting international interest. Attendees usually comprise representatives of other international publishing houses looking to make a deal and agents and brokers hunting down potential new clients and partnerships.

It's fair to say that for most authors publishing independently, exhibiting at these massive trade shows is probably out of their financial reach (the smallest stand sells for upwards of €400 per square metre) although there is nothing to stop you from attending as a visitor as the shows are usually open to the public at weekends.

A far more affordable option for local authors is local events. These are obviously not on the grand scale of international trade fairs, but nevertheless, they offer opportunities for promotion and exposure. New events are being organised all the time, so it's best to research your options.

The annual **South African Book Fair**[9] forms part of the National Book Week, which takes place in the first full week of September. It's usually held in Johannesburg and is organised by the South African Book Development Council (SABDC), which is the representative body of this country's book sector. The event aims to provide a strong promotional platform for publishers, authors and other players in the book trade.

The annual **Open Book Festival**[10] is held at The Fugard Theatre in Cape Town, in September. This literary festival presents a variety of events featuring mainly local and some international authors.

---

9   www.southafricanbookfair.co.za
10 www.openbookfestival.co.za

The annual **Jozi Book Fair**[11] takes place in Johannesburg, also in September. This is a four-day festival that promotes reading and writing in all South African languages. Exhibitors typically comprise NGOs and publishers, and there are a number of author-participation events. Each annual festival has a different theme – in 2017 it was 'Women and Literature'. The Jozi Book Fair also features special skills programmes for school children.

The annual **Franschhoek Literary Festival**[12] is held in May in the small village of Franschhoek, near Cape Town. In an incredibly picturesque setting, the festival aims to bring together a broad cross-section of mainly local authors to present a variety of events that inspire and inform. The emphasis is on informal discussions and debates between authors, as well as on talks and one-on-one conversations. It also hosts book launches, so it may offer a real opportunity for new authors to promote their work.

TIP Club together for a book fair stand

Many of the larger book fairs charge a lot for a stand – more than most authors are ever able to afford or recoup at the event from book sales. With literally thousands of books available for sale, consumers are spoilt for choice and competition is high. If you would like to take a stand to exhibit your book, consider partnering with other self-published authors to share the cost and limit the risk. It also means that you can share the responsibility of dealing with customers, take breaks to grab some food, visit the other stands, and network with exhibitors who could benefit your book. It provides an excellent opportunity to make important connections, learn more about the industry, and gain some much-needed exposure.

Finally, to make the most of your stand and attract people to it, think of ways to grab the attention of passersby. This is usually not difficult because most book fair stands are frequently understated or look the same. Think outside the box – do something different – be memorable. You're paying good money for your space so make every penny count.

---

11   www.jozibookfair.org.za
12   www.flf.co.za

FORTUNE FAVOURS THE BRAVE

You have spent hours researching and writing your book, poring over words, analysing carefully-chosen phrases, rearranging structure and finally creating compelling content. You will need to spend just as much time marketing and promoting your book.

So be brave, get yourself out there and promote, promote, promote!

If you just write your book and hope for the best, you will fail. If you market and promote your book, you have a fighting chance of succeeding.

19

IT'S ALMOST, BUT NOT QUITE, THE END

"It's none of their business that you have to learn to write. Just let them think you were born that way."

– ERNEST HEMINGWAY

And so we approach the end – just as we began – with the words of one of the greatest writers of all time.

It's true that some people are born to write, but even they need to learn their craft. It is a skill just like any other, and it requires practice, discipline, resolution, perseverance and passion. Getting your book published requires the same discipline. You owe it to yourself and your readers to find the right publishing channel for your book and to produce the best possible book that you can afford without putting yourself in debt or financial danger.

We always remind our authors about the 2 Ps – Passion and Purpose. Our most successful authors have been passionate about their topic, whether it has been poetry, nutrition or business.

They have also been passionate about seeing their work transformed into a high-quality, attractive and readable book.

Writing and publishing with passion means that you are happy to continue with the torture and slog of completing your book because it's something you believe in. Writing and publishing with purpose means that you are setting out to achieve something and you won't stop until you have achieved your goal. Nor will you settle for anything less than the best.

Combining passion and purpose results in a better book and personal satisfaction.

We have written this book with passion and purpose, pooling our collective years of experience in the book publishing environment. We are passionate about making authors' dreams come true, and our purpose is to equip you with the best possible information and skills to write and publish your book.

Hopefully, we have achieved this, or at least prompted you to think about the processes and intricacies of publishing a book.

But it never really ends. As soon as you have published your first book, you need to start thinking about writing your second one. A second book cements your reputation as a writer and an expert in your field. It demonstrates that you are seriously committed to your craft. It helps persuade bookstores to stock your titles. It lures readers and book buyers into looking at your first book if they have not already done so. It's a double win! Best of all, you can leverage your efforts off your first book because much of what you will need to do to make your second book successful has already been set up – the foundations have already been laid.

Also, having been through it before, the publishing process should be easier the second time around because you know what to expect, where you need to look, what you need to consider and what you need to provide.

For now, we give you permission to pour all your effort, time, passion and purpose into writing and publishing your first book and making it the best it can possibly be.

Good luck!

SECTION 6

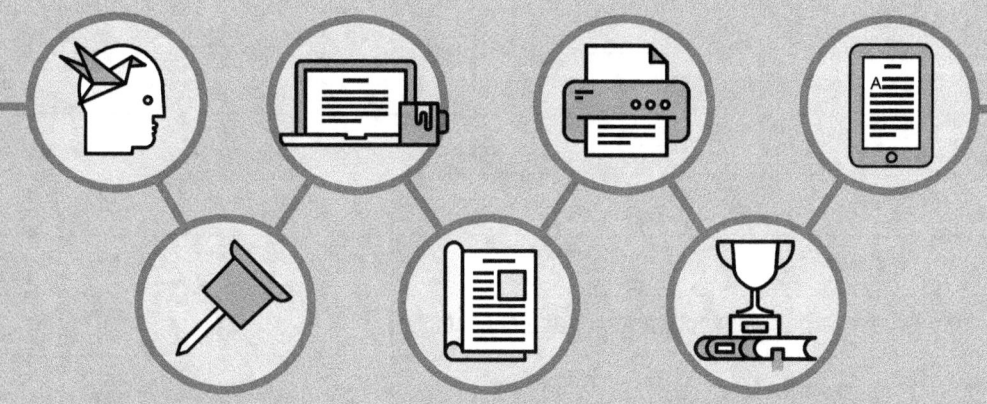

APPENDICES

APPENDIX A

Chapter 1: The write stuff – getting it together

1. What are your reasons for writing your book?

2. What do you want your book to achieve?

3. Who is your target audience (primary and secondary)?

4. Who is your competition?

5. What are your book's unique selling points?

6. What are your best marketing and promotion ideas?

7. With whom can you work to help you sell and promote your book?

APPENDIX B

Keywords and title names

Keywords for your book

Potential title names

SECTION 6 | APPENDICES

APPENDIX C

An example of prelim pages for non-fiction

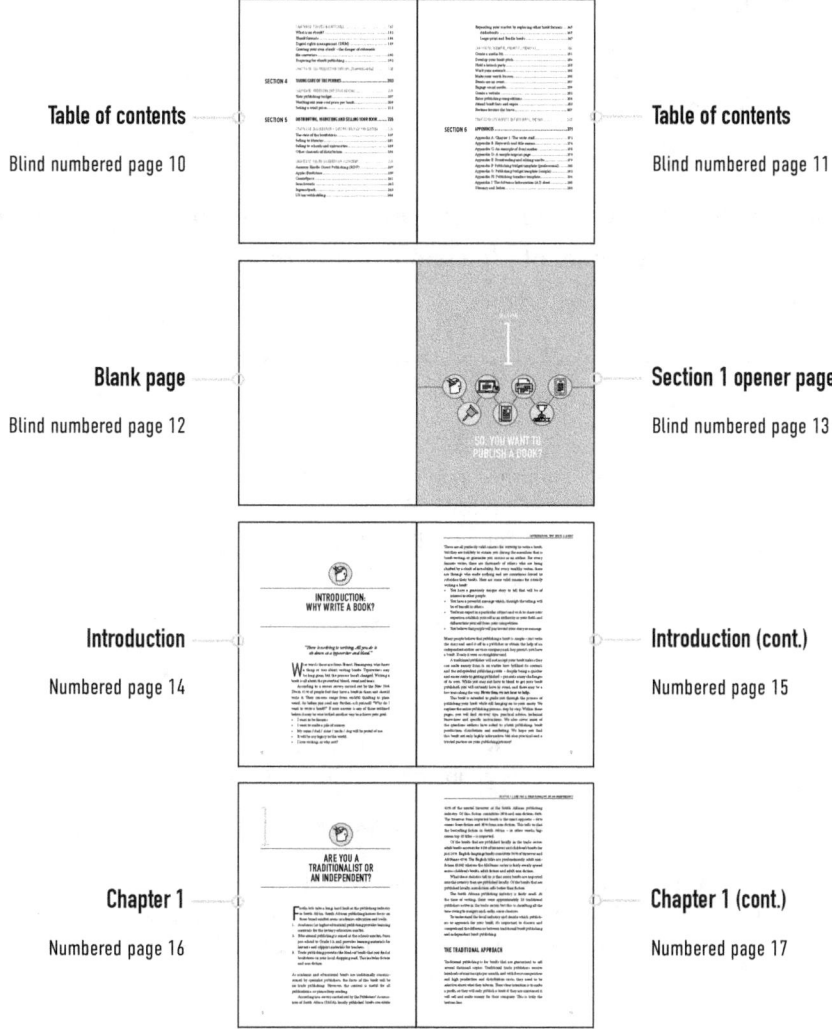

This is an example of prelim pages, also called front matter. There are no hard-and-fast rules concerning where certain pages should be positioned within the prelim section. The only two rules are that: 1) the first page of the book is a right-hand (recto) page; and 2) all left-hand (verso) pages are even-numbered pages, and right-hand pages are odd-numbered pages.

In our example, we have used blind numbering for our prelim section and our section opener, which is the 13th page (you may prefer to number your section opener page, if you have one). Visible page numbering, using numerals, starts on our Introduction page on page 14, a left-hand page. Your book may have a preface and foreword. If so, these could come before or after the table of contents. You might also prefer to start your introduction or first chapter on a right-hand page.

APPENDIX D

A sample imprint page

Adapt and complete this sample imprint page (also called a copyright page) as needed. You can also include the names of professionals and companies who worked on your book, as well as image and text credits.

Published by [Publisher name]
[Postal address]
[Your website address]
[Your email address]

First edition [Year]

[Full book title]
ISBN Print Edition [ISBN]
ISBN Kindle Edition [ISBN]
ISBN ePub Edition [ISBN]

Copyright © [Year] [Your name]

All rights reserved. No part of this publication may be reproduced, stored in a retrieval system, or transmitted, in any form or by any means, without the prior written permission of the author.

[Your email address]

Editor: [Editor name/s]
Proofreader: [Proofreader name/s]
Cover design: [Designer name]
Illustrations and DTP artwork: [Artist name/s]
Photographer: [Photographer name/s]
Typesetting: [Typesetter name]
Printed by [Printer's name]

Credits
[Copyright owner's name] p. X; [Copyright owner's name] p. X;
[Copyright owner's name] p. X; [Copyright owner's name] p. X;

APPENDIX E

Proofreading and editing marks

∧	Insert something (the text to be inserted will likely be provided in the margin)	⊙	Insert colon	⌐	Move left
℮	Delete	=	Insert hyphen	⌐	Move right
⌒	Close up space	/N/	Insert en dash	⊓	Move up
℮	Delete and close up	/m/	Insert em dash	⊔	Move down
#	Add space	˅	Insert apostrophe	⌐⌐	Centre
∼	Transpose	?	Insert question mark	¶	Begin paragraph
sp	Spell out	!	Insert exclamation mark		
≡	Make uppercase	(/)	Insert parentheses		
/	Make lowercase	[/]	Insert brackets		
stet	Let stand (do not implement change)	(( )) or (,)	Insert quotation marks		
eq#	Make equal space	bf	Set as bold		
ʌ,	Insert a comma	ital	Set as italics		
⊙	Insert a period	wf	Wrong font		
;/	Insert a semicolon				

Reproduced with kind permission from Wordy.com – https://www.wordy.com/writers-workshop/proofreading-marks-symbols

APPENDIX F

Publishing budget template for professional projects

SERVICE	COST
PRODUCTION COSTS	
Manuscript evaluation	R
Translation (if required)	R
Editing	R
Second edit (if applicable)	R
Book interior design and style sheet set-up	R
Typesetting and layout	R
Illustration costs	R
Photographic costs (e.g. photographer or photo library)	R
DTP artwork costs (e.g. tables, graphs, graphics)	R
Preparing images, if not included in the typesetting fee (touching up photos, converting RGB to CMYK, resampling dpi, etc.)	R
Author's corrections (normally three sets are included in the typesetting fee but confirm this with your publisher)	R
Cover design and make-up, including print-ready PDF files	R
Cover artwork cost (commissioned or purchased)	R
Writing or editing back cover blurb	R
ISBN application and barcode generation	R
Proofreading	R
Printing file preparation and generation of print-ready PDF files	R
Author photo cost (for 'About the author', and/or the back cover)	R
Printed and bound sample book for signing off, including delivery	R
Printing	R
Delivery costs to national distribution warehouse or your home	R
Print-on-demand file creation and upload for international distribution	R

SERVICE	COST
Ebook conversion and online distribution	R
Project management and administration costs (if applicable)	R
Miscellaneous production costs	R
TOTAL PRODUCTION COSTS	R
OTHER COSTS	
Delivery costs (warehouse, media, launches, etc.)	R
SAPnet / Nielsen BookData listing*	R
Marketing / promotional services fee (if using a promotional company)	R
Book launch	R
Publicity and social media	R
Website	R
Marketing pack (flyer, banner, launch invite, etc.)	R
Book reviews (e.g. Kirkus reviews, etc.)	R
Consumables (e.g. stationery, paper, photocopies, etc.)	R
Miscellaneous (all other expenses)	R
	R
	R
	R
	R
	R
	R
TOTAL PUBLISHING COST	R

*To find out more about Nielsen BookData, refer to page 150 of this book.

We recommend adding an extra 10–15% to your total budget to cater for unexpected expenses. Some books also carry additional costs, which will need to be factored in. For instance, when producing a cookery book, you will likely require a food stylist, kitchen and utensil hire, prop hire, assistant chefs and ingredients.

APPENDIX G

Publishing budget template for simple or private publishing projects

SERVICE	COST
PRODUCTION COSTS	
Manuscript evaluation	R
Editing	R
Typesetting (book interior formatting)	R
Cover design and make-up, including print-ready PDF files	R
Writing or editing back cover blurb	R
ISBN application and barcode generation	R
Proofreading	R
Printing file preparation and generation of print-ready PDF files	R
Printed and bound sample book for signing off, including delivery	R
Printing main consignment of books	R
Delivery costs of the printed books to your home	R
Print-on-demand file creation and upload for international distribution (optional)	R
Ebook conversion and online distribution (optional)	R
Miscellaneous production costs	R
TOTAL MANUFACTURING COSTS	R
OTHER COSTS	
Book launch	R
Consumables (e.g. stationery, paper, photocopies, etc.)	R
Miscellaneous (all other expenses)	R
	R
	R
TOTAL PUBLISHING COST	R

Notes

APPENDIX H

Publishing timeline template

Ask your service provider/s for their service turnaround times and complete the workflow chart below. Then, using the worksheet opposite, translate this workflow chart into specific handover and completion dates to ensure that your project stays on track.

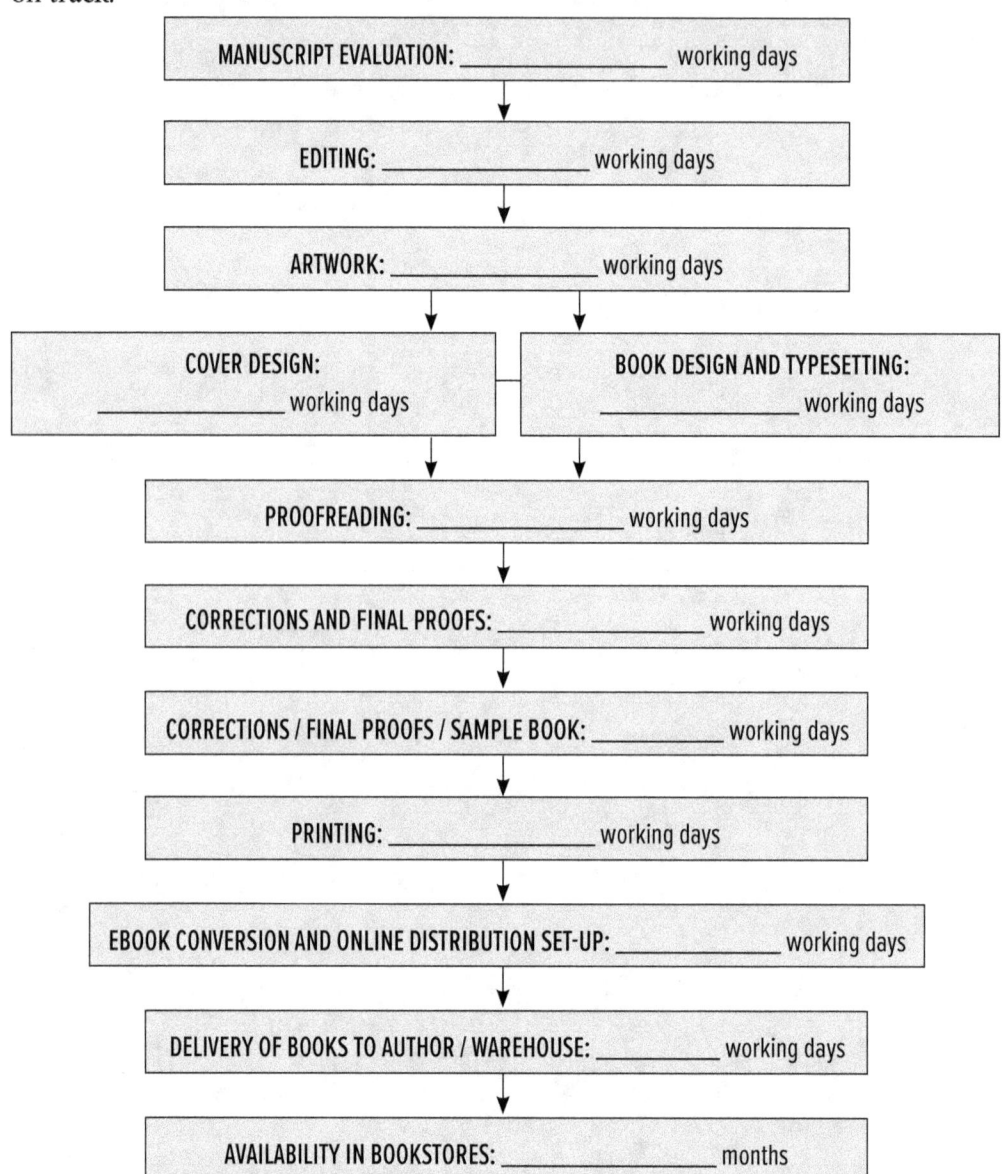

Worksheet for managing your timeline and setting deadlines

Managing your production schedule will help you to plan your book launch date and other promotional activities. Adapt this template as needed.

Service	Duration	Date handed over	Due date
Manuscript evaluation			
Editing – First edit			
Editing – Second edit			
Cover design			
Book design and typesetting			
1st page proofs to author/editor for proofreading			
1st page proofs to typesetter for corrections			
2nd page proofs to author for checking			
2nd page proofs to typesetter for corrections			
3rd page proofs to author for checking and signing off			
Printed and bound sample book/s			
Book printing			
Ebook conversion			
Online distribution set-up – ebook			
Print-on-demand distribution set-up – print edition			
Delivery of books to author/distributor			
Availability in retail outlets/bookstores			

APPENDIX I

The Advance Information (AI) sheet

The Advance Information (AI) sheet provides retailers and libraries with important bibliographic information about your book. If you're selling to libraries and stores, you will need to provide your book distributor with an AI sheet.

The AI sheet should be no longer than one A4 page. It should also be concise and simple. In a traditional publishing environment, AIs are typically produced four months ahead of publication as bookstores order ahead of publication. Book reps are not always able to see the shop buyers, and sometimes have to leave material for the buyers' consideration. It is important that your AI is professional and does the job of providing good information.

The AI sheet typically features the following information:
- An image of your book's front cover
- Book title and subtitle
- Author's name and contributors' names
- Publisher
- Year of publication
- Size of book and orientation (in mm or inches, portrait or landscape)
- Number of pages
- Book format (e.g. hardcover, hardcover with dust jacket, softcover, softcover with cover flaps, etc.)
- Subject area – you can include the BISAC code

The main body of the AI sheet will contain:
- A good description of the book
- Key selling points
- Readership/target audience
- Brief information on the author, listing previous books published and anything that might establish the author as an authority in the subject field of the book; if the author does talks and presentations or will be actively involved in promoting the book, this should also be mentioned
- Ordering details

An example of an AI sheet is provided opposite.

PUBLISH LIKE A PRO:
The Complete Guide to Successful and Profitable Self-Publishing
(South African Edition)

ISBN: 978-0-6399466-0-3
Authors: Vanessa Wilson and Georgina Hatch
Publisher: Quickfox Publishing
Publication date: June 2018
Size: 244 x 170mm
No of pages: 304
Format: Softcover
Categories: Language Arts and Disciplines, Reference Handbooks
BISAC code: LAN027000 / REF015000
Price: R295

BOOK DESCRIPTION
Written by two experts in the publishing industry, **Publish Like a Pro** is a comprehensive guide to navigating the world of self-publishing in South Africa today. The authors explain in detail exactly what one should consider when choosing to go this route. It empowers authors to create better quality books and avoid costly mistakes. Every aspect of the publishing process is explored, with professional advice and best practices provided along the way. Equipped with the insider knowledge that **Publish Like a Pro** offers, self-publishers will have a greater chance of making the right decisions and reaping the rewards and profits that self-publishing can offer.

KEY SELLING POINTS
- Self-publishing is a booming industry, with many South African authors choosing to go this route.
- This book provides accurate, previously hard-to-come-by information in the South African publishing space.
- Every aspect of self-publishing is explored, making it the most comprehensive reference book available.
- The authors are experts in the field, providing credibility to the content.
- Practical worksheets, templates, "Did you know?", and "Tip box" features have been included for added value.
- The authors will be actively promoting the book through public talks, workshops and the media.

READERSHIP/TARGET AUDIENCE
Anyone thinking of writing a book, whether they are yet to start, or already have the process underway. Secondary market: Authors who would like to publish another book or update their books; professionals in publishing, design and journalism looking to gain a broader understanding of the industry; business owners, entrepreneurs and companies looking to establish their brands and expertise in the market.

ABOUT THE AUTHORS
Vanessa Wilson is the founder and owner of Quickfox Publishing. She has a design and production background spanning 30 years and has freelanced for South Africa's largest traditional publishers as a production specialist. As an author who has successfully published independently, she understands the challenges and rewards when going the independent route. She has immense experience in all aspects of independent publishing, from both a business and production point of view. **Georgina Hatch** is a multi award-winning journalist with extensive experience in newspaper and radio journalism, as well as magazine and book publishing. Her resume includes five years as Publishing Director at Struik Publishers and a position as general manager of Independent Newspapers' property publishing division. Georgina has also successfully published independently, and now specialises in editorial consulting and coaching, as well as manuscript development assistance and evaluation.

HOW TO ORDER
Quickfox Publishing – Orders Tel: 021 531 1913 or Tel: 0861 234 256, info@quickfox.co.za, www.publisher.co.za (online store with discount options for retailers – email us for your discount code)

GLOSSARY AND INDEX

1984, 41

A3 – a paper sheet size measuring 420mm × 297mm (double A4), 159

A4 – a paper sheet size measuring 297mm × 210mm commonly used in laser printers and office copiers, 44, 133, 155, 158, 159, 286

A5 – a paper sheet size measuring 210mm × 148.5mm (half of A4), 114, 197

academic publishing – publishing that provides learning materials for the tertiary market, 70, 148, 169

acknowledgements – a note of thanks to others for their assistance and support, 52, 278

Adobe Digital Editions – cross-platform software used for reading ePub and PDF ebooks, 188

Adobe Reader – free, downloadable software created by Adobe Systems to open and read PDF files, 143

advance copy – a free copy of a book given to a bookseller or library, or released to the media before the book is printed and made available to the public

Advance Information (AI) sheet – a publisher's information sheet providing book and ordering information, 229, 230, 286, 287

Agatha Christie, 54

aggregator – a distributor who sells through multiple channels, 236, 237

Amazon, 42, 64, 185–189, 192, 193, 197, 226, 237–239, 245

Amazon Kindle Direct Publishing (KDP), 188, 192, 193, 214, 236–239

Among Ash-heaps and Millionaires, 41

Animal Farm, 41

appendix – extra information near or at the end of a book, 53, 145

Apple iBooks Store, 236, 239, 240

arabic numerals – a decimal numeral system in which numbers are written as 1, 2, 3, and so on, 145

art paper – a finely-grained coated paper used for high quality black and white or colour printing, 171, 176

audiobook – a digital recording of a reading of a book, 236, 241, 245-247

Audiobook Creation Exchange (ACX), 246

Audioshelf, 246

AZW – an Amazon ebook format, 185-187, 238

Baa, Baa Black Sheep, 41

backorder – a customer order that cannot be filled because the item is temporarily unavailable or out of stock, and for which the customer is prepared to wait

Barnes & Noble, 185, 186, 188, 236, 241

bibliographic detail – the description of a book, including authorship, edition, publisher, book format, price, 150, 288

bibliography – a list of other books to read, 53

BISAC codes – Book Industry Subject and Category codes used by retailers and libraries to help them accurately categorise books into subject areas, 150, 194, 195, 288, 289

bleed – the print area that extends beyond the trim edge of the page; it is used when a background or image 'runs off' the page, and ensures that there are no white gaps at the page edge if the trimming is slightly off, 158, 159, 178-181

blind numbering (blind folios) – pages that are numbered but the numbers are not printed on the page, 145, 279

BlindSA, 248

Blurb, 236

BMP – a bitmap image file format typically used on PC-based printing and publishing platforms, 112, 127, 128, 151

bond – standard white paper used in South Africa known commonly as photocopy or laser paper, 165-170

BookBaby, 236

book block – this is the inner section of the book after it has been printed, folded and trimmed, 162, 165

book distributor, the agent responsible for getting books from the publisher to the bookstore or book buyer, 61, 226, 227

book interior design – designing the style of the inside of a book, 78, 94, 131, 132, 134, 282

book production – the processes used to manufacture the book, which typically include editing, design and layout, printing and ebook conversion, 17, 20, 29, 91-93, 99, 139, 173

book synopsis – a summary of the book outlining the plot and key ideas and events, 45, 46, 54, 76, 79, 97

Braille book – a book that has been translated into Braille for the sight-impaired; the Braille lettering is embossed on each page, 247-249

Building Your Book for Kindle, 193, 197, 241

business plan – a formal statement of business (or publishing) goals and the plans for reaching them, 70, 72, 89

Calibre – Mac and PC software that can be used to read and convert a variety of ebook formats, 188

camel case – the first letter of each word is capitalised, also called title case, 130

cartridge paper – a white uncoated paper that is often used to replace bond when extra bulk is needed in a book; it is more lightweight than bond, 165, 169, 170, 176

caselining – the fabric or printed image that wraps around and is glued to the raw cover board of a hardcover book, 160, 161, 176

Chicken Soup for the Soul, 54

Claim of Treaty Benefits, 244

CMYK – the four colours used in full-colour printing – Cyan (C), Magenta (M), Yellow (Y), Key/Black (K) – also called process colour; full-colour images are made up of a combination of these four colours, 127, 136, 151, 154, 157, 179, 180, 282

Coates colours – pre-mixed colours used for printing that form part of the Coates colour system, 114

content plan – an outline of your book showing the content that will be included and where it will be placed, 36–38

copy editing – an edit that checks primarily for grammar, spelling, punctuation and style, 99

copyright – the legal right to print, publish, perform, film or reproduce literary, artistic, dramatic or musical material, 100, 104–106, 278, 280

copyright holder – a person or entity with the legal right to use literary, artistic, dramatic or musical material, 104, 106, 117, 118

copyright infringement – using literary, artistic, dramatic or musical material without permission from the copyright holder, 104

CorelDraw – vector graphics design and editing software developed by Corel Corporation, 127, 136

cost price – the publishing cost per book, 61, 207–210, 212, 213, 216, 218–221

cover design – designing the front and back cover of a book, 63, 64, 66, 67, 70, 72, 76, 78, 137, 138, 152, 201, 280, 282, 284, 286

cover flaps – the flaps found on the front and back covers of a book featuring a blurb about the book, endorsements, or a photo and information about the author/s, 154, 161, 288

covering letter – the introductory letter that accompanies your manuscript when you submit it to a publisher, 45, 46, 128

creamy bulky paper – an imported hi-bulk, off-white or cream-coloured paper that is very lightweight, yet offers good bulking capabilities; it is also easier on the eye, so makes a good choice for text-heavy books, such as fiction, 168, 170

CreateSpace, 243, 244

Creative Commons – an online organisation that allows users to freely and legally share and use knowledge and creativity under a Creative Commons copyright licence, 105, 115, 117

crop marks – the marks that indicate where printed pages should be trimmed; crop marks are also called trim marks (*see* trim size)

crowdfunding – a form of funding in which small amounts of money are raised from a large number of people, typically through the Internet, 88, 89

CustomFlix Labs, 243

custom publishing – a publishing process that is tailored to the author's or client's specific requirements; the author pays the full cost of publishing but earns all profits from the sale of the books, 58–63, 72, 73, 79, 80, 94, 123, 126, 132, 147, 151

Dan Brown, 35

debossing – the process of recessing type or an image on a book cover using an uninked block (like a stamp); *see* embossing

dedication – a message at the beginning of the book to honour or express gratitude to a person or people, 52, 145, 278

Deon Meyer, 32, 228

digital printing – a printing technology that uses toner instead of ink, requires minimal set-up, and can be used to print a very small number of books cost-effectively, 79, 109, 114, 147, 153, 157, 158, 161, 174-178, 201

Digital rights management (DRM) – copyright protection for digital media, 183, 184, 187, 189, 190, 238, 241

double-page spread – two facing pages in a book, 122

dpi – dots per inch; a measure of the resolution of an image for printing, 109-116, 194, 282

Draft2Digital, 246

drop cap – a large letter used as a design feature that drops below the first line of a paragraph at the start of a chapter or section, 186

DTP (desktop publishing) – designing and formatting documents on a personal computer using layout and design software, 180, 282

duplication – making multiple copies from one master copy, 248

dust jacket – the printed, detachable cover that has front and back flaps and that wraps around the casing of a hardcover book; also called a book jacket or dust wrapper, 160, 161, 288

Ernest Hemingway, 16

ebook – an electronic format of a book that can be read on computers, tablets, cellphones and e-readers, 20, 22, 94, 204, 212, 214, 217, 222, 233, 284, 287

economy of scale – the cost benefit derived from producing many items as opposed to just one item in one manufacturing session, 251

edit/ing – correcting or modifying material for publication, 20, 22, 23, 29, 35, 43, 48, 58, 61, 63, 65-67, 70, 72, 73-77, 79, 92, 94, 95, 199, 207, 231, 250, 284

educational book, 18, 133, 161, 163, 165, 169

educational publishing – publishing aimed at the school market, 18, 101, 132, 148

electronic files – digital files, usually in PDF or Word doc format, but could be in other digital formats, 23, 24

embossing – the process of raising text or an image on a cover using an uninked block (like a stamp); see debossing, 154, 251

end matter – the content found at the back of a book, after the main text has ended, such as the glossary, index, references, appendices, and so on, 52, 53, 127, 145, 179

endpapers – the papers found at the front and back of a hardcover book. The one side of the leaf is glued to the hardcover itself, while the other leaf serves as the very first page of the book; endpapers may be plain or printed, 160, 176

EPS – an encapsulated PostScript file format compatible with PostScript printers and often used for transferring files between various graphic applications, 121, 127, 128

ePub – an ebook format that can be read on devices such as e-readers, smartphones, tablets and computers with ePub reading software installed, 146-149, 184-188, 190, 194, 197, 238-243

Ernest Hemingway, 16, 268

extent – the total number of pages in a book, 79, 156

fiction – literature that is invented or imaginary, 18, 19, 31-33, 37, 39-41, 45, 46, 50, 52, 133, 228

First Impressions, 41

Findaway Voices, 246

fixed layout ebook – an ebook in which the layout is fixed and does not change or reflow to accommodate the screen size of the device on which it is being read, 183, 185-187

foiling – a finishing process applied to covers using a stamping technique and thin metallic or coloured foil, 154, 161

folio – number, as in page number

font – a displayable or printable character in a specific style and size, 66, 132-134, 179, 182, 183, 186, 187, 197, 250

foreword – a short introduction to the book usually written by someone other than the author, 50-52, 88, 279

front matter – the content found at the beginning of a book, before the main text begins, such as the title page, table of contents, and copyright page, 144, 174, 177, 179, 278

F. Scott Fitzgerald, 41

full colour – using all four process (CMYK) or all three screen (RGB) colours, 71, 113, 122, 124, 151, 154-157, 160, 161, 170, 176, 185, 219, 242

genre – a book style or category, e.g. poetry, romantic fiction, business, historical, etc., 31, 32, 47, 70, 75, 78, 79, 132, 144, 168, 172, 174, 195, 215, 222, 253, 264, 266

George Orwell, 41

ghostwriting – someone who is hired to write on behalf of another person under the name of that other person, 22

Global Connect Programme (GCP), 242

glossary – an alphabetical list of definitions and pronunciations of special or unusual words, 53, 134

Gone with the Wind, 41

gross margin – what you earn before costs are deducted

gsm (grammage) – paper weight in grams per metre, 161, 166, 168-171, 176

gutter – the additional margin on the bound edge of the page to ensure that text isn't obscured by the binding

half-title page – usually the very first page in a book carrying nothing but the title name, 52, 145, 278

halftone – different tones of colour or grey produced by small dots of varying sizes of ink or toner

hard-copy – printed on paper, 48, 114, 140

hardcover – a stiff, inflexible cover board primarily used for coffee-table books, reference books, cookery books, and collectors' editions; it is usually covered with printed or textured paper, cloth, or leather, 65, 159-161, 164, 176, 201, 215, 244, 288

Harry Potter, 54

iBooks – an Apple app that is used to read ebooks on Apple mobile devices, 185, 187, 188, 240

iBooks Author – Apple's ebook authoring software, 240

iBooks Store, 236-241, 243

illustrative style – the type or style of illustration, 119

illustrator – someone who creates artwork for publishing, design and advertising, 52, 108, 116-123, 137

Illustrator – professional illustration software created by Adobe Systems, 127

image library – a collection of pictures or photographs held by a particular company that can be used for a fee, 116, 117

imposition – the unique arrangement of multiple pages on one large flat sheet of paper; different page counts and binding methods require different impositions, 156, 163, 175

In Black and White, 26

InDesign – desktop publishing software created by Adobe Systems, 136

index – an alphabetical list of topics and their page numbers placed at the very end of non-fiction books, 53, 63, 127, 145

IngramSpark, 188, 214, 236, 237, 242, 243

ISBN – International Standard Book Number, a unique numeric commercial book identifier, 22, 52, 53, 64, 67, 78, 146-151, 230, 242, 250, 254, 280, 282, 284, 289

iTunes – a media player by Apple that is also used to purchase digital files such as music, videos and books; an iTunes account is needed for ebook publishing through iBookstore, 240

iTunes Connect – an Apple service that allows content producers to manage content distributed through the iTunes Store and iBooks Store, 240

iTunes Producer – Apple's submission tool for music and books to the Apple iTunes Store, 240

Jack Canfield, 54

Jake White, 26

Jane Austen, 41

Jay Artale, 236

J.K. Rowling, 54

John van de Ruit, 26

JPEG – a file compression format and an abbreviation for Joint Photographic Experts Group, 112, 113, 121, 127, 128, 194

KDP Select, 238

keyword – a word or phrase that describes something; used to search online, 128, 138, 150, 194, 195, 261

Kindle app – an application used to read Kindle ebooks on Apple, Android and Windows mobile devices and desktop computers, 238

Kindle Book Lending, 239

Kindle Direct Publishing (KDP), 188, 192, 193, 214, 236-239, 243, 244

Kindle ebook – an ebook format that can be read on Amazon's proprietary ebook devices and apps, 135, 146, 148, 149, 182, 184-190, 193, 194, 238, 239

Kindle e-reader – an Amazon proprietary device that is used to read Kindle ebooks, 238

KF8 (Kindle Format 8) – a reflowable and fixed layout ebook format that can be read on Amazon's proprietary Kindle Fire ebook reader, 185-187, 238

Kindle MatchBook, 238, 239

Kobo, 241

Kobo Writing Life, 236

large-print book – a book that uses a large font size to make the book easier to read for sight-impaired readers, 247, 248

Lauren Beukes, 32

lead time – the time between the start of a process and the finish, 163, 256

legal deposit – a legal requirement to submit copies of published materials to a repository, usually a library, 78, 146, 150

line edit – looks at the creative content, writing style, and language used in written content, 78, 146, 150

literary agent – someone who acts on behalf of an author to represent the author's work to a publisher, 13, 47

lithographic (litho) printing – a printing process that transfers an image from an inked plate to a rubber blanket (roller) and on to paper, 76, 153-158, 162-164, 168, 174-179, 201

lpi – lines per inch is a measurement of printing resolution that shows how close together lines in a halftone grid are, 180

Lulu, 236

manuscript evaluation – a critical assessment of a manuscript, 22, 58, 60, 64, 72, 75, 77, 86, 87, 94-97, 201, 206, 282, 287, 289

margin (book) – the blank space around the type area on a page, 44, 132, 133, 141, 142, 144, 177, 178, 180, 181, 185

margin (profit) – the amount you make in profit as a percentage of the selling price, 242

Margaret Mitchell, 41

Market Access (IngramSpark), 242

mark-up – the percentage you add to the cost price to get your selling price, 216, 218-221

Mark Victor Hansen, 54

metadata – data that describes or gives information about other data, 42, 67, 238

Microsoft Publisher – an entry-level desktop publishing application from Microsoft used mostly in business environments for non-professional publishing, 136

MOBI – a cross-platform ebook format that can be read using Kindle, Calibre, Stanza Desktop, Mobipocket Reader, and smartphones that support the format, 185, 187, 188

multi-channel distributor, 236, 237

net profit – what you make after all costs have been deducted, 71, 211, 212, 222

net receipt – the trade price after bookseller discounts and VAT have been deducted, 24, 25, 28

New York Times, 16, 96

Nielsen BookData – an international bibliographic database, 150, 283

non-fiction – writing that is based on facts rather than imagination, 18, 19, 26, 31-34, 37-43, 46, 50, 52, 53, 60, 78, 82, 133, 138, 144, 145, 165, 169, 170, 176, 177, 184, 185, 194, 196, 197, 245, 258

offset printing – a process that transfers an image from an inked plate to a rubber blanket (roller) and on to paper, 153

out of print – no longer available from the publisher, 25

overwriting – rewriting text where necessary to improve comprehension and the quality of the writing, 22

page proofs – a set of printed or electronic (PDF) proofs that authors and editors use to check for editorial and layout errors, and to ensure that corrections requested have been implemented, 102, 139, 282, 284, 287

Pantone colours – pre-mixed colours used for printing that form part of the Pantone colour system, 114

paperback – a soft, slightly stiff yet flexible book cover, also referred to as softcover, 159, 162, 165, 176

PASA (Publishing Association of South Africa) – the official body for South African publishing and publishing professionals, 19, 228

Payoneer, 239, 240, 243, 245

PayPal, 241, 243,

PDF – a portable document format that enables users to capture and exchange electronic documents in exactly the format intended, 118, 121, 127, 128, 131, 132, 139, 140, 143, 146, 149, 153, 157, 178-180, 184-188, 241, 243, 282

PDF/X-1a, 178, 179

Penguin Books, 26

Penguin Random House, 246

perfect binding – loose, inner pages that are trimmed, stacked, pressed together and glued into the spine, 143, 144, 162, 164, 177

permissions – an official document giving authorisation to republish material owned by other copyright holders, 20, 22, 58, 104–107, 114, 116, 118, 126, 199

Photoshop – image-editing software created by Adobe Systems

Pioneer Printers, 248

pixel, 109, 110

pixelation, 111

plagiarism – taking someone else's work and passing it off as your own, 35, 103

POD – *see* print-on-demand

point size (pt) – font size, e.g. 10pt

ppi – pixels per inch; a measure of the resolution of an image for the Internet, 109

preface – an introduction at the beginning of a book by the author or editor explaining the book's purpose and acknowledging assistance from others, 52, 279

preflight – a production term for 'checking' an electronic file to ensure that it meets industry printing requirements, 136, 195

prelim pages – the pages that come at the beginning of the book before the main body of text starts, also known as front matter, 144, 145, 278, 279

Premium Catalogue, 241

pre-selling – selling a book before it has been printed or released, 89

Pride and Prejudice, 41

primary market – the main consumer market likely to buy the book, 34

print finishing – all the activities performed on printed material after printing, such as binding, foiling, embossing, trimming, additional tooling, gilding, etc., 59

printing plates – the plates used by offset printers to transfer printing inks to rubber rollers that then transfer the ink to the paper, 23, 29, 156, 157, 175

print-on-demand (POD) – a publishing process whereby books are printed on digital presses as and when orders are received, even if the order is for only one book, 58, 66–69, 78, 98, 108, 123, 126, 132, 133, 135, 144, 147, 151, 153, 158, 161, 166, 174, 176–181, 235, 236, 238, 241, 243–245, 250, 287

print-ready PDF – the final PDF file used for printing, made up to the printer's specifications, 94, 132, 153, 178, 241, 282, 284

process colour – the colours used in full colour printing, also known as CMYK (Cyan, Magenta, Yellow and Key/Black), 157

proofreading – reading printer's proofs or other printed material and marking any errors, 20, 76, 78, 94–96, 102, 103, 127, 199, 250, 281, 102, 201, 284, 286, 287

PSD – an Adobe Photoshop file format extension (e.g. image.psd), 112, 128, 151

publishing – the activity of preparing books and other material for sale, or making information available to the general public

publishing contract – a legal contract between a publisher and an author to publish material written by the author, 21, 23, 29

PUR binding – a form of perfect binding where the pages and cover are glued at the spine using a highly durable glue called Polyurethane Reactive (PUR), 162, 164, 172

QuarkXpress – desktop publishing software developed by Quark Software, 136

query letter – a formal letter that an author sends to a literary agent, publishing house or magazine to propose a writing idea or manuscript, 47

recto – right-hand page, 279

reflowable ebook – an ebook that reflows to accommodate the screen size of the reading device and the font size chosen by the user, 135, 182, 184, 186-188

resampling – changing the size of an image by changing the resolution (dpi/ppi), 109-111, 282

resizing – changing the physical dimensions of an image without changing the resolution (dpi/ppi), 109, 111

resolution – the number of dots or pixels per inch in an image; written as dpi (dots per inch) or ppi (pixels per inch), 109, 110, 113, 114, 117, 120, 123, 178-180

resources – a list of materials used when writing the book, 53

retail price – the price the public pays for a book, also called the list price or selling price, 24, 25, 28, 175, 237, 242, 244, 245, 254, 258

RGB – TV and computer screen colours – Red, Green and Blue; all screen images are made up of a combination of these three colours, 127, 151, 282

rights-managed images – a type of image purchase and use that grants you the right to use images in very specific ways, 114-116

roman numerals – a Roman numerical system that uses letters to represent numbers, for example: I = 1, V = 5, X = 10, L = 50, C = 100, D = 500, M = 1 000, etc., 145

roundback hardcover – hardcover binding with a rounded spine, often used for fiction, poetry, law and reference books, and collectibles; it is also suited to books that have a dust jacket, 160, 176

royalty-free image – a type of image purchase and use that grants you the right to use an image in multiple ways, with few restrictions, 114, 115, 116

royalty-free library – a repository that stocks royalty-free images, 114–117, 122

royalty threshold – the minimum royalty earnings that must be met before payment is made to the author, 240, 241, 244

RRP (recommended retail price) – the recommended selling price of the book as set by the publisher; bookstores can override this price if they choose, 214

RSP (recommended selling price) – the same as the recommended retail price, 214

saddle-stitching – book pages are folded in half and wire-stapled at the spine, 162-165, 177, 178

Samuel Johnson, 35

SAPnet – South African Publisher's Network, the South African agents for Nielsen BookData, 50, 283

sans serif font – a font that has no serifs (little feet) finishing off the strokes of letters, for example, Helvetica (*see* serif font), 134, 135

secondary market – another consumer market, other than the main consumer market, who will likely buy the book, 34, 289

self-publishing – a form of publishing in which the author pays the publishing costs and earns all the profits from sales

serif font – a font with serifs (little feet) finishing off the strokes of letters, for example, Times New Roman (*see* sans serif font), 134, 135, 144

sheet size – the size of the paper sheet that fits on a printing press; different presses use different sheet sizes; the sheet size dictates the number of book pages that can be printed together in one pass (*see* imposition), 158, 159

show through – when images or text on one side of a leaf of paper show through on the reverse side of that leaf

signature – a group of pages printed on both sides of a sheet of paper, 154–156

single-channel distributor, 236, 237

Smashwords, 236, 241, 246

softcover – this is a slightly stiff, yet flexible book cover referred to as a paperback, 143, 146, 148, 149, 151, 159–161, 164, 201, 215, 241, 288, 289

spine – the section of perfect bound and thread-sewn books that lies between the front cover and the back cover that faces you on a bookshelf when the book stands upright, 59, 120, 124, 143, 158, 160, 162–165, 177, 179–181

spot colour – a special pre-mixed ink created by mixing other colours together that can be used instead of, or in addition to, process (CMYK) inks, 114, 143, 154, 157, 176, 179, 180

Spud, 26

squareback hardcover – hardcover binding with a flat spine, usually used on full-colour coffee-table and cookery books, 160, 176

stock images – a collection of images that are usually licensed for specific uses, 114–116, 123

stock photos – *see* stock images

subsidy publishing – a form of publishing in which author and publisher co-invest in the production and publishing of the book; also called partnership publishing, 70, 71, 73

substantive edit – a comprehensive edit; the editor considers the book's aim, intended use, organisation, style, flow and content design, 99, 100, 104

subtitle – a subordinate title giving more information about the book, 41–43, 53, 150, 288

sulphate board – a high-bulk, lightweight board that is coated on one side and uncoated on the reverse. The coated side is the printed side; commonly used for softcover (paperback) books, 161, 176

table of contents – a list of chapters or parts of a book presented at the beginning of the book in the order in which the chapters or parts appear, accompanied by the corresponding page numbers, 36, 52, 177, 182, 194, 278, 279

target audience – the group of people at whom the book is aimed, 30, 34, 82, 97, 124, 274, 288, 289

target market – the group of people likely to buy the book, 26, 28, 29, 33–35, 62, 71, 76, 79, 85, 100, 134, 172, 184, 210, 223, 233

tautology – saying the same thing twice in different words, 100

testimonial – words of praise about your book by people who are respected or have influence, 50–53, 139

The 4-Hour Work Week: Escape 9-5, Live Anywhere and Join the New Rich, 41

The Alliance of Independent Authors (ALLi), 236

The Great Gatsby, 41

The Last Man in Europe, 41

The Smashwords Style Guide, 193, 197, 241

The South African Booksellers Association, 227

The South African Library for the Blind, 248

thread-sewing – the book pages are folded into 8-, 16- or 32-page sections and then sewn along the fold of each section for binding, 143, 155, 162, 163, 164, 172, 177, 244

TIFF – a common file format for raster graphics (bitmap) images commonly used in printing and publishing, 112, 121, 127, 128, 151

Timothy Ferris, 41

title – the name of the book, 40-43, 52, 53, 288

title case – the first letter of each word is capitalised, also called camel case, 130

title page – a page at the beginning of a book giving the title name and the names of the author/s and publisher, 52, 132, 145, 194, 278

top and tail bands – small fabric bands at the top and bottom of the spine of hardcover books that hide the binding and give the book a finished look; they are sometimes accompanied by a ribbon that can be used as a bookmark, 160

trade price – the price that bookstores pay publishers or wholesalers to purchase the book, 160

trade publishing – general fiction and non-fiction publishing for the bookstore market, 18, 169, 205

traditional publishing – a form of publishing whereby a publisher funds, produces, prints, and sells the book, and pays the author royalties on sales, also called royalty-based publishing, 13, 17-33, 33, 50, 53, 56-58, 61, 63, 69-72, 81, 83, 87, 94-96, 100-102, 108, 128, 129, 131, 132, 137, 139, 151, 154, 172, 175, 198, 205, 208, 209, 211, 226, 250, 264

translating – converting text from one language to another, 58

trim marks – marks that indicate where a printed book should be trimmed (*see* trim size)

trim size – the actual size after the book has been trimmed, 132, 155

typeface – a set (or family) of fonts of a specific style in various weights and sizes, 133

typesetting – formatting and laying out type and book content for printing, 20, 70, 78, 94, 95, 99, 102, 127, 129, 131, 135, 136, 139, 140, 198, 201, 282, 284, 286, 287

typo – a typographical error, 101

vanity publishing (press) – a form of publishing in which the author pays to have their book published with no prior vetting or evaluation process, 58, 61-65, 72, 78, 87, 107, 108, 123, 126, 132, 147, 150, 151, 166, 173, 200, 207, 212

US Letter – a common American paper sheet size, 157

US Tax Interview form, 240, 244

US tax withholding, 244,

USP (unique selling point) – the special quality that differentiates your product from other, similar products, also called the unique selling proposition, 30

verso – left-hand page, 279

wiro bound – loose pages bound together using spiral bounding made of wire, 249

Work-for-hire – a copyright that is assigned at creation to the person for whom the work is being created, such as an employer or a client, 24, 61

Worcester, 248

Zebra Press, 26

Acknowledgements

A very special thank you to my partner, Bruna Dessena, for your constant support, and for always wanting the best for me.

Thank you to Gill Marshall, who took a chance and gave me my first lucky break and introduction to the world of publication design when I knew absolutely nothing. You opened the path. You remain the best designer I've met.

To my co-author, Georgina: when we first met, I had a feeling we'd do something big. Thank you for starting and driving this project. It wouldn't have happened, otherwise.

To Rachel Bey-Miller and Michelle Bovey-Wood: you have produced miracles over the years and have been instrumental in getting Quickfox Publishing to where it is today. Thank you for volunteering your time and expertise to help review this book. And Nadine Dove, thank you for donating your time and doing an excellent job with the proofreading.

To Lindsay Green, who joined me as a publishing intern – you were born for this! Your efficient and reliable management of our office, projects and admin freed me up to finish this book. Thank you, also, for your research assistance and willing ear.

To our key suppliers who have provided excellent service over the years – Angela Voges; Andrea Willmore; Aziza Pillay; Portia Almano; Anita Minaar; Grant Walton (Digital Action SA); Linda Kay (Tandym Print); Lesley Ackerman; Deon Martin and Siseko Sodlaka (Novus Print Solutions); Suzette Hamman and Laura Fortuin (Sula Books); Magret Kibido and Nelisa Lunika (NLSA); Yolanda Alexander and Shafeeka Waggie (Castle Graphics); Glen Witbooi (Shumani Printers); Craig Hughes (RSA Litho); the late Johan Pretorius (Symcom) – a huge thank you for your support.

To all our brave clients, past and present, who took the plunge and trusted us with their babies. You are exceptional people. And thank you, especially, to Dyan Belonje – you were our first!

To all who have worked for, or contributed to, Quickfox: Wendy Lloyd; Neil de Jager; Lana de Jager; Veronica Washaya; Lisa Wilson; Maggie Flynn; Courtney North; Nazli Allie; Paula Fonseca. With blessings and much gratitude.

About the authors

Vanessa Wilson founded and manages Quickfox Publishing, a leading custom publishing company based in Cape Town.

She has a graphic design and book production background spanning almost 30 years, having started as an apprentice with Gill Marshall, a prominent, award-winning graphic designer in Johannesburg. After cutting her teeth in magazine and publication design, she later became a book production specialist for South Africa's largest traditional publishers.

Since the inception of Quickfox in 2007, she has gained immense experience in all aspects of independent publishing, having adopted a very hands-on approach with each project and, with her team, assisting hundreds of authors reach their goals. She is committed to producing professional, trade-quality books, earning her company a solid reputation in the book trade.

She has collaborated on two bestselling books, one of which was self-published. This is her third book.

Irish-born **Georgina Hatch** is a multi-award-winning journalist whose career in publishing began when she was just 14 and became a youth correspondent for her community newspaper. Since then, she has gained extensive experience in newspaper and radio journalism, as well as magazine and book publishing. Her résumé includes five years as Publishing Director at Struik Publishers (now Random House Struik) and a position as general manager of Independent Newspapers' property publishing division. Georgina particularly enjoys editorial consulting and coaching, as well as manuscript development assistance and evaluation. She runs her own editorial business, Write It Right. She also offers personal brand development and image consulting – successfully merging her two passions to help authors promote their brand and expertise through publishing.

She now lives in Ireland but continues to consult with, and assist, South African authors. This is her second book.

Notes

Notes

Notes

www.ingramcontent.com/pod-product-compliance
Lightning Source LLC
Chambersburg PA
CBHW051147290426

44108CB00019B/2637